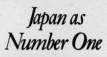
Japan as
Number One

Japan as Number One
Lessons for America

EZRA F. VOGEL

HARPER COLOPHON BOOKS

HARPER & ROW, PUBLISHERS

NEW YORK, CAMBRIDGE, HAGERSTOWN, PHILADELPHIA, SAN FRANCISCO

LONDON, MEXICO CITY, SÃO PAULO, SYDNEY

A hardcover edition of this book is published by Harvard University Press. It is here reprinted by arrangement.

JAPAN AS NUMBER ONE. Copyright © 1979 by the President and Fellows of Harvard College. All rights reserved. Printed in the United States of America. No part of this book may be used or reproduced in any manner whatsoever without written permission except in the case of brief quotations embodied in critical articles and reviews. For information address Harvard University Press, 79 Garden Street, Cambridge, Mass. 02138. Published simultaneously in Canada by Fitzhenry & Whiteside Limited, Toronto.

First HARPER COLOPHON edition published 1980.

ISBN: 0-06-090791-6

82 83 84 10 9 8 7 6

To David, Steven, and Eva
May they live in a better America

Preface

IN 1958, fresh with a Ph.D. from Harvard University in Social Relations, I set out as a social scientist seeking generalizations about the family and mental health that would hold true cross-culturally. I chose Japan not because I was a Japan specialist, for my ignorance was vast, but because Japan of all the modern countries seemed most different and hence the most critical for testing hypotheses about modern society. I was convinced that to make meaningful statements about the family and mental health in Japan I first had to become immersed in Japanese life. By the time my wife and I had been engulfed in two years of language study, research, and Japanese-style living apart from foreigners, I found myself far more interested in Japan itself than in social science generalizations. In my field work report, *Japan's New Middle Class*, I tried to delve into the inner life of Japanese families who were first our research subjects and later our friends, leaving generalizations to others.

For the next two decades I could not satiate my curiosity about Japanese society. I went to Japan almost every year, continued to revisit old friends, read the research reports of others, and kept reorganizing my thoughts each time I taught my course on Japanese society at Harvard. New mysteries, new subtleties, new dimensions of Japan kept appearing, and its constant change was a seemingly inexhaustible gold mine for intellectual curiosity.

In the last several years, however, I have found myself, like other Americans, increasingly preoccupied with what is happening in America, with the decline of our confidence in government, with our difficulty in coping with problems such as crime, urban disorganization, unemployment, inflation, and government deficits. When I first returned to the United States from Japan in 1960, I had not even questioned the general superiority of American society and American institutions. In almost every field we were substantially ahead of Japan, our capacity for research and creativity was unexcelled, and our natural and human resources seemed more than adequate. By 1975 I found myself, like my Japanese friends, wondering what had happened to America.

In the meantime the country I originally chose to study for other reasons had become extraordinarily successful. Japan still does not have the world's largest gross national product, nor is it the leading country in the world politically or culturally. Yet the more I observed Japan's success in a variety of fields, the more I became convinced that given its limited resources, Japan has dealt more successfully with more of the basic problems of postindustrial society than any other country. It is in this sense, I have come to believe, that the Japanese are number one.

Astounded by recent Japanese successes, I found myself wondering why Japan, without natural resources, was making substantial progress in dealing with problems which seemed so intractable in America. Convinced that Japan had lessons for other countries, I was no longer content to look at Japan only as a fascinating intellectual mystery. I wanted to understand the success of the Japanese in dealing with practical questions. My first inclination was to examine how such Japanese virtues as hard work, patience, self-discipline, and sensitivity to others contributed to their success. But the more I examined the Japanese approach to modern organization, the business community, and the bureaucracy, the more I became convinced that Japanese success had less to do with traditional character traits than with specific organizational structures, policy programs, and conscious planning. For several years I have been wrestling with the problem of understanding Japan's successes, and this book is the result of my intellectual labors.

I have wondered why it is that the full scope of Japanese successes has not been presented more forcefully to the American people, especially since the most knowledgeable American business, government, and academic specialists on Japan are so acutely aware of them. I have concluded that the answer is deceptively simple. Most Japanese understate their successes because they are innately modest, and more purposive Japanese, wanting to rally domestic forces or to reduce foreign pressures, have chosen to dramatize Japan's potential disasters. On the American side, our confidence in the superiority of Western civilization and our desire to see ourselves as number one make it difficult to acknowledge that we have practical things to learn from Orientals. I am convinced that it is a matter of urgent national interest for Americans to confront Japanese successes more directly and consider the issues they raise.

Since my message departs from conventional wisdom about matters of great importance, it is vulnerable to criticism. Some will say I have seen Japan only through rose-colored glasses, that I can see harmony but not conflict, that I think more of the privileged than the underprivileged, that I am concerned with efficiency but not democracy, that I underestimate the difficulty of borrowing from a different culture, and that my faith in America is wanting. I hope the reader will conclude that I make no effort to conceal Japan's difficulties, but the aim of this work is not to present a rounded, balanced picture of how Japanese society works and how the individual is shaped. Its purpose is to describe selected aspects of the Japanese national system that are so effective that they contain lessons for America. Japan has many institutions America would not want to copy, and these will be mentioned. The successes Japan does have come at a price, and the price needs to be considered. Japan is by no means a utopia and to some extent shares the full range of problems found in every modern society. If at times my description of Japanese practices sounds like a model rather than an empirical description with all its complexities, distortions, and imperfections, it is not because I desire to idealize Japan but rather because I wish to elucidate the essential features of a model we might consider for adoption. The desirable features of the Japanese system are often based on cultural traits different from our own which are not easily adopted, but deep structural changes are possible, as the Japanese proved in borrowing from the West. If anything, this book is written because of faith in America, a faith that we do not shirk difficult problems, that we will not be satisfied to hide behind "the American way" to preserve indefinitely undesirable remnants of the past, and that we can make necessary adaptations, even if they fly in the face of once-conventional wisdom and require learning lessons from people we had not regarded as mentors.

I am indebted to the following people for helpful comments on the manuscript: Walter L. Ames, Hans Baerwald, David Bayley, John C. Campbell, Robert E. Cole, Albert C. Craig, William G. Cummings, Richard Dyck, Glen Fukushima, William L. Givins, Nathan Glazer, Andrew C. Gordon, Carl Green, Thomas Hout, Charlotte Ikels, Robert Immerman, Alan Jehlin, Eugene J. Kaplan, Yoshio Karita, Donald Klein, Thomas Lifson, George C. Lodge, David MacEachron, Gary Marx, Terry C. McDougall, Michael McMullen, James C. Morley, Richard Neustadt, Kazuo Nukazawa, Daniel C. Okimoto, T. J. Pempel, David Plath, Lee Rainwater, Martin Rein, Edwin O. Reischauer, David Riesman, Thomas Rohlen, Patricia Steinhof, Katsuhiko Suetsugu, Keizo Takemi, Ray Vernon, David Vogel, Donald Warwick, and John Wheeler. I am especially indebted to George C. Lodge for his stimulating discussions of American business and to Manabu Hara, Yoichi Funahashi, Suzanne H. Vogel, Nicole Seligman, and Anna Laura Rosow for cooperation in research. I am indebted to countless numbers of Japanese friends for offering their help, especially to Tsutomu Ouchi, Seizaburo Sato, and Yoichi Miyazawa. I am indebted to Aida Donald and Susan Wallace for editorial advice and assistance.

Contents

PART ONE

The Japanese Challenge

I

A Mirror for America

IN 1976 WE AMERICANS celebrated our bicentenary with fitting fanfare, but we let the year pass without seriously reflecting on the suitability of our institutions for the next century. Our press and television have dramatized the difficult problems our nation is straining to contain, but they offer little analysis. We know that institutions that once served us well are now less effective, but it is more manageable and certainly more interesting to personalize the cause, to attack someone's corruption or secrecy or his failure to provide proper leadership, than to search for institutional alternatives. Our response is to make a new proposal, enact a new regulation, or bring in a new charismatic figure to clean up some organization, quickly.

We are at a loss to understand why these efforts are not more successful. Public-spirited politicians, although sensitive to the inadequacies of government, must respond to short-range political pressures, having no mandate to consider fundamental changes. Business leaders are acutely aware of the increasingly complex problems created by the political, social, and economic environment surrounding the traditional business arena, but they have neither the leisure nor the organization to respond to them. Academics, falling victim to their own specialization

3

and having little personal experience in management, are inadequately prepared to confront problems which are in essence systemic and holistic.

One of the best vantage points for looking at our institutions, for reexamining our assumptions and considering alternatives, is from another place that faces similar problems but finds different solutions. As world leadership is shared by more countries, we will have more to learn by studying their successes. Of these other countries, Japan, the world's second largest economy, a modern democratic nation with a free enterprise system similar to our own, offers us the best perspective.

Considering the nature and scope of Japan's successes, it is remarkable how little interest Americans have shown in profiting from the Japanese example. As Japanese institutions begin to function more effectively than foreign ones, many Japanese now return from foreign study tours discouraged that they found so little to learn, but they still scour the world for useful lessons or hints of lessons. Where American institutions lag behind, America is still unprepared to learn from countries outside Europe. Japan is studied by some Americans as a fascinating culture with an interesting history, a subtle literature, intriguing customs, and profound religious thought. But those who seek to learn from Japan are from the world of culture, not from the world of affairs. It is perhaps understandable that the Japanese, in the habit of looking abroad for things to learn, continue studying, while Americans in the world of affairs, in the habit of teaching the rest of the world, find it difficult to assume the posture of the student, even when such indifference to or casual dismissal of foreign success blinds us to useful lessons.

Japanese institutions provide a particularly illuminating mirror for America for several reasons. For one, Japan, unlike Western countries, has consciously examined and restructured all traditional institutions on the basis of rational considerations. America's political system was designed almost two hundred years ago for a premodern agricultural society, and it has not undergone any consciously designed major reorganizations since then. New institutions have grown up piecemeal, with no overall conceptualization of their desirability. Japanese institutions have undergone two major explicit reexaminations in the past 110 years to determine which institutions were desirable. In 1868 Japan began a two-decade-long study of the best institutions in the world in each sector: government, business, education, military, and the arts. After World War II, under the direction of the Allied Occupation, Japan again undertook a basic revamping of institutions to make them more democratic and more effective. Although the Occupation ended in 1952, the Japanese continued reorganizing for several more years, particularly in commerce and industry, which had not yet modernized when the Occupation ended. In both the late-nineteenth and mid-twentieth centuries Japanese leaders attempted to select institutions appropriate for a country in their circumstances and with their cultural tradition. The resulting institutions more closely resemble foreign models than those of traditional Japan, but Japanese leaders endeavored to select the best models and then to make additional improvements. In preparation for this selection, Japan developed specialists who analyzed the strengths and weaknesses of comparable institutions in each modern country; no country is more experienced in evaluating the effectiveness of existing institutions and in creating or reshaping institutions by rational planning to meet future needs. By looking at Japan we can make use of this detailed evaluation of modern institutions.

A second reason why Japan is a useful mirror is that of all the fully industrialized democratic countries, Japan, as the only non-Western one, is the most distinctive. One should not overstate its uniqueness: many of the practices to be discussed in this work can be found to some extent in Europe, Canada, or Australia, and Japanese institutions were molded as much by conscious decisions as by tradition. But Japan drew creatively on its own tradition and adapted a variety of European institutions in new and different ways. Because of Japan's efforts to recombine different traditions, no modern fully industrialized country presents a greater contrast to American institutional structure and provides greater opportunities for examining underlying assumptions.

Third, circumstance has forced Japan to pioneer in confronting problems that are just beginning to distress America. America established its patterns of government–business relations in an era when natural resources were, for practical purposes, unlimited and people could dispose of their refuse without devastation to the environment. In the future, it could be disastrous if the government made no effort to control energy resources and environmental pollution. When America was a loosely populated country with ample land and economic opportunities, people could have maximal independence with minimal governmental interference. Now with increased crowding it is desirable for the government to give some direction in the distribution of population. Before modern transportation and communication, many decisions were wisely decentralized to states, but with increasing mobility it is desirable for the national government to bring some order to increasingly complex, overlapping, and inconsistent state regulations in fields such as taxation, welfare, and education. In an earlier era when American trade and commerce were overwhelmingly geared to internal markets, it was not essential to have a foreign trade policy. Foreign trade has by now grown so rapidly that some American industries are in danger of being eliminated and workers unemployed unless America develops a trade policy consistent with the comparative advantages of our economy.

The Japanese Challenge: A Mirror for America

In all these spheres Japan faced the same problems earlier and responded more energetically. With almost no natural resources, Japan decades ago had to adopt energy policies to confront shortages that America is just now acknowledging. With population overcrowding, Japan had to find collective arrangements that represent everyone's interest and reduce the individual's disruption to society as a whole, a problem less serious in America before urban congestion. In 1868, with over two hundred fifty local lords, Japan had more difficulties in responding to the competition of other nations than America did in 1776 and therefore worked harder to provide central authority. For over a hundred years, to avoid foreign conquest and catch up with the modern West, the Japanese government had to assume leadership in dealing with broad issues in planning, restructuring, modernizing, and phasing out declining industries, a leadership America is only now beginning to consider desirable. As a small island dependent on international trade for resources and markets, Japan decades ago began developing a foreign trade policy that America now regards as necessary. In short, Japan pioneered in developing policies appropriate for America's new circumstances.

A fourth reason why Japan is a useful mirror is that Japanese institutions have been extraordinarily successful. These successes are not only economic but political and social as well. While many are worthy of emulation, this is not to say that Japan has an overall higher quality of life than America, a judgment that would be subjective at best. Even though the Japanese are dealing with many problems more effectively, they suffer from excessive crowding and serious shortages of resources, problems from which America is happily spared. Japanese institutions may not ensure even Japanese success decades from now, because the Japanese are highly vulnerable to world energy shortages, protectionism against Japanese exports, and growing competitiveness from developing countries with lower labor costs, all of which could have serious effects on Japan regardless of the effectiveness of its institutions. It is difficult to argue that the present form of Japanese institutions is best even for Japan in the future, for they must be adapted to an era of slower growth rates and increasing protectionism. One cannot conclude that adopting Japanese institutions will enable America to escape serious difficulties, because even the best Japanese institutions are imperfect and many other factors aside from those considered in this book will affect our success. And not all Japanese institutions are desirable and worthy of emulation. However, using measures America has traditionally used to determine success, it is readily demonstrable that in many areas Japanese institutions are coping with the same problems we confront, more successfully than we are. Could we not profit by showing the same eagerness to learn from the East that Japan has shown in learning from the West?

Many readers who note the Japanese successes in the pages following will find ways to ignore Japanese patterns on the grounds that they are costly, that they have inherent even if not clearly unidentifiable weaknesses, or that they do not easily fit the American tradition. I ask only that the reader who is wont to say, "It won't work here," suspend his final judgment until the last chapter.

2

The Japanese Miracle

IF JAPAN WERE an American state, it would rank fifth in geographical size, following Alaska, Texas, California, and Montana. A population of 115,000,000, half the size of America's, lives in this area, making Japan the most densely populated major country in the world. About one-sixth of its land is arable, and even with high productivity per acre, well over thirty percent of its food supplies must be imported. With virtually no petroleum, iron ore, coal, or other mineral resources, Japan is dependent on imports for almost eighty-five percent of its energy resources. It imports more timber from North America than it produces. Producing Japanese foodstuffs requires more farmland in America than is available in Japan. From 1945 to 1947, as six million soldiers and civilians, some of whom had been overseas for decades, returned to be supported by the home islands, food shortages and malnutrition were widespread. One might properly wonder, as many Japanese did, whether a country the size of Montana with virtually no physical resources could support over one hundred million people.

By 1952 when the Allied Occupation ended, Japan had almost recovered its prewar levels of production, but its gross national product was little more than one third that of France

9

or the United Kingdom. By the late 1970s the Japanese GNP was as large as The United Kingdom's and France's combined and more than half the size of America's. The Japanese were producing approximately as much steel as the United States, but in more modern and efficient plants. In 1978, of the world's twenty-two largest modern blast furnaces, none was in the United States and fourteen were in Japan. With more modern plants and higher productivity, Japanese steel was outcompeting American steel in American as well as foreign markets. Making good use of its comparative advantage first in labor costs, then in economies of scale, modern technology, and organization, Japan built up highly competitive industries in field after field.

In the early 1950s Japanese radios, tape recorders, and hi-fi equipment were less competitive than their American counterparts, but before long they dominated the market. The Japanese watch industry eclipsed the justly famous Swiss watch industry. The British motorcycle industry was virtually eliminated by the Japanese motorcycle industry, and of the several most successful motorcycle companies in America, only one, Harley-Davidson, is non-Japanese. The German dominance in camera and lens production before World War II has given way to the Japanese. In optical equipment the Japanese are similarly dominant. Even in fields remote from Japanese tradition Japanese companies often outperformed their Western counterparts. By the 1970s the sales of Steinway and other American piano manufacturers were no match for Yamaha; Muramatsu's Western flutes were competing favorably with American ones. Japanese dominance extended into such diverse fields as bicycles, ski equipment, snowmobiles, cut pottery, and zippers. In the late 1970s, as the cost of new Japanese ships ran twenty to thirty percent lower than European ones, European countries were forced to resort to nonmarket mechanisms to limit the number of ships purchased from Japan. This forced

The Japanese Challenge: The Japanese Miracle

Japanese shipbuilding companies, in the wake of the oil crisis, to operate at much less than capacity, but even then Japan outdid Europe and America combined, for it produced about fifty percent of the world's shipping tonnage.

In 1958 Japan produced fewer than one hundred thousand passenger cars, and through the early 1970s Volkswagen was the major foreign car exporter to the United States. Soon thereafter Toyota's and then Nissan's (Datsun) American sales surpassed the German manufacturer. By 1978 Volkswagen was replaced by Honda, which became the third largest automobile exporter to the United States. During 1977 Japan exported over four and one-half million cars, while America exported only a small fraction of that number. Japan sold almost two million cars in America, while about fifteen thousand American-produced cars were sold in Japan. If market forces alone were operating, Japanese car exports would have increased substantially in 1978, but Japan chose to restrain its exports artificially to avoid political repercussions in Europe and America.

The effort to explain these Japanese successes as a result of cheap labor is out-of-date, for by 1978 with devaluation of the dollar, Japanese wages were slightly higher than those in the United States.* If anything, modernization of facilities and productivity increases are more important in explaining Japanese superiority. Economist Dale Jorgenson surveyed various factors in industrial production and concluded that on the average the modernity of technology used in Japanese manufacturing had edged past the United States by 1973. In 1975 one Japanese worker could produce about one thousand English pounds worth of cars every nine days, whereas at Britain's Leyland Motors, to produce the same value a worker took

* Since changes in dollar values do not always reflect changes in yen values, dollar values throughout the book are calculated at 180 yen per dollar, the approximate exchange rate in October 1978.

forty-seven days. In 1976 none of the major European car producers (Fiat, Renault, or Volkswagen) was able to produce as many as twenty cars per man-year of labor, but Nissan employees produced forty-two cars per man-year and Toyota turned out forty-nine. In 1962 the Japanese produced roughly one hundred tons of steel per worker, compared to four hundred in England; but by 1974 Japanese productivity in steel was estimated to be two to three times that of England. By 1976 a typical Japanese worker in a ball-bearing factory produced about three and one-half times as much as a worker in RHP, the leading English manufacturer.

In several major fields such as computers, industrial chemicals, and film, Americans are still more successful than their Japanese counterparts, and in these fields Japan still protects its industries. In computers Japan already constitutes the most serious challenge to IBM and other multinationals of American origin, and Japanese-made computers are already gaining an increasing share of their domestic market while their protectionism declines. In copying machines, Japanese market share is growing rapidly. America is clearly superior in military and nuclear technology, although Japanese technology has improved so rapidly that Japan and the United States are now engaged in large joint research projects. The Japanese have at least temporarily given up their effort to manufacture large airplanes, partly because of pressure from the United States to buy American planes and ease the trade imbalance. Nonetheless, many parts for American planes are produced in Japan.

One measure of Japanese and American competitiveness is in the trade balance. America's trade imbalance with Japan approached ten billion dollars a year by the late 1970s with few signs of abatement despite dollar devaluation and political pressure. But if anything the imbalance understates Japanese industrial competitiveness, for much of America's exports are in agricultural products and raw materials. Japan's trade policy until the late 1960s was among the most protectionist in the world, and that once greatly impeded American attempts to penetrate Japanese markets. Despite rapid trade liberalization in most areas, Japanese ministries still occasionally create special difficulties for competitive American products, and until the mid-1970s the United States government did not adequately represent the interests of American companies in their efforts to break into Japanese markets. But the primary reason for the trade imbalance, as the Boston Consulting Group's 1978 study for the United States Treasury Department has shown, lies not in Japan's protectionism but in America's inferior competitiveness and lack of interest in cultivating exports to Japan. America's competitiveness has declined compared not only to Japan but to other countries. From the late 1960s to the late 1970s, of goods purchased by Japan from overseas, America lost about forty percent of its market share to Australia, Korea, Taiwan, and other Asian countries.

The extent of Japanese superiority over the United States in industrial competitiveness is underpublicized in America, but the true state of affairs was reflected by a high official of a leading Japanese research center who privately acknowledged that the United States with its highly competitive agricultural sector has by now taken the place of Japan's prewar colonies, supplying agricultural products and raw materials to a superior modern industrial machine.

Unless America's competitiveness is improved, short-range palliatives—including devaluation of the dollar—are likely to have little effect and the imbalance may well increase. Given the decline in America's research capacity compared to Japan's growing interest in research, the lack of encouragement by the United States government to American business compared to Japan's encouragement of its businessmen, and America's shortage of foreign capital compared to Japan's growing surplus, there is every reason to expect that the competitive gap will continue to widen.

In areas where Japanese competitiveness has increased so rapidly as to threaten large American industries, the United States felt it necessary to impose nonmarket mechanisms to reduce the Japanese threat. In the 1960s when Japanese textiles threatened to overwhelm the American textile industry, political pressures from America eventually led to "voluntary quotas" by Japanese companies to avoid formal tariff barriers. In the 1970s when it appeared as if several major American television companies might be forced out of business by Japanese competitors, Japanese companies similarly held back on sales to the United States. In the case of steel, a complicated formula, a trigger-price mechanism, was used to restrain steel imports, a substantial part of which came from Japan. In the late 1970s, as Japanese automobiles became so competitive that they were already outselling American-produced automobiles in California, Japanese car manufacturers raised prices to restrain exports to the United States and thereby avoid more serious American protectionism. In textiles, steel, television, and automobiles, informal restraints on Japanese exports to the United States relieve immediate trade tensions, but as long as this informal protection continues, it reduces pressures for American industries to rise to Japanese standards of competitiveness.

In international trade the Japanese have had to learn to communicate in English and to adopt patterns of trade developed and originally dominated by Western countries. Despite these obvious disadvantages, the Japanese have begun to dominate international commerce as they dominate industrial production. Mitsubishi Trading Company, Mitsui Bussan, Sumitomo Trading, C. Itoh, Marubeni, and Nissho Iwai are rivaled only by each other, not by any foreign trading company. For example, these six companies, to say nothing of other large Japanese trading companies, conduct over half the two-way trade between the United States and Japan. Because of their superior information and contacts around the world, a sizable portion of international trade not involving Japan is now channeled through these large trading firms.

Japanese investment in the United States already exceeds American investment in Japan and is growing at a much more rapid rate as more Japanese companies establish plants and purchase stocks and property in the United States.

Stagnation has been a serious problem in most modern countries, and both the American and Japanese governments are reluctant to stimulate their economies substantially for fear of inflation. In the wake of the oil shock of 1973 the Japanese government erred by overstimulating the economy, leading to a very high rate of inflation for over a year. Except for this brief period, however, in recent years Japan has not only maintained a higher growth rate than the United States but has kept its increase in wholesale price index lower.

During the 1950s, economic success was partly at the expense of the Japanese consumer, and the social infrastructure for wage raises lagged behind growth and productivity increases. However, in recent years per capita income and ownership of consumer goods have grown about as fast as the gross national product and therefore far more rapidly than in other countries. So striking has been the growth in consumer purchasing power that foreigners in Japan now have difficulty maintaining the standard of living of their Japanese counterparts without special allowances, and Japanese in America consider luxury goods and restaurants very moderate in price. There are many ways to calculate personal income, but if one includes subsidized housing, by 1978 Japanese wages had already surpassed American levels and are continuing to grow at a faster rate. To be sure, sewage systems are not yet universal and house size and car ownership still lag behind the United States although the gaps are narrowing. The retail distribution sector is not as efficient as America's and prices are high by international standards. Using conventional price indices, Japanese wages as of 1978 still buy less, but the average Japanese spends less than public rates on housing and uses less beef and other products that are high priced on these indices. Japanese lead the world in household diffusion of television sets (especially color sets) and cameras. In possession of videotape recorders, Japanese consumers are substantially ahead of the United States not only in percentage but in absolute numbers of owners. The quality of ski equipment on an average Japanese ski slope compares favorably with the equipment on the most exclusive ski slopes of Europe or America. Although some may disagree with the subjective judgment that quality of clothing in Japan is superior, on average, to that in the United States, there is widespread agreement that the variety and quantity of sports uniforms, clothing for weddings and other ceremonial parties, company wear, and casual wear exceed that of any other population, probably by a substantial margin. If anything, the Japanese maintain their belongings in a better state of repair than do Americans.

Transportation and communication systems within Japan are rapidly pulling ahead of their Western counterparts. With short distances Japanese use fewer airplanes than Americans, but in rail transport the Shinkansen bullet train route from Tokyo to Kyoto, opened in 1964, is more rapid and comfortable than anything the United States is currently considering even on the most heavily traveled routes, although in 1977 America purchased some of this fifteen-year-old technology. This line has already been extended to Fukuoka in the southern island and, though delayed by objections to the noise, is being extended toward the very northern tip of the main island.

Rapid and convenient rail service throughout the country is superior to European as well as American service.

The speed of the mail service undoubtedly compares favorably with world standards, but it is in the application of new electronic communications systems that Japan excels. Video machines and facsimile reproduction machines attached to telephones are more widely used than in any other country. It took some one hundred computer specialists four years to devise the system, but by the mid-1970s a customer could go into any regular local branch bank and have funds transferred to any other account in any local bank in the country by computer in the same day. The computer systems for controlling steel production are more sophisticated than any Western counterparts. The idea of putting all books and magazines on computer tapes and having this information available through a telephone or television system to every household in a nation is not unique to Japan, but Japan is far ahead of the United States in working out the organizational, technical, and legal problems. It is not impossible that Japan might begin to implement this system in not much more than a decade, far ahead of the United States.

With the extraordinary movement of Japanese from the countryside to the city after World War II and the un-paralleled rapidity of change caused by industrialization and Westernization, one might expect social disorganization to be immense, for the strain on many people has been substantial. It is difficult to find meaningful cross-cultural measures of social disruption, but one such indicator is the extent of crime. Observers uniformly note that people walk anywhere in Japan at all hours of the night, fully confident of their personal safety. To an extent that would shock Americans, the Japanese carry a great deal of cash with them because they pay large bills with cash rather than checks. Taxicab drivers give no indication of worrying about their personal safety. These subjective judgments are supported by the data available. Americans studying Japanese crime records, which are more complete than American records, indicate that around 1960 the rates for major crimes such as homicide, assault, theft, and rape were several times higher in America than in Japan. From 1960 to 1973 American crime rates rose 110 percent and other modern countries' crime rates went up also, except for Japan, where they declined further.

One might suspect that the Japanese neglected culture and education in their efforts to obtain rapid economic growth, but if anything cultural imports have proceeded as rapidly as technological imports and have been diffused among the population with equal speed. Japan leads the world in percentage of young people who complete high school, about ninety percent. Although a higher percentage of Americans enter a university, a higher percentage of Japanese complete universities. Although the average number of years of formal schooling is very similar in the two countries, Japanese children attend school slightly longer hours each day and about sixty more days per year than their American counterparts. They spend far more time in supplementary educational classes, and most do substantial extra studying in preparation for high school or university entrance examinations. Westerners familiar with the Japanese educational system observe that Japanese students, on the average, are more familiar than most Western students with world history and current events. In mathematics and science, the only areas where there is reliable quantitative information on comparative international skills, Japanese youth substantially outperform their counterparts in modern Western nations. The Japanese also rank high in music and artistic capacity and in physical agility. The Japanese young people's knowledge of English far surpasses the American student's knowledge of a foreign language, although their knowledge of spoken English cannot compare with that of most Europeans. But given that virtually no Japanese knew English in 1945, the progress of Japanese in learning a foreign language within a generation has perhaps been unique among large nations, and the progress continues.

It has often been noted by foreign observers that the Japanese absorb an extraordinary amount of factual information for entrance examinations at the high school and university level. Despite sometimes intense cramming, Japanese adults retain an unusual eagerness for data on topics as diverse as international affairs, politics, history, science, and the arts. Although one or two countries rank ahead of Japan in readership of daily newspapers, if one combines readership of books, magazines, and newspapers, Japan is clearly ahead of any other country. Whether, as some foreigners would argue, the programs of the two national TV channels, NHK and NHK Educational Television, are qualitatively superior to public network programs in other countries is difficult to evaluate, but they are in any case outstanding. Through the major dailies, the ordinary Japanese reading public gets a breadth of information about basic world developments that compares favorably with the best of foreign newspapers.

With an industrial output which has now surpassed that of the Soviet Union concentrated in such a small area, the Japanese have confronted a most severe pollution problem. Since the early 1970s when the problem gained prominent attention, the Japanese have responded with pioneering techniques now being studied by Americans seeking new solutions to their pollution problems. The standards for pollution control for new plants and the amount spent on pollution control by the mid-1970s surpassed that of any other country. By the late 1970s the most serious sources of pollution had been substantially reduced; for example, American and European auto manufacturers had to make special appeals to be allowed to sell new cars in Japan for they did not meet Japanese standards for emission, which by the late 1970s were the most rigorous in the world.

The Japanese national health insurance program does not offer high benefits by Western European standards. However, an observer in Japan is impressed that people seem lively and wear their age well, that obesity and debilitating illnesses seem uncommon. These impressions are supported by the statistical data that is available. By the mid-1970s Japan had the lowest infant mortality rate of any country in the world. Perhaps the best overall measure of a nation's health system is the longevity of the population. In 1955 Japan's average life expectancy was over four years shorter than America's. By 1967 Japan's average life expectancy surpassed America's, and in 1977 it surpassed Sweden's, to become the longest of any nation in the world.

The question of satisfaction with life requires more subjective judgments. If one looks at international public opinion data on complacency and self-satisfaction, the Japanese rank low. They seem to have aspirations for betterment as high or higher than any country in the world. But foreigners who observe the Japanese in public commonly conclude that in a sense of involvement in purposeful activity, of dignity in performing their work role, and of pride in personal appearance, the Japanese rank very high. It is tempting to dismiss the Japanese as automotons who know nothing but work. According to the 1977 International Labor Organization Yearbook of Labor Statistics, in 1976 the average American work week was 40.0 hours and Japan's average work week was 40.2 hours. If one took full account of unreported overtime, a typical Japanese may work an average of three or four more hours a week, but even then the total work week is in the range of Western European countries. Those who have observed Japanese families and other groups in private have concluded that in zest for life, delight in carefree relaxation, and enthusiasm for recreation, the Japanese are no laggards. As they say of themselves, they like to work hard and to play hard. Many thoughtful Americans visiting Japan express amazement at the tidiness of urban facilities, the reliability of public transportation, the courtesy of commercial personnel, the affluence of department stores, the quality of restaurants, and the virtual absence of derelicts and alienated slums. They end by wondering, like Japanese vistors to America, why Americans cannot make their cities and their organizations work as well.

In gross national product, standard of living, political power, and cultural influence, Japan is not number one in the world today. In gross national product per person, Japan surpassed the United States in 1977 or 1978, according to varying estimates by economists; but barring significant yen revaluations, even if present trends continue it will take well over a decade before Japan's gross national product surpasses that of the United States. With all fringe benefits added in, the average Japanese family income has surpassed that of its American counterpart, but in purchasing power, as measured by conventional economic estimates, the average Japanese in 1978 had not yet surpassed his American counterpart. Although measures of purchasing power are subject to question, because the package is geared to American tastes and the Japanese are more frugal, pay less interest because of fewer debts, and draw more income from savings, there is no doubt that Americans enjoy more housing and yard space.

Japan has thus far chosen to maintain a low posture in international political affairs, to cooperate with other nations rather than take initiatives, to defend its own interests rather than assume responsibility for preserving peace and order around the world. Its political influence cannot now compare with that of the United States.

In cultural affairs, national influence tends to lag decades behind economic power. Western European nations that can no longer match Japan in economic power still enjoy greater cultural respect and influence than Japan, and the Japanese still pay respect to the manners and arts of Western Europe. More Japanese take piano lessons than Americans, to say nothing of the number of people studying Japanese arts and music. However, in Western art and music, despite rapid Japanese advances, America still enjoys a preponderance of outstanding artists and musicians. The Japanese lag far behind in the number of Nobel prizes received for science and literature, although there may be grounds for wondering whether they receive the recognition they deserve. The Japanese on the average engage in more physical exercise than their American counterparts, but Americans clearly outperform the Japanese in most international athletic competitions. The gap between the United States and Japan in political power and cultural and athletic performance is narrowing, but not as rapidly as the gap in economic capacity. At present, in political and cultural influence and even in gross national product Japan is not the number one power in the world.

Yet in the effectiveness of its present-day institutions in coping with the current problems of the postindustrial era Japan is indisputably number one. Considering its limited space and natural resources and its crowding, Japan's achievements in economic productivity, educational standards, health, and control of crime are in a class by themselves. This success is more striking when one considers how far behind Japan was in many of these areas not only in 1945 but even in the mid-1950s, after recovery from World War II was essentially complete.

Many Americans seem interested in finding some explanation of how the Japanese have used unfair tactics to outperform other countries; charges that they are imitators, narrow economic animals, and dumpers and that their government and business have illicit intimacy are not uncommon. Such facile attempts to explain Japanese success may ease American anxiety about our performance, but not only are they unfair to the Japanese but they blind us from learning about Japanese success and condemn us to falling further behind.

Japan has serious problems aside from crowding. Its universities are generally mediocre, discrimination against Koreans and the descendants of Tokugawa-period outcasts (*burakumin*) widespread, defensiveness against foreign contamination relentless, government bumbling in planning projects such as Narita airport sometimes distressing, and big business treatment of public complaints often arrogant. Since the focus of this book is not on a rounded picture of Japan but on practices potentially useful for Americans wanting to improve our country, such problems will be considered in detail only where relevant to the question of whether these problems are essential parts of institutions we might want to borrow. The institutions that follow were chosen because they are crucial for understanding overall Japanese success and because they could be models that America would do well to emulate.

PART TWO
Japanese Successes

3

Knowledge: Pursuit and Consensus

IF ANY SINGLE FACTOR explains Japanese success, it is the group-directed quest for knowledge. In virtually every important organization and community where people share a common interest, from the national government to individual private firms, from cities to villages, devoted leaders worry about the future of their organizations, and to these leaders, nothing is more important than the information and knowledge that the organizations might one day need. When Daniel Bell, Peter Drucker, and others hailed the coming of the postindustrial society in which knowledge replaced capital as society's most important resource, this new conception became a great rage in Japan's leading circles. But these leading circles were merely articulating the latest formulation of what had already become conventional Japanese wisdom, the supreme importance of the pursuit of knowledge.

It is not always clear why knowledge is needed, but groups store up available information nonetheless on the chance that some day it might be useful. Information gathering is general and specific, long-term and short-term, formal and informal. Organizations send out observation teams and invite in experts. They gather information from classrooms and golf courses, from conferences and bars, from think tanks and television. They gather it from professionals and amateurs, friends and foes. New friends are cultivated because they might provide access to information, and new groups are formed to select and process the information. Potential sources are carefully nurtured so that further queries can be processed as needed. New areas of knowledge are explored to provide new clues, and people are assigned to spend several years mastering potentially profitable specialties. The process is nothing if not thorough.

GROUP LEARNING: ROUTINE AND URGENT

Whenever two people are together, the one imparting information is accepted as the teacher, and the listener becomes the student. Everyone is expected to be a student part of the time, and a good student is admired at any age. The good student displays modesty, humility, persistence, and forbearance. In a group setting, if the student thinks the teacher less than fascinating, he may doze discreetly; if he finds the teacher less than outstanding, he conceals it. He may not challenge the teacher's wisdom. He accepts the framework of assumptions of the teacher, and if encouraged to ask a question, finds one that will enable the teacher to demonstrate his abilities. The student is bound by his role as a learner and seeks to learn what he can; he does not try to impress others with his cleverness.

Study is a social activity which continues throughout life. By the time Japanese youth complete formal schooling, not only have they acquired general information, but they have acquired the habit of studying in groups. Even if they read alone, they discuss their reading with peers. University education may be more important for certification than learning, and the social atmosphere may impede probing, but it does not impede groups of students from continuing to learn, nor does it impart such confidence that students can consider themselves expert before they begin their employment. After he is employed, the school graduate is prepared to receive his specialized training and he remains receptive to broad generalized training. At his work place the new employee first undergoes long periods of specific training as an apprentice with properly humble status and throughout his later career frequently participates in a variety of study groups. An employee is encouraged to engage in work-related study even when there are no study groups, and a housewife, young or old, is encouraged by family and friends to study how to be a better housewife, mother, and, later, a better mother-in-law and grandmother. Adult education courses, offered by local communities, companies, newspapers, and department stores as well as universities, are extraordinarily popular.

.Off the job, an employee is constantly looking for opportunities to learn what might be useful for his work; but he also tries to learn important things with no apparent immediate relationship to his work, for they might prove useful in the long run. When a foreign visitor comes to Japan, most Japanese almost instinctively think, "What can I learn from him?" and the three million Japanese who now travel abroad each year look for little hints of new ideas they might apply at home.

The penchant for study may be rooted in groups, but in no arena is it more clearly manifested than in the mass media. Sports magazines, adult comics, some weekly magazines, and some television shows are almost exclusively for entertainment, but newspapers, magazines, and television are also expected to convey generous amounts of information. Not only do Japanese spend more time reading than their American counterparts—whether it be newspapers, magazines, or books—but a higher proportion of the media they encounter is designed to enhance knowledge and skills. Each of the two largest Japanese newspapers have a circulation of about six million, much larger than that of the largest American daily. The several largest Japanese newspapers, each with more specialized reporters and more foreign correspondents than any American paper, can provide their readers with highly detailed background information. Because these large newspapers are national rather than local, public awareness of national and international issues is greater than in the United States. Japanese newspapers in 1976 had a circulation of sixty-one million, the same as the United States or almost twice as large a circulation per population.

Numerous serials inform Japanese specialists in an almost infinite variety of areas of interest. Herbert Passin, chairman of Columbia University's sociology department, commented that when he wishes to give new ideas an airing in Japan, he and Japanese intellectuals can find many publications where their ideas will be immediately printed, whereas in America it would at best take many more months to find an outlet. Some thirty thousand new books are now published in Japan each year, about the same as in the United States. Since World War II approximately one hundred fifty thousand books have been translated into Japanese. Not all of these are for conveying information, but the amount of information flowing into English from other languages is miniscule compared to that translated into Japanese.

Educational television is generously funded, and a significant proportion of programming time is devoted to basic educational courses rather than to elite entertainment. Courses on five foreign languages—English (at several levels, from "Sesame Street" to adult programs), German, Chinese, French, and Russian—are available on the regular weekly schedule of the national education network. In recent years special programs for farmers, small businessmen, and mothers of children of various ages have appeared. The audience for educational television expects charts, graphs, and illustrations but is prepared to watch programs that in the United States would not be seen as particularly fascinating. In the late 1960s, for example, when computers first gained widespread attention, over one million copies of the textbook to accompany the educational television program on computers were sold in one year. Even on commercial channels, information programs abound and several programs a day present favorite foreign television shows dubbed into Japanese.

Although basic learning continues everywhere and at all ages, information gathering becomes focused and takes on a special campaign-like intensity when an organization recognizes an issue as preeminently important. During the course of the several years that a given issue such as planning a railroad or promoting venture capital or revising local tax systems is dominant, nearly every member of the organization works with some aspect of it, exploring new angles and seeking and relaying new bits of information.

The process usually begins long before the exact nature of the issue has been precisely defined. At this early stage, government or business leaders may begin to consult knowledgeable individuals or may assign representatives from their organization to an exploration of approaches to the problem, the subissues that are involved, and the resources and people who might best be asked for advice. After a period of consultation, they begin to send out people to do more intensive observation and study. The researchers assemble, summarize, and, when necessary, translate books and articles. Study groups begin to confer on subissues. Later meetings are held to evaluate what has been learned and to define what else needs to be learned. People are sent out again to ask the same questions in order to verify certain points and to focus on new, slightly different problems. Staff members consider all important relevant options and at later stages redefine issues and select especially promising approaches for restudy with more thoroughness. They mull over, digest, recognize, and redigest their information as their options gradually narrow and decisions emerge.

BASIC LEARNING ILLUSTRATED: SPORTS

The process of learning skills on a national scale may be illustrated by the Japanese approach to studying sports. When China began to expand its contact with non-Communist nations in the early 1970s, the first sports team it sent abroad was table tennis, the one sport in which the Chinese were world champions. China next sent out men's and women's volleyball and basketball teams, sports in which they are almost as strong.

The standard Japanese approach is different: they choose instead a prominent Western sport they hope to master. The first major sport selected was baseball, introduced in 1873 five years after the Meiji Restoration, and popularized at the turn of the century when it was clearly the preeminent American sport. Japanese sent observers to watch the strongest American teams and to undergo training under their tutelage. They invited the best players to Japan for demonstration games. It is no accident that America's most celebrated pre-World War II baseball player, Babe Ruth, received a tumultuous welcome in Japan and remained one of the great Japanese heroes. After World War II the Japanese were quick to invite to their country whole demonstration teams. Gradually Japanese teams arranged to recruit one or two American players each. To be sure, some of the American players were past their prime, but that was not the point. Their own playing might help the team only a little in the short run, but they could help to train other team members, imparting know-how that would make the Japanese teams strong in the long run. The Japanese invited the best American big league teams to Japan to play Japanese teams. In the early years the American teams overwhelmed their Japanese counterparts, but it was no shame to lose badly at that time. It was seen as the way to build up skill. Gradually the Japanese teams lost by smaller margins, and, despite the American advantage of greater physical size, the Japanese began occasionally to beat American professional teams.

When a group of young girl swimmers from the United States dominated the Tokyo Olympics of 1964, they caught the eyes of the world, but in Japan they became a sensation. Young Japanese and their coaches made pilgrimages to the United States to study the system for developing that talent. The American girls were invited to put on exhibitions in Japan and to give occasional pointers to their Japanese counterparts. Aside from the coaching given talented Japanese swimmers, the major lesson in Japanese eyes was that the United States had developed an intensive program to single out swimmers with competitive potential at junior high school age, providing a reservoir of talent from which championship swimmers could develop. The statesmen of the Japanese sports world concluded that if Japanese grade schools throughout the country were to teach swimming, Japan could create an even larger group of talented young swimmers with an earlier start, possibly compensating for small physical size and a population base smaller than the United States' and Russia's. The government did not require that primary schools provide swimming pools, but local "PTAs," caught up in the mood, began to demand that their schools build pools and offer swimming programs. Within several years swimming pools dotted the Japanese countryside, usually alongside elementary schools, as well as urban and suburban areas. This enthusiasm began to fade somewhat when it was found that some elementary school pupils were spending too much time in swimming, to the detriment of their studies and sometimes their health, but the basic programs continued. Soon after the 1976 Olympics the East German girls who had dominated the swimming competition toured Japan not just to demonstrate their skills but to offer pointers to aspiring Japanese swimmers and their coaches. The Japanese girls may not yet be able to defeat their East German and American competitors, but in a short span of time they have successfully climbed into the ranks of international competitive swimming in spite of their smaller physical size.

The actual decision to introduce a new sport is a complex one. No factor is more important in the timing than international popularity. Guiding the process is a kind of sports community with sports statesmen, business sponsors, coaches, leading players, sports writers, sporting-goods store owners, and allies in the government bureaucracy. The community does not necessarily have a fixed membership, but there is a recognized community of specially interested people who work together effectively and who know how best to develop a new sport. They know how to whip up the enthusiasm that makes the new sport a kind of fad, but they also know how to direct the careful acquisition of know-how that is essential for creating popularity and competence.

Interest in a new sport does not derive only from international competitive ambitions. Shortly after the war, business leaders discovered that the golf course was an ideal locale for creating informal contacts with their counterparts in different countries. Some Japanese businessmen concluded that for them to play well it was advisable to develop professional golf, for professional Japanese golfers could then give them helpful tips. Foreign professional players were invited to Japan, and before long budding Japanese professionals were on the international circuit. Once golf became popular in Japan, it took on a life of its own, with special privilege going to those who belonged to fashionable country clubs. In certain Japanese businessmen's circles, a person's golf handicap is almost as important an item of information as his company's gross sales. The stylishness only added to the seriousness with which Japanese studied golf.

Whatever the sport, the basic approach to learning has been and remains the same. For another example, one notes that bowling, learned from America, became so popular in the 1960s that for a time the world's two largest bowling alleys were in Tokyo and more Japanese were bowling than Americans. The Japanese learned gymnastics from the Soviet Union, hockey from Canada, tennis from Australia and the United States, soccer and rugby from England, skiing from Austria, basketball from the United States, table tennis originally from the United States and now from China. A newcomer to the Japanese sports repertory is American football. No country's efforts to learn football can compare with those of Japan, which has hosted entire American professional football teams that come to Japan to play one another, since no Japanese teams are yet up to American competitive levels.

While new sports are being added to the Japanese repertory, traditional sports are not ignored. Sumo, judo, karate, and aikido remain popular despite occasional faddish swings; when a new fad strikes and study of a new sport reaches a peak, the old sports nonetheless retain their niche in the expanding sports panorama.

It has been a matter of keen disappointment to the Japanese that their athletic teams have not had the extraordinary success that their companies have enjoyed in international economic competition. There has been continual self-criticism and analysis of the causes of their failure. They do not take refuge in the excuse of their small physical size, nor do they let up in their efforts at self-improvement, even though they have reached international competitive levels in virtually all sports and are not far behind the Soviet Union, the United States, and East and West Germany. Foreign sports specialists observing the Japanese expect continued progress in their mastery of Western sports.

The same ingredients found in the sports field (group

leadership, group-oriented study, humility, long-term perspective, and high ambition) are also present in other cases of learning, whether organized by the government, private companies, or the local community.

BUREAUCRATS AS INFORMATION MANAGERS

From the beginning of the Meiji period in the mid-nineteenth century, Japanese government leaders had sent abroad missions to study foreign governments and societies to prepare for a state with the most effective modern constitution, army, industry, science, technology, and agriculture. After World War II, government-sponsored study abroad extended into extraordinarily diverse fields, from philosophy to politics, atomic physics to toy making, business management to household management, and from medical science to jazz. As the spectrum of learning widened, the process of acquiring information became increasingly elaborate.

Japan's elite officials from the various ministries have the preeminent responsibility for guiding the acquisition of knowledge. They themselves are constantly analyzing information and deciding what further information needs to be gathered, playing a role that in the United States is partly played by academics and the White House staff. Within each ministry large numbers of experts spend a major part of their time following developments abroad within their respective spheres. They are expected not only to keep track of developments in general but to search for examples that Japan could usefully emulate.

The Japanese government's financing of foreign training is concentrated not on young university students but on elite young bureaucrats who have already spent at least a year or two in their respective ministries. Government officials remain in the same ministry until retirement, and therefore it pays the ministry to provide them with years of specialized training in areas basic to their future responsibilities. Because each age cohort rises together and at its peak holds all key positions within the ministry, an effort is made to ensure that some bureaucrats in every age group are trained to tap each of the major bodies of knowledge relevant to the minstry's basic work. After receiving general training in ministry affairs, young bureaucrats within each age group are divided into separate specialties to be trained in appropriate languages, technical work, and theory in the best universities in the world, with all expenses and allowances paid by the ministry. These bureaucrats studying abroad have a clear sense of what knowledge their ministry needs and can concentrate their studies in these spheres. The system ensures that those who receive valuable training will be in key positions to make maximum use of it.

In the Foreign Ministry, for example, two or three young officers are selected each year to work on China. After a two-year tour of duty in Tokyo within the ministry, they are commonly sent for a two-year course in the language in Taipei or Peking. After Tokyo recognized Peking in 1972, the first exchange students Tokyo sent to Peking for language study were not bright university students but these young Foreign Ministry officials. After language study one or two in the age group may be sent to American universities to become familiar with Western scholarship on China and another to Moscow to become familiar with Soviet work on China. After this assignment, the officer may be sent to Peking or Hong Kong to work on analysis of current events. Although he begins work after three or four years of full-time study, he is in many respects still an apprentice until after his tour of duty in Hong Kong or Peking. Throughout his career the China specialist in the Foreign Ministry is expected to keep in touch with important research and analysis by the institutes under whom he was originally trained. This system thus guarantees that the most important channels for potential information will remain open.

Staff preparation for other specialties within ministries is not ordinarily so extensive, but the basic approach for training elite bureaucrats is the same. The Finance Ministry sends promising young officials overseas to study tax systems, tax laws, business administration, theoretical economics, and econometrics. The Ministry of International Trade and Industry (MITI) sends officials abroad to study development of specific industries, theories of economic development, and energy economics. The object of study changes depending on an estimate of the future seriousness of certain issues. During the 1960s, for example, when Japan was reluctantly internationalizing its trade, a MITI official was assigned to France to study ways in which France had successfully resisted the advance of British manufactured goods. After 1973 the number assigned to study energy problems immediately increased.

Bureaucrats consider no responsibility greater than keeping well informed. When the scope of information gathering exceeds the ministry's span of control, they help mobilize private institutions most directly concerned to set up task forces to fill in gaps in informaton. Within the ministry considerable effort is made not just to collect information but to sift it and to ensure that key actors in the ministry are neither flooded with more information than they can control nor inadequately informed on matters of import. Within ministries, it is not the top-level who are expected to take initiatives in processing information as in America but the key bureau and section leaders within the ministry. In MITI, for example, the bureaus responsible for the respective industrial sectors all gather information that might be useful for guiding Japan's industrial development in that sector. For its respective sector each bureau wants to know world market trends, the state of technology, the likely timing and nature of new technological breakthroughs, the nature of the most successful industries in the world, and the reasons for their success. These bureaucrats erect formal and informal timetables as to when issues are likely to come to the fore, and they focus their information gathering accordingly. For example, in the decades after World War II, MITI officials considered it extremely important to develop basic Japanese industries like steel and electric power, and they concentrated their information-gathering efforts in these sectors. Interest in gathering know-how about the automobile industry began to develop in the 1950s, whereas computers did not emerge as a high priority until the late 1960s. After the oil shock in late 1973, energy problems took on top priority. Officials concerned with Middle Eastern oil, for example, recognized that paying for the oil and investing capital would not be sufficient to ensure the continuous flow of oil from the Middle East to Japan. They decided therefore to organize major technological development projects in the Middle East, which would make the oil-producing countries dependent on Japanese know-how and technological assistance. To do this well required vast amounts of information about Middle Eastern business patterns and social customs. It led to a rapid increase in the number of Japanese studying Arabic and Middle Eastern culture in general, with the goal of building a broader base of relations that would provide a more reliable source of natural resources.

When an issue rises to prominence, the Japanese do not hesitate to overlap and duplicate their efforts to gather relevant information. As James Abegglen of Boston Consulting group put it, "They smother a problem." Bureaucrats stationed abroad not only gather information directly but mobilize private Japanese who can assist in the process and identify foreign locals, be they newsmen, scholars, bibliographers, influential business friends, or free-wheeling entrepreneurs, who can open channels of information. The government helps finance research if necessary, but in most cases the gathering of information requires little or no financial support by the government. Companies finance research, and the media, sensitive to the heightened interest in the particular issue, invite academic and professional specialists to speak or write, without government financing. Informative speeches or conferences are not only reported but often printed in full in magazines. Editing may be hasty and at times sloppy, but the ideas and information are widely available at great speed.

Especially knowledgeable foreign specialists receive invitations through Japanese friends or acquaintances for attractive opportunities to speak, write, or visit Japan. Prominent Americans may be under more pressure from Japanese than American media to get their main ideas out to a broader public with great speed. Foreigners invited on such occasions are extraordinarily impressed with Japanese hospitality, generosity, and appreciation of their intellectual contributions. In the process, the information gatherer acts within the bounds of courtesy due a distinguished teacher. He listens carefully, absorbs whatever he can and asks questions, but rarely challenges or shows off his own knowledge. If anything, he underplays his own understanding of the issue.

The scope of government information gathering is breathtaking. At the height of the student turmoil in various countries during the Vietnam War, Japan's Economic Planning Agency dispatched an official to America to talk with radical American economists about various potential crises of capitalism. The purpose was to enable the Economic Planning Agency to be more sensitive to potential contingencies in drawing up its multiyear plans. A Japanese-speaking American student, the only foreigner on a mission sponsored by the Japanese government to consider developments in a third country, was detached for part of the time to interview various local residents about their attitudes toward Japan. In the mid-1970s when it appeared that Japan might be moving toward a coalition government, a mission was sent to Europe to study the conditions under which coalition governments of European countries since World War II became immobilized and what kind of problems this created. The purpose: to explore mechanisms for avoiding such immobilization if coalition government came to Japan.

"Think Tanks": Maximum Information at Minimal Cost

Japanese government agencies have long supplemented their own research institutes with support to a small number of private institutes in order to obtain more specialized and detailed information. Some of these outside institutes, like the Institute for Developing Economies, with several hundred researchers studying other parts of Asia, have a staff and a collection of current materials as large as any research institute in their field in the world. However, in the 1960s as the complexity of problems facing Japan multiplied, the Japanese moved to create many more institutes to cope with the knowledge explosion. In characteristic fashion, large numbers of Japanese delegations traveled abroad to study foreign research institutes and then advise on the optimal development of Japanese "think tanks." Think tanks became a new fad and dozens of new ones sprang up, as the proverbial phrase goes, "like bamboo shoots after the spring rain." Before long there was even a federation of think tanks. Japanese observers concluded that American research centers were often too independent from the original financing organ and hence less than optimally responsive to requests for relevant information. Therefore, in Japan each research center is assigned to a certain ministry which controls the annual appropriations and supervises information collection. Government agencies also help sponsor other research centers with a small core of permanent staff capable of expanding through short-term contracts in order to obtain special kinds of information in their field of expertise.

By American standards many of these research organizations conduct relatively little basic research and their studies lack originality, analytic depth, and thoroughness. But the Japanese have had a different vantage point. The goal of these research groups is not to be original. It is not that Japanese lack the creativity to be unique, for in some priority areas like forecasting and analysis of energy problems the Japanese have in fact conducted high-quality original research. The task of the Japanese think tank is to serve as an information sweeper, bringing in all the best knowledge in the world on certain issues. The institutes summarize the information not to form conclusions or even to display individual analytic virtuosity but to suggest a variety of possible approaches potentially useful to their sponsoring organization. What the sponsor buys in a research center is not the beautifully prepared definitive major report but continuing access at an informal as well as formal level to relevant information on important pending issues. The researchers are generally not identified with any political point of view, and they do not defend particular intellectual positions. They accept their service role of providing all the facts, ideas, and visions that might conceivably be useful on a given issue.

One weakness of ministry-sponsored research institutes is the parochialism which stems from the specific ministerial interests. In the early 1970s the government set up the National Institute for Research Advancement (NIRA) to provide inter-ministry coordination and to see that large issues would be dealt with in an integrated fashion, not simply from the points of view of the specific ministries. NIRA makes an effort to coordinate the selection of topics and to guide the division of labor between various think tanks under different ministries so that all important topics receive rounded treatment.

Some think tanks are temporary creations that can be closed down depending on their performance record and the needs of government sponsors. Those with an expandable core of permanent staff are given assurance of long-term support by the appropriate government agencies. A small number of substantial research groups, most similar to large American ones, like Nomura Research Institute, Mitsubishi Research Institute, and the Japan Economic Research Institute, meet the needs for sustained quality research. They have secure private and government funding and a permanent research staff. When an issue becomes salient, competing research projects are assigned to several research institutes, but when issues become less important, the government terminates contracts with the less effective think tanks.

In short, think tanks, like most information-gathering units in Japan, draw on resources throughout the world, orient themselves to general and specific missions in defined policy-related areas, adjust to current needs of sponsors, and digest the information flowing to them to make it useful to government decision makers.

COMPANY INFORMATION STRATEGY

Individual companies sponsor information-gathering activities with no less enthusiasm than government ministries. Some American companies have programs in training and information gathering not totally different, but on the average Japanese companies collect and process information more thoroughly than their foreign counterparts. The leading Americans considered most innovative in thinking about the future, like

Herman Kahn, Peter Drucker, John Kenneth Galbraith, and Daniel Bell, are given more time and attention by businessmen in Japan than in America.

The Japanese general trading companies (like Mitsubishi, Mitsui Bussan, Sumitomo, Marubeni, C. Itoh, and Nissho Iwai) are unparalleled by other companies, Japanese or foreign, in their international information network. In part their success comes simply from their size, since most of Japan's foreign trade is conducted through these six companies, each of which is represented in virtually every country in the world. But success comes also because information gathering has such high priority. In gathering detailed economic information, private companies are superior to the Japanese government, but their superiority is especially pronounced in areas where they have a substantial economic interest. Even in political information gathering they sometimes outdo the Japanese Foreign Ministry. When a Japanese airliner was highjacked in 1973 in Abu Dhabi, for example, the Foreign Ministry relied on Mitsubishi Trading Company telexes to keep informed. And a Japanese magazine referred to one company official with high-level political contacts as the "Mitsubishi Ambassador in Washington." The trading companies' presence in small cities in major countries provides them with more detailed regional information than is obtained by the Foreign Ministry.

In 1973 the American government was shocked to learn that Soviet officials in the United States had arranged with an American company for a large sale of wheat to the Soviet Union, but a Japanese trading company was not surprised. Officials in the Moscow office of the trading company had wired the Tokyo office that several high trade officials who would make such agreements were suddenly absent from the Moscow scene. Upon request from the Tokyo office, company employees stationed in New York found that these officials were going through a New York airport en route to Colorado, and regional trading company officials were able to confirm that they were meeting with the American company. It was not difficult to surmise what the meeting was about. The purpose of the Japanese company's research was to make some adjustments to the grain market before information about the purchase became public and caused a rise in the price of grain. Although such thoroughness is not unusual, the basic long-range effort lies not in such intelligence coups but in the continued collection and analysis of nonsecret material relevant to company interest, all the way from macroeconomic theory to the price of hog bristles in rural China.

Other Japanese companies undertake training and information gathering with comparable vigor. In middle-sized family companies, for example, it is common for the owner of the company to select one or two sons or sons-in-law for special training with the expectation that they will later acquire senior managerial responsibility, possibly becoming president of the company. Usually the father first sends the sons to a prominent private university like Keio, both to receive a general liberal arts background and to meet other future business leaders. These young men then form a network of friendships which can, among other things, contribute to the informal information flow once they assume responsibility in the company. After Keio a preferred pattern is to become fluent in spoken English and then enroll for a masters in business administration at a major American business school. The Japanese believe that American business management training is superior to that of any other country, and experience in America also helps future leaders to develop friendships and knowledge of American business. After graduating from business school the student is expected to work several years in America or Europe in companies in the same field as his father and often in companies where his father has developed some business contacts. Since the aim of this period abroad is to receive an apprenticeship training, salary is not a serious consideration. After several years of such experience, the young man returns home, where he is expected first to reestablish himself with the workers and employees in his father's company, usually by taking on routine jobs in various parts of the company. Only later does he begin his management apprenticeship, gradually putting his training to work, all the while keeping open channels of communication with former fellow students and work associates.

In larger nonfamily corporations, officials rise slowly through the ranks. Because employees tend to remain in large corporations until retirement, it is rational for Japanese companies to invest far more heavily in training than do Western companies, where employees with such special skills would be more attractive to other employers. Employees on the management track customarily are rotated to a wide variety of departments and sent to outside training centers to acquire skills in various areas and to develop the close personal relationships that will later facilitate the flow of information needed for effective management decisions. Even if American companies can acquire new talent from the outside to bring skills to the company, the lower turnover of Japanese companies permits a more intimate nexus of personal relations between officials and other employees throughout the company.

When an issue is defined as the current top priority, the company, like a ministry, may frantically intensify its quest for information; but even in slack periods information gathering never stops. Japanese companies that have surpassed their Western counterparts in overall levels of technology and organizational know-how do not stop learning. They continuously search out weak spots where another company, Japanese or foreign, might have more strength and provide clues as to how they can continue to improve. A small dye maker in Western Japan with fifty employees, for example, follows appropriate journals to determine which dye-making plants anywhere in the world have made the most important recent innovations. One or two employees are dispatched each year to spend a month or more observing these innovations.

Large Japanese companies hedge their bets by keeping open all potentially important channels of communication. For example, whenever a young politician becomes so prominent that he is considered to have a great future, each major daily newspaper identifies one or more young staff reporters who by reason of personality, style, and political persuasion get along well with him. This reporter may be assigned to a variety of posts, but one of his responsibilities is to retain a special personal relationship with that politician, to keep his confidence, and if necessary to become his advocate within the newspaper and in public as well. Therefore, regardless of which politician becomes prime minister or a leading cabinet member, when critical stories break, a newspaper has some reporter who can draw on a thorough knowledge of and special access to that leader. Other companies informally assign certain employees to maintain a comparable range of potentially important contacts, be they with potential buyers, sellers, suppliers, financiers, bureaucrats, or politicians, domestic or foreign.

Japanese companies also keep open channels to former senior executives who are believed to possess a priceless accumulation of knowledge and good judgment. By granting former high officials special honors and privileges and avoiding disruptive coups that would alienate them, present officials maintain easy access to their predecessors. Although ordinary workers in a large company retire at an average age of fifty-seven, the highest executives remain later. Directors and managing directors are generally in their late fifties and sixties, presidents in their sixties or even older, and chairmen of the board in their late sixties or seventies. The company board generally consists of former executives rather than outside directors as in an American company. Japanese organizations may err on the side of granting too much authority to retired high officials, but by so doing they retain use of their advice, judgment, special expertise, and range of connections.

While most information is open, some is treated very sensitively. Where there is a danger of giving away competitive advantage to another company, Japanese company employees fight like samurai in preserving secrets. Companies prefer in-house specialists or special friends rather than outside consulting companies—lawyers and auditors, for example—to diminish the risk of passing on information to competitors. Stories of geisha passing on secrets obtained from businessmen in one company to those in another are a favorite comedy theme, but in fact geisha, like select newsmen taken into confidence by a given company, have proven to be reliably discreet. Even within a company it is accepted that certain important matters will be known only at higher levels, although the company's major goals and plans are generally widely understood by all company employees.

At the same time, competing companies are alert to opportunities where they can profit from joint study. When new management approaches were being introduced in the 1950s, all major companies, whether competitors or not, sent personnel to common study sessions. In the late 1960s when companies were introducing computers on a large scale, their representatives attended a variety of study sessions to discuss the impact of computerization on office organization and personnel policy. Joint study sessions cover an almost limitless range of issues from energy policy to government tax policy, to regional development, to welfare programs, to wage programs, to accounting procedures, to pollution problems.

In the late 1950s and during the 1960s the initiative for cooperative study sessions often came from the Japan Productivity Center, which represented government, business, and labor organizations. Sometimes the study sessions are encouraged by ministry officials in a given sector who want to raise the general level of expertise of companies in their sector or who, because of busy schedules, cannot brief everyone individually. Initiative may come from Keidanren (the Federation of Economic Organizations), from a trade association, from an ad hoc gathering of companies in the sector, or from think tanks or business schools concerned with promoting their own institutions. In any case, despite the basic competitiveness between companies, employees of rival companies can be perfectly cordial and even friendly as fellow students while discussing issues which, while only marginally important for competitive advantage, are nonetheless useful for all concerned. Companies have thus taken great care to distinguish when they can and cannot engage in cooperative study, for while highly competitive, they also want to cultivate every possible channel for information gathering.

To keep their employees optimally informed, virtually all sizeable companies organize study groups for senior management, middle management, new employees, and, not uncommonly, for dependents of employees. The company not only calls on in-house experts, but invites outside lecturers on topics of interest and sets up study groups focusing on new books or articles of unusual relevance. If a company cannot provide its employees with appropriate specialized training, the employees are encouraged to take correspondence courses or to take a brief leave of absence to attend proper training programs.

COMMUNITY INFORMATION GATHERING

The same kind of intensive broad-gauged information gathering takes place in a community that is undertaking a program of local development, be it a middle-sized city or a small village. Leaders of a middle-sized city considering a new transportation system, for example, are likely to study cities of comparable size to determine which have the most modern transport systems in the world. Local government officials, local businessmen, educators, technical specialists, or, more often, some combination of the above would then form an inspection team that would travel abroad to observe the best systems in detail. The findings would be publicized in great detail in the local community through meetings of specialists and in larger public gatherings. After the community had thoroughly digested these reports, the world's most promising two or three transport systems for a city of that size would be selected for further study and the same or similar inspection teams would return to the model system for reassessment. When this team returned its findings would be discussed again. Usually one system would begin to emerge as the most promising and appropriate, although certain modifications would be suggested in order to avoid the minor problems of the best system or to adapt it to particular local needs. The result: a system as modern and up-to-date as any in the world and a local citizenry well-informed as to why a particular system was chosen.

A village considering a new swimming pool, community hall, or granary does not undertake the planning with the same sophistication as a larger community or company, but it undergoes comparable periods of information gathering and discussion, for the usefulness of information gathering has become part of the conventional wisdom of Japanese society.

KNOWLEDGE FOR CONSENSUS

The Japanese approach to information gathering did not originate entirely in Japan, but drew heavily on techniques borrowed from Western countries. These Western models were most fully developed in Japan, for it is unlikely that either the pervasiveness of general study and information gathering or the intensity of the search for focused information is rivaled in any other country.

If one examined all the research institutes, universities, and government and private research organizations in America studying any given issue, it is likely that the sum total of basic information would surpass that in Japan. But quantity alone is not the key to Japan's success in handling information. It derives rather from the long-term commitment of organizations to their employees and vice versa, for this permits a level of training and retraining that is simply not rational for organization with higher rates of mobility. And this continuity in membership means that not only is information better retained but the core of key employees are constantly reprocessing information and looking for new opportunities to add key bits of understanding. Information gathering is not an end in itself. It is a group-directed process closely linked to long-range organizational purposes, permitting an impressive range of information to be concentrated where and when the organization can best use it.

The Japanese assume that differences of opinion can best be resolved not by adversary procedures and brilliant argument but by further gathering of information. When two units cannot resolve an issue they may take it to a higher authority for resolution, but when higher authorities weigh possible courses of action, employees are dispatched to gather further data to tilt the decision in one direction or another. This increases the chance of reaching a wise decision, but perhaps even more important it reduces the need for anyone to make the difficult decisions that favor some and alienate others. People avoid posturing and advocating until the information is gathered and analyzed. The decision comes not so much from arguing, persuading, and contending but from joint efforts to arrive at the best solution, and the process of reaching the decision in this manner leaves the organization with fewer bruised egos, less contentiousness, and more good will. In decision making the Japanese endeavor to concentrate on the overall goals of the organization, minimize polarization, and find the one solution most likely to succeed. Information gathering is ideally suited to these goals.

Furthermore, the widespread participation of all levels of a group in the process helps to increase group members' commitment to a decision. When a company decision is made to enter a certain market or start a new production line, the employee does not need to be told the explanation, for he already knows it. A citizen of a community may not expect to have as much input into decisions as specialists, but when he learns of the final decision about the new transport or construction project, he typically knows enough about the reasons for the decision that his confidence in the basic civic institutions are reinforced. When the ordinary citizen hears about an important national decision, he knows enough about the basic reasons to identify very strongly with his government and be ready to implement the decision. Japanese loyalty and patriotism are not inherited but are constantly recreated by organizational practice, and perhaps no practice is more important than the shared search for more information and the optimal solutions to which it leads.

4

The State: Meritocratic Guidance and Private Initiative

IN PUBLIC OPINION POLLS the Japanese express dissatisfaction with almost everything. The government is too dominated by big business, politicians are selfish, bureaucrats are arrogant, academics are impractical. Modern civilization is too materialistic, inflation is rampant, housing is crowded. Even at the height of economic growth, when households were polled respondents expressed dissatisfaction with the economy. But ask the informed Japanese who has traveled abroad if America and European governments have handled problems like economic growth, urban renewal, pollution control, and crime with greater success, and the reply is likely to be a sigh of benevolent sympathy, ending with a rhetorical query as to why those countries have become so decadent. Other countries are of course much worse off, the speaker reluctantly acknowledges—and then quickly returns to what really interests him: what is wrong with Japan. A foreigner can only wish his government had such problems.

What factors explain how the Japanese government handles contemporary problems with such relative success? How do the Japanese select their leaders and train them to deal with these problems so well? How do leaders avoid becoming overextended while assuming responsibility for almost all developments affecting Japan in the entire world? How does the bureaucracy maintain the power to accomplish all this without becoming corrupt and without alienating the people? How is the central government able to control national developments without destroying local initiative?

FUNNEL TO THE TOP: HIGHEST ABILITY,
BROADEST EXPERIENCE, LONGEST SERVICE

One can distinguish two key groups of decision makers in the Japanese government: the top politicians, including the prime minister and other key cabinet members, and leading bureaucrats. As in other parlimentary democracies, the prime minister is elected by Diet members, but since the conservative Liberal Democratic Party (LDP) has dominated the Diet since 1955, in fact the Diet merely approves as prime minister the man LDP leaders (mostly Diet members) choose. The prime minister in turn selects his cabinet members, almost all of whom are also Diet members, who serve also as heads of various ministries and other agencies. By custom, leading cabinet members are generally LDP politicians who have their own factions.

The politicians make many important political decisions, but compared to the American government the top politicians have little leverage over the bureaucracy. The prime minister may appoint one politician to be minister and another parlia- mentary vice-minister in each ministry, but there are no other political appointments in the ministry, and the person who really runs it is the administrative vice-minister, the highest career officer in the ministry. The key decisions in the ministry are made by the permanent bureaucrats rather than by the politicians of the Diet and the cabinet.

Not only is the central bureaucracy much more powerful than in the American system, but other parts of the govern- ment, like the judiciary and local government, are much weaker. The top cabinet officials have considerable power, but the Diet is relatively weak compared to the American Congress, and most of the legislation is in fact drafted by bureaucrats rather than by Diet members.

Leading bureaucrats invariably have attended the best universities and have risen through the ranks in a carefully prescribed fashion. Tokyo University students are acknowledged to be at the apex of the two million students in Japanese universities. Entrance to Tokyo University is strictly by achievement tests that demonstrate uncommon ability and consummate determination. Within Tokyo University, the ablest students enter the Law Faculty, which in fact provides broad training for public administration, with secondary emphasis on political science and law. The top graduates of the Law Faculty enter the most prestigious ministries (Finance, International Trade and Industry, Foreign Affairs) and agencies (Economic Planning, Land, Environmental), providing they pass the ministerial written examination and demonstrate poise, breadth, and commitment in interviews. Of the twenty-odd students entering a key ministry in the elite track each year, perhaps fifteen come from the Tokyo University Law Faculty. This reflects greater openness than in the past, when that figure might have been as high as eighteen or nineteen. Now five or six might have been top students at other national universities like Hitotsubashi and Kyoto, at private universities like Keio and Waseda, or at the Economics Faculty of Tokyo University. This selection procedure ensures that elite bureaucrats are not only extremely able but are also protected by an aura of respect, rivaled perhaps only by the elite bureaucrats of France. America has elite political appointees commonly paid more than the highest paid Japanese bureaucrats, but they are not meritocratically selected, professionally trained, or subject to career discipline. Perhaps the closest American analogy would be law school graduates selected to clerk for Supreme Court

Justices, but in Japan this talent is disciplined within an organization and kept together until retirement.

The five-hundred-odd elite-track bureaucrats in a given
ministry are generalists, stratified by seniority based on year of
entry to the ministry. By custom they come to work as late as
ten o'clock every morning, an hour or so later than ordinary
ministry employees. Ordinary employees leave at five or six,
but the elite rarely leave work before nine or ten o'clock at
night. It is difficult to get ordinary bureaucrats to work on
Saturday without special compensation, but elite bureaucrats,
who are not officially required to work on weekends, rarely
miss a Saturday and rarely leave before two or three o'clock
in the afternoon. They are always available for extra duty,
and when the work load is especially demanding, they sleep
overnight at the ministry on specially provided cots. Although
their salaries rise with seniority, they are paid less than their
counterparts in private industry. Their offices are modest, and
they have only minimal entertainment allowances. There is no
statutory retirement, but elite bureaucrats invariably retire by
their mid-fifties at the latest. Ordinary bureaucrats sometimes
continue working even past sixty-five. Equally dedicated bureaucrats may be found in other countries, but all Japanese
elite bureaucrats in major ministries are expected to display
such dedication. The bureaucrats are fully aware that they are
dealing with important problems, and they take pride in their
successful handling of difficult issues.

The esprit that unites a ministry's five hundred or so elite
bureaucrats rests on their sense of group mission. Although not
immune from political pressures, bureaucrats do not hesitate to
unite against politicians who obstruct their perceived mission.
Responsibility for success in any important matter rests with
a work unit, and all in the unit are judged by their unit's
contribution to the ministry. Superiors do not promote someone who cannot win the liking and cooperation of his peers,

for an individual's value to his unit is determined by his capacity to work effectively with his peers, his superiors, and his subordinates. Each bureaucrat is personally identified with the mission of his work unit and of the ministry as a whole.

Ministries rotate all elite bureaucrats through a prescribed course, with terms of two to four years. After an initial apprentice position in the ministry, the future leaders are commonly assigned to regional posts, overseas study posts, and a variety of key sections within the ministry. After two or three terms of this kind, the elite are subdivided into ordinary elite and especially promising elite. Especially promising elite rotate through a term as a special assistant in the ministry secretariat or another highly prestigious position. By the time ministry officials reach their thirties they can identify those in their age group who are most likely to fill the top posts two decades later. At about age fifty, the top several in the age group advance to become chiefs of the most important divisions, and all others who entered the ministry the same year retire. Several years later consensus begins to jell about who would make the best vice-minister in his age group, and the administrative vice-minister chooses his successor, who becomes the most powerful person in the ministry. All remaining peers resign, not because of an official rule but because of custom and because they will receive high positions in private firms or public corporations or will become politicians. They are chosen by these other organizations for their access to the ministry as well as for their ability, and therefore the ex-bureaucrat wants to keep good relations with his former co-workers.

As an age group progresses through the ministry, the field of candidates for eventual vice-minister narrows rapidly, so that the top three or four contenders have about twenty years to prepare themselves once they know they are serious candidates for the office. Japanese bureaucrats are constantly amazed at the power the American government grants to cabinet

members and department heads who have so little governmental experience and so little preparation for the position.
How can the outsider, whether he is a lawyer, academic, or
businessman, know enough to do his job well? How can he
successfully make use of so much authority when he lacks the
intimate personal relationships in every section to ensure that
absolutely reliable information will be channeled to him? Or
as they put it to American visitors, not entirely cynically, "We
are amazed how much talented outsiders can achieve in your
system and what fresh ideas they bring to their organization."

Over the years leading bureaucrats develop close relationships with their age peers in other ministries as well as their
own as they all rise simultanously. In many cases these relationships began among classmates at the Law Faculty of Tokyo
University or even among classmates at the small number of
elite high schools. To be sure, the intimacy among bureaucrats
of different ministries is rarely on the same level as that among
those within a ministry, but there are a variety of formal and
informal events that enable the elite of the ministries to get to
know one another. This makes possible a level of understanding and exchange of information that goes well beyond formal
documents and formal meetings. It also facilitates more accurate predictions of the actions and responses of other ministries.
By the time they are in their forties, leading bureaucrats in one
ministry try to find occasions to socialize with leading bureaucrats of the same age in other ministries, for it makes their
work go more smoothly, and this will become even more important when they reach really top positions.

In Washington, D.C., it is conventional wisdom that a
new administration should appoint new department secretaries
with a new vision that can overcome bureaucratic lethargy. In
the Japanese view, the American president's power to make
political appointments for the top positions in the departments
of the American government renders them completely depen-

dent on the president and robs the bureaucracy of its daring, autonomy, and, in the long run, talent. High-level Japanese bureaucrats, having complete job security and a group esprit, are able to achieve a self-confident and dynamic leadership that, in their view, would be destroyed if they had to toady to high-level outside appointees; yielding top authority in ministries to outside amateurs would be a disaster.

How then does a Japanese ministry achieve the freshness and receptivity to public opinion for which Americans feel they must look to outsiders and periodic shakeups? First, since the elite core is relatively small, it is not bogged down in the many administrative details confronting the larger group of lower-level officials. It has the security, the ability, and an ethos that enable it to concentrate on what is good for the nation as a whole. Second, Japanese bureaucrats constantly meet with journalists, politicians, and deliberative councils, and these meetings force them to account for their ministry's performance and planning. Top leaders often gather in interministry groups like the weekly meeting of administrative vice-ministers, where they confront common problems. For their ministries to maintain prestige in such meetings, the vice-ministers must be responsive to the demands of the public and the other ministries. In general they have enough authority and success so they do not need to become defensive, but their performance in areas under their jurisdiction is constantly evaluated, and every ministry strives to be known for its achievements. With constant intimate, informal interaction, a climate of opinion develops among leaders in business, politics, and the media which bureaucrats inevitably share. They do not want to stand apart, and no one needs to threaten bureaucrats with loss of job, for the approval of others and the internal desire for achievement provide more than adequate motivation.

How do Japanese ministries assure this vigor and morale among their employees? Because retirement of the elite is at an early age, power is invariably in the hands of young officials at the prime of their life who expect to live to see the consequences of their policies. In addition, in a small group of elite with close personal contact, the esteem of co-workers is of extreme importance, and maintenance of this esteem requires hard work and sensitivity to others. Frequent informal activities like mahjong, bar hopping, parties, golf, and weekend trips provide tension release, and fellow workers tend to offer more emotional support than in an American office, where options for pursuing one's career without going through the immediate work group create conflicts with group commitment. Furthermore, the elite bureaucrat enjoys a prestige that extends far beyond mere utilitarian acceptance of his authority. His family are buoyed by his status and share in his success, and in turn they are able to provide him with support and tolerate his extraordinarily long hours of work.

Politicians respect the ability of bureaucrats and recognize that they need their good will. Diet members have no independent research staff and rely on bureaucrats for specialized staff work. Politicians who try to work around a bureaucrat are likely to have the whole bureaucracy poised to retaliate by embarrassing the politician at the first opportunity. A Diet member may, for example, be given incomplete briefings by bureaucrats so that he can easily be made to appear foolish and ill-informed in Diet interpellation. It rarely comes to such a showdown, however, because politicians realize the advantage of maintaining the cooperation of the bureaucrat. They will want the bureaucracy to support construction projects in their locality or stand up for rice price supports. The two political appointments in each ministry, the minister and parliamentary vice-minister, have certain prerogatives on certain ministry issues like local construction projects, rice price supports, aid to small businessmen, and increase in welfare payments that are close to the heart of the politician. When it comes to the

balancing of interests between farmers and small and big business, the politicians have considerable say if it does not greatly
affect the budget. However, when it comes to the basic
administrative work of the ministry, politicians know they
must defer to the administrative vice-minister and the bureaucrats beneath him.

Even the prime minister's office has only a limited research
capacity, and while it has considerable say in large issues close
to the heart of politicians, it rarely tries to second-guess the
bureaucracy. Lacking the staff to make independent analysis,
the prime minister's office must ally with the ministries rather
than work around them. The three or four leading special
assistants to the prime minister, in the fields of Finance, Foreign
Affairs, and Home Affairs, are selected by the respective ministries to represent them and serve as a liaison between themselves and the prime minister. To be sure, they must be able
to work closely with the prime minister, but they are not
perceived as special assistants primarily loyal to the prime
minister but as representatives of their ministries who provide
the liaison to the prime minister in their areas of specialization.
Indeed, the prime minister is not expected to formulate policy
statements of his own. Rather, he works closely with the
bureaucracy and enunciates what various ministries advise him
to. In short, the bureaucracy is granted the prestige and authority necessary to sustain high group morale and achieve a
high level of performance.

The grooming of leading candidates for prime minister is
as thorough and almost as free of surprise as the grooming of
leading bureaucrats. The route is not necessarily connected to
university attendance, but the potential prime minister must
have approximately twenty years of prescribed positions behind him. The specialized training begins when he becomes a
faction leader in the LDP. The faction is, in effect, a personal
support group for a potential prime minister, for faction

members are pledged to vote for him as prime minister and the leader in turn gives financial assistance to the members and helps place them in good assignments within the Diet.

People who become faction leaders are one of two types. One, the "pure politician," becomes a Diet member at a young age and rises within the Diet. By his third or fourth term, with six or more years of Diet experience, a promising young Diet member may be selected by senior leaders of the LDP to be parliamentary vice-minister of one of the ministries. After serving successfully as parliamentary vice-minister in several ministries, he may inherit a faction from its retired leader or split off and form his own faction. Although factions were theoretically abolished in 1976, old faction alignments have not disappeared, and promising young politicians now head clubs which operate like factions, looking after their members' interests while cooperating with other LDP factions against opposition parties.

The second type of potential prime minister, the ex-bureaucrat, enters the Diet later, after serving in the bureaucracy. After some years in the Diet, a promising ex-bureaucrat may inherit a faction or split off from a senior faction leader to form his own. In recent years those who have aspired to be politicians and who have the qualifications to be bureaucrats have first served some years in the bureaucracy to acquire prestige and experience. At an early age, often in their thirties, they respond to a good opportunity to become a Diet member in order to gather Diet seniority and become a major leader. Of the several faction leaders, generally the ex-bureaucrats have the greatest chance of becoming prime minister. They have a wealth of experience in the actual operations of the government as well as impeccable credentials and university training, and they are freer of the petty political obligations that weigh down politicians who rise through the ranks. Since the mid-1950s only two prime ministers, Miki and Tanaka, were not former bureaucrats. They rose to power under special circumstances, and the experience of the Liberal Democratic Party under their leadership makes it likely that prime ministers in the near future will be ex-bureaucrats.

Whether he is a pure politician or an ex-bureaucrat, the promising faction leader must first serve a minimum of several months, but usually longer, in at least half a dozen key positions before he may be considered for the prime ministership. These positions include secretary-general of the Liberal Democratic Party and minister of the top ministries (Finance, Ministry of International Trade and Industry, Foreign Affairs, Economic Planning Agency) and perhaps some other ministries. As secretary-general of the party, he acquires experience in money raising and party affairs. As a minister, he does not direct the basic work of the ministry, which is the responsibility of the administrative vice-minister, but he must be aware of the major policy lines within the ministry, and he must work closely both with senior men of the ministry and with party leaders in affairs related to the ministry. As minister, he must be sufficiently familiar with ministry affairs to make policy addresses and answer questions in public on important issues confronting the ministry. While serving in these positions, the aspiring prime minister also gains experience directing his faction and looking after the interests of the faction members.

Which faction leader already rotated through these positions is selected to become prime minister depends on seniority and capacity to work with other top leaders as well as political considerations such as factional power and alignments, mood, timing, and public popularity. The final selection of the prime minister is de facto made by certain elder statesmen in the party, but their choice is narrowly circumscribed by these political considerations. In the past twenty years one compromise candidate has been elected: Prime Minister Miki. There had been a draw between two leading nominees, and the party selected Miki as the third choice. Yet even he had served in each of the various positions considered to be prerequisites to high office.

By the time a prime minister takes office, therefore, he has served in all the most prestigious ministries, in the top party position, and in key Diet positions. Unlike equally homogeneous Great Britain, where party leaders and bureaucrats have virtually no informal social interaction, he will have benefitted from decades of close contact between politicians and bureaucrats. He is familiar with the issues and knows key bureaucrats and party leaders personally, having served over many of them. For informal information and advice he can draw on his former personal assistants in each ministry and on his friends in the media who formerly covered his activities and now cover various parts of the government.

By letting LDP leaders select the prime minister from among themselves, the Japanese do not risk the election of a top official who has charismatic appeal but is unable to work effectively in the central government. Rather, they choose a politically experienced and highly able leader who is a known quantity, one who can work harmoniously with the various ministries. His knowledge of policy and personnel may not be fully adequate for him to act independently in matters of important policy, but he can make excellent use of experts beneath him. The Japanese marvel that in the United States a man may be elected president who has no experience in the Washington bureaucracy, or no experience in the national capital at all, and that such an outsider can set policy and tell experienced bureaucrats what to do. Such a pattern, in their view, would destroy the pride and enthusiasm of leading bureaucrats. It could lead to amateurish decisions and to policies tied too closely to a single viewpoint. The lack of seasoned judgment and predictability that such a pattern might produce could jeopardize stable alliances with foreign countries.

Boundless Scope and Measured Encouragement: The Approach to the Private Sector

Since the late nineteenth century, when it became clear that competition alone did not sufficiently serve the public interest, the burgeoning American bureaucracy has developed and administered increasingly numerous and complex regulations designed to tame monopolies and curb the evils of business. The assumption has been that many businesses, if left to their own devices, would take advantage of the government and the people. The job of the regulatory agencies is to oversee the business community and uncover deceptions; the spirit of the regulated organization is to provide the minimum of information and to comply with as few rules as it can legally get away with. If at times former regulators enter the ranks of the regulated and the regulated corrupt the regulators, this is seen as merely an imperfection. When in industry related to the military the Defense Department encourages and strengthens certain firms, this is not considered fully legitimate, but it does not alter the fundamental stance of the government concerning business, which is to curb evils by regulation.

By contrast, the bureaucratic elite of Japan, which since the late nineteenth century has been trying to encourage modernization, tries to provide a framework that best enables business to prosper in the long run. Japan is not without regulatory agencies, and indeed parts of the American bureaucracy encourage business; but the Japanese elite bureaucrats' sense of responsibility for overall economic success is broader and deeper. Each ministry puts out one or more annual white papers which provide a tour of the horizon in each major area of the economy and society, reporting on annual developments and giving guidelines for future projects. Bureaucrats in a given agency accept responsibility for everything that occurs in Japan within their sphere of jurisdiction and sometimes outside Japan as well. If terrorists explode a bomb at Narita Airport, the highest officials in the National Police Agency are held accountable; if the yen is revalued, Ministry of Finance officials are criticized; if a senior White House advisor makes a surprise visit to Peking, American specialists in the Foreign Ministry suffer for not knowing; if steel is in oversupply, MITI officials are blamed; if trading companies withhold goods from the market to raise prices, the cabinet is in trouble.

Japanese bureaucrats in each sphere are expected to think through all major issues in their sphere and to develop and implement long-term plans. Since 1975 the annual volume on directions for the economy published by MITI, the most important ministry supervising industry, has been called *Long-range Vision*, but the title merely formalizes what has long been a basic mission of all Japanese bureaucrats concerned with the economy. The government rarely subsidizes private business directly, but bureaucrats are relentless in their efforts to create conditions for business that are necessary to realize their long-term visions.

The constant interaction among elite bureaucrats reinforces concern with long-range issues. When they assemble, formally and informally, what they have in common is the mission of the ministry as a whole. Since they are a small group and know each other intimately, and since they are rotated frequently and interact constantly, they cannot avoid being aware of one another's responsibilities. Compared to America's Department of Commerce, for example, where an official can become lost in the work of his section without considering all relevant parts of the department, the elite Japanese bureaucrat inevitably thinks about how his work fits in with that of his colleagues he sees every day. Just as inevitably, permanent employment leads him to think about the long-range issues confronted by his ministry, and interaction between seniors and juniors ensures stability of ministerial leadership, institutional memory, and continuity of policy.

Because political leaders also have considerable continuity and in any case rarely interfere with the main trends of ministerial policy, the continuity of policy is unimpaired by elections, cabinet shuffles, or short-range political pressures. Finance Ministry officials who make up the budget, for example, make marginal allowances for requests of politicians, but if politicians endeavor to go beyond these margins, bureaucrats are known to denounce cabinet interference, proclaiming that the budget "is not a political matter and politicians should not interfere with the government." Japanese bureaucrats yield to no one in the passion that can be generated when their jurisdictional authority is challenged. In America, on the other hand, the White House, drawing on requests from various branches of the government, puts together annual budgets that are less insulated from political pressures. The Office of Management and the Budget, located within the White House, does not have a strong independent authority that would enable it to resist political pressures that greatly disturb the budgeting process. Japanese bureaucrats, less buffeted by sudden new proposals by political leaders and special political interests, are able to provide predictable leadership for the private sector, which can then plan accordingly.

Japanese priorities for economic growth are undiluted with concern for military security. In America, since World War II military security has been judged to be of preeminent importance, consuming a high proportion of our national budget and of the time of our ablest leaders. In Japan the military has claimed less than one percent of the gross national product each year and commanded correspondingly little attention. Because of its small geographical area, Japan is the country most vulnerable to nuclear weapons, and hence Japanese defense specialists have concluded that possessing weapons invites more risks than not possessing them. Of all the major powers, Japan is the only one that has constitutionally renounced the use of offensive forces and prohibited stationing forces overseas. It is tempting to argue that Japan has had a free ride in defense as a result of the American defensive umbrella, although Japan does bear a high portion of the costs of American personnel stationed in Japan. As the junior partner in a military alliance, the Japanese are appropriately deferential, but they are nevertheless convinced that Americans have assumed too forward a military posture and have spent too much on military hardware. Japan is much closer to China and Russia than the United States, but with some minor exceptions, as when the Soviet Union attacks Japanese fishing boats and its airplanes invade Japanese air space, the Japanese perception of military threat is lower than America's. For years Americans appeared more anxious to keep troops in Japan than the Japanese were to have them there. In the view of Japanese leaders, raising Japan's military expenses above the level of one percent of its GNP would not appreciably increase security. They see maintaining good relations with other countries to guarantee the flow of natural resources as more important for national security than military weaponry. In a sense Japan's military policy is a bold enterprise, an effort to be the only major power that is not a major military power. It is a boldness that has high payoffs, direct and indirect, for the private sector.

For over two decades after World War II, Japan, pursuing economic growth with a passion that America reserved for fighting Communism, turned a higher proportion of its GNP and intellectual effort toward basic internal development than did the United States. Parts of the American electronics industry, for example, found it desirable to produce for government contracts which guaranteed a certain amount of profit rather than for the consumer market. They therefore neglected the international competition in consumer electronics, whereas Japanese firms were forced to be competitive and captured an increasing share of the market. When the American government invests in research and development, the highest proportion goes to military, space, or basic research. The Japanese government, on the other hand, concentrates research expenditure in areas where there is a high probability of a substantial return for Japanese companies but where investment costs are sufficiently great and risky as to be otherwise unattractive to private industry. The goal of the government's own research institutes is not to increase governmental control over these areas but to make the research results available to companies that can best use them to enhance the competitiveness of the economy or the industrial sector as a whole. This is true for those institutes that are part of the government, such as MITI's Agency of Industrial Science and Technology, as well as those institutes financed by other sources, such as those institutes under MITI, the Ministry of Transportation, and the Ministry of Agriculture that are financed respectively by bicycle racing, boat racing, and horse racing.

While accepting responsibility for virtually all developments in society, Japanese bureaucrats try to avoid becoming overextended, maximizing the areas where they provide guidance and minimizing the activities they manage directly. Like the United States and unlike many European countries, Japan has few government-controlled companies in basic industries. Iron, steel, mining, and petroleum are all in the hands of private companies. Furthermore, an even larger share of the Japanese economy is in private hands than in America. Even during the rapid growth period of 1955 to 1964, with considerable government investment in construction to support economic growth, the Japanese tax burden was only 18.5 percent of the GNP, compared to 26.5 percent in the United States and much higher rates in Western Europe. In 1973 it was 22 percent, compared with 28 percent in the United States and much higher rates in Western Europe. In part this is because of the low defense and welfare budgets but also because bureaucrats try to keep government expenditures low in order to keep the Japanese economy competitive internationally.

The branches of the bureaucracy concerned with the economy all play a role in providing guidance to this large private sector. The Economic Planning Agency, established in 1955 when economic priorities shifted from recovery and control of inflation to economic growth, provides indicative planning for the entire economy. The agency's original staff included bureaucrats drawn from MITI and the Finance Ministry, and it continues to work closely with these ministries. Its multiyear plans help provide flexible guidelines for priorities of financing, foreign exchange, and technology transfer. It does not try to manage the economy directly but to provide targets reflecting long-term trends and specifying what would be necessary for balanced national development. It is in effect a point of communication, coordinating estimates of future growth made by government branches and the business community. It helps draw attention to various needs and helps shape the thinking of the Development Bank, the Export–Import Bank, the Bank of Japan, the Finance Ministry, MITI, and large corporations about what is required for a certain level of growth. Since it does not really plan the economy, it is very flexible in adjusting its estimates to changing conditions, and these changes are therefore quickly known by all concerned so they can make appropriate adjustments.

The ministry that takes the greatest initiative in guiding industrial growth is MITI. MITI officials are so persistent in their efforts to look after the welfare of Japanese industry that they are dubbed by their countrymen as *kyōiku mama*, overanxious mothers who hover over their children and push them to study. They endeavor to push the pace of modernization ahead of market forces by setting high standards for modernization of plants and equipment and by promoting mergers of companies that lack the capital to meet those standards. They boldly try to restructure industry, concentrating resources in areas where they think Japan will be competitive internationally in the future. As wages rose to Western levels in the late 1960s, MITI bureaucrats tried to reconcentrate resources in industries that were capital-intensive rather than labor-intensive. After the 1973 oil shock they greatly accelerated plans to push Japan into service- and knowledge-intensive industries rather than energy-intensive ones. MITI officials consider it their responsibility to assist companies in declining industries to merge or go out of business while encouraging new ones to move into the localities and employ the personnel who were laid off. If conditions are not serious enough to shut down a whole industry, they work out a "depression cartel": agreement among companies in a depressed sector to reduce production capacity, with the reduction distributed relatively equally among the companies. MITI also tries to rescue basic industries that have been harmed by some exogenous forces, like petrochemicals after the oil shock.

To strengthen Japan's competitive power and increase Japan's independence, MITI promotes oil companies that are strictly Japanese, not affiliated with "foreign majors." It encourages cooperation among Japanese companies to exploit opportunities for economic development abroad, to ensure the supply of raw materials into Japan, and to help secure markets for Japanese firms abroad. In the mid-1970s, as foreign capital became plentiful and markets for manufactured goods saturated, MITI helped form consortia of Japanese industries to undertake large construction projects and encouraged private insurance companies to provide appropriate coverage, reducing the risks of such ventures. When foreign countries demand restrictions on Japanese exports, MITI officials consider it their responsibility to help formulate an agreement among Japanese companies in an industrial trade sector to restrict exports proportionately across the board. In areas where Japan has no choice but to liberalize, MITI officials nudge industries to prepare themselves for the threat of the international market and exert their influence to postpone liberalization in growth sectors until the companies become fully competitive on the international market.

MITI's aim is not to reduce competition among Japanese companies but to create the strongest possible companies with the greatest competitive potential. Perhaps the nearest American analogy is the National Football League or the National Basketball Association. League officials establish rules about size of team, recruitment, and rules of play that result in relatively equally matched teams of great competitive abilities. They do not interfere in internal team activity or tell a coach how to run his team, although they do try to provide information that would enable the coach to improve. MITI is divided into branches corresponding to the major industrial sectors, and firms generally specialize in a particular industrial sector. In each sector, the MITI branch tries to create the most effective league of competing companies. Through these branches, MITI considers the overall prospects of an industrial sector and the potential of companies within that sector. It helps ensure that the promising companies get the necessary capital, land, foreign exchange, technological know-how, and access to resources and markets to make best use of their potential. When necessary, MITI officials help to arrange funding from such semigovernmental organizations as the Development Bank, the Export–Import Bank, and the Asian Development Bank. More commonly, banks, whether semigovernmental or private, take the initiative themselves. MITI approves of strong, promising companies, and banks compete eagerly to give loans to the companies that have MITI's blessing. When the government sells reclaimed land or refilled land to private companies, priority goes not to the highest bidder but to companies that can best make use of it. When foreign technology is available for purchase, MITI officials try to see that it is bought at the lowest possible price by the company that can best utilize it without overwhelming its competitors. MITI uses the same criterion in deciding which firms should be allowed to affiliate with which foreign firms.

MITI relegates to itself the right to enunciate very detailed rulings about what companies can and cannot do, but it does so only with a broad base of support from leading firms in an industrial sector. It deals with the dangers of monopolistic restraint of competition by requiring handicaps for big companies that control too large a share of a given market. So as to contain the damage to small commercial businesses and bring order to their gradual decline, it decrees how large a department store may be and where it can be located. Since pollution became an issue, it decrees whether the economic benefits of a given factory outweigh the potential harm to the environment before it grants plant construction permits.

MITI's statutory power to control these developments is very limited, and efforts to extend that authority were rebuffed by the business community, other ministries, and the Diet. It does have some statutory power in limited areas: its officials can reserve licensing for companies that meet certain standards; new plants that pollute must have MITI approval before construction; it is allowed to form depression and modernization cartels, albeit with some counterpressures from the Fair Trade Commission; it controls some research expenses; and it grants approval to licensing agreements and to companies that affiliate with foreign companies. But overwhelmingly the success of the ministry is derived not from statutory rules but from its efforts at administrative guidance and from the voluntary cooperation of the business community.

How then does MITI achieve this "voluntary" cooperation? In the first place, companies know that MITI is primarily
interested in the welfare of companies in the respective industrial sectors. Second, MITI provides superior information
and analysis. Third, within a given industrial sector MITI
bureaucrats and company officials at a variety of levels meet
constantly, formally and informally, and develop mutual
understandings. MITI officials of a given rank generally interact on an equal level with company officials who are slightly
older, higher in rank, and far better paid. A bureau chief in
MITI responsible for a given industrial sector may be in his
late forties but he may confer with company managing directors and presidents fifteen years his senior. Section chiefs and
section members may meet as equals with division chiefs in a
company. And while they may drink together in a comfortable
private room, stretching out on the *tatami* floor of a private
restaurant, the parties on both sides are fully aware that their
purpose is business. The relaxed, intimate atmosphere is a means
to achieve frank exchange of information and views. A mid-
level MITI official not uncommonly spends three or four
evenings a week in such informal gatherings with appropriate
business representatives. In America, a private company's foot-
ing the bill might be considered conflict of interest, but in
Japan it is clear that these MITI officials are not in collusion
with a specific company. Rival companies entertain them
similarly, but officials do not base their ultimate decision on
the quality of the entertainment or their personal preferences.
They are human and admittedly not immune from tilting close
decisions, but decisions are made by groups in consultation
with the industrial sector organization so that favoritism is
difficult; the main criterion for all decisions is the long-term
contribution to Japanese industry as a whole. Many leading
MITI officials go to work for private companies after retirement, and while outright collusion is difficult, they can be very

useful in facilitating communication between MITI and companies in need of improved channels.

Fourth, company officials know that when they request licenses, permits, choice locations, and tax breaks, MITI will respond more favorably to cooperative companies. Even if MITI eventually grants the necessary permissions to an uncooperative company, the harassing tactics of delaying, requesting more information, raising new questions, and creating uncertainties are ordinarily enough to inspire companies to be more cooperative.

Finally, MITI generally works in harmony with the consensus in an industrial sector or in the business community as a whole. In a given industrial sector there exists a social community of leading firms whose opinions carry great weight in many circles—with politicians, bankers, and other businessmen. Everyone asumes that the companies in an industrial sector and the corresponding branch of MITI have sufficient continuity in personnel to maintain, in effect, an institutional memory. Cooperative companies are eventually rewarded, uncooperative ones punished. Through cooperation with the Finance Ministry, MITI may determine a company's allowable deductions and the amount of depreciation permitted. Also in cooperation with the Finance Ministry, which directs the Bank of Japan, which in turn lends money to commercial banks, MITI maintains leverage over lending. Banks could refuse to extend loans to a company not supported by MITI and a trade association. However, banks rarely need to consider the ultimate sanction of recalling loans, MITI rarely needs to consider refusing permits, and an industrial sector organization does not often need to consider threatening a company with expulsion. Whatever implicit sanctions are conveyed in granting or withholding goodwill, it is the maintenance of goodwill that consciously motivates the company leaders. Since MITI generally acts in concert with the industrial sector organization or the business community, it can ordinarily count on the support of the majority of firms in disciplining an unreliable member. Indeed, many decisions made by MITI might more properly be viewed as MITI enunciation of a consensus among the most significant actors.

To provide feasible goals and issue such detailed decisions intelligently, MITI officials regularly collect an extraordinary amount of information. They keep up with foreign developments, especially in business, technology, and economics, reading not only foreign publications and government reports but unpublished papers by foreign scholars and researchers at think tanks. In addition to basic financial statements and other regular reports of developments in Japanese firms from various sectors, they require knowledge of the personal, social, and political relationships within a company and between companies. The agreements they promote among companies in a given industrial sector require a higher level of trust than can be achieved through formal contacts. When a specific issue arises, interested parties schedule even more informal gatherings than usual. When necessary, bureaucrats from other ministries join these meetings and other knowledgeable experts and men of influence are called in. Businessmen convene parallel meetings on related topics without bureaucrats present to reach understandings to be presented in later meetings with MITI officials. As a result, American government officials and businessmen negotiating economic matters feel at a great disadvantage because Japanese officials are much better informed, not only about Japanese companies but often about American companies, which are more reluctant to share information with government officials who may be more interested in regulating than assisting.

Some of the most intensive interaction between MITI and companies in a given sector occurs when a declining industrial sector needs help or a growing industry needs financing and other resources for modernization. In both cases, because companies alone cannot solve the problem, MITI officials naturally think of mergers as part of the solution. The process of exploring various possible mergers and organizing several strong companies from many smaller ones commonly takes several years and may take more than a decade. This kind of process requires very detailed knowledge of and constant interaction with all the key personalities involved. Even in the end MITI is not always entirely successful. It tried valiantly, for example, to reduce the number of major auto companies to two or three rather than the present six: Toyota, Nissan (Datsun), Honda, Isuzu, Mitsubishi, and Tōyō Kōgyō (Mazda). The primary question is how well the personnel, capital, and plants of the various companies supplement one another and how these resources can best be combined. Although MITI may help arrange tax breaks, capital funds, and technology transfer for merging companies and create obstacles for companies especially resistant to a reasonable merger, in the end companies merge only when they consider it in their interest to do so. In the course of this process, MITI encourages companies within the sector to hold discussions about possible merger and prods companies toward merger faster than they may wish to go. MITI officials generally approve any reasonable mergers worked out by the companies themselves. But the strong ties within a Japanese company make it difficult to discharge excess personnel even at a time of merger, and the fusion of two formerly tight-knit companies can result in cleavages between the two groups of personnel that remain for years or even decades. Personnel in a smaller company, naturally wary of being absorbed by a larger company, may offer formidable resistance. A foreigner observing the interaction between MITI and a resistant company would be hard put to describe the process as part of the cozy government–business partnership of "Japan, Inc.," and mighty MITI is not always victorious.

Whatever the issue, MITI officials do not approach their task legalistically. Their view is that rapidly changing conditions require more adjustment to individual predilections and special circumstances than is permitted by relying on legal precedent. They may draft a host of specific regulations that are later approved by the Diet, but such regulations serve as guidelines for standards and procedures without greatly restricting the scope of bureaucrats' decision making. They want to avoid too many minute regulations that might hamper their effectiveness and distract attention from the major issues affecting the larger purposes of their ministry. Important issues therefore are not resolved by courts or even by legal criteria but are settled on the basis of more complex judgments about world trends, market potential, political and financial support, and individual company capacity. Whereas in the United States, regulatory functions are usually independent of departments like commerce and work at cross purposes, in Japan the combination of regulatory and advisory functions within MITI helps ensure that regulations are administered in a way consistent with the ministry's overall purpose.

The pattern of relationships between MITI and the manufacturing sector is also found in the relationship of other ministries and the private sector in their jurisdiction. Other economic ministries like Finance, Construction, Transport, Posts and Telecommunications, and Agriculture, Forestry, and Fisheries accept broad responsibility for all developments in their sectors. The relationship between the Finance Ministry and banks and security companies is very similar to that between MITI and manufacturing companies. Its "window guidance" is analogous to MITI's administrative guidance, and it supervises a major league of twelve large commercial banks (city banks) and a host of smaller regional banks. Among the responsibilities of the Construction Ministry, for example, is ensuring that there are several strong companies to offer attractive bids for civil engineering and other construction projects.

The Ministry of Transport is mandated to develop modern air, railway, shipping, and motor transport. Japan Airlines, All-Japan Airways, and Toa Domestic Airlines monopolize air travel, but they operate as private companies, and government bureaucrats constantly encourage these airlines to provide efficient and modern domestic services at low costs, despite their strong support for Japan Airlines in international negotiations. In the 1950s a number of the private railway companies competed to become private airway carriers, but the Ministry of Transport determined that the domestic airline market (aside from special helicopter services, sight-seeing planes, and the like) was too small to support several competing companies and that one major international and two major domestic carriers could meet the demand with the greatest effectiveness. The Transport Ministry later established another international airline when Taiwan refused to permit Japan Airlines to service both Peking and Taiwan, but the Japanese airlines are essentially monopolistic. However, Japan Airlines requires the close cooperation and support of the Ministry of Transport, which therefore is able to encourage the company to supply inexpensive and efficient service.

The superiority of Japan's rail service to that of the United States cannot be attributed to superiority of government planning alone, although the programs of technology importation, research, planning, and construction required impressive coordination. Japan's population concentration, the high volume of intercity travel, and the interest in public transportation compared to American preference for automobiles permits a capital investment in rail services that the American public is not prepared to support. But even given this financial support, the Shinkansen bullet trains are a model of passenger transportation that may yet influence American patterns as energy problems affect passenger car travel.

A number of Japanese private railway companies (like Tōkyū, Seibu, Tōbu, Hankyū, Meitetsu) compete with the national service in regions where there are large numbers of commuters. The Ministry of Transport helped plan these regional systems, which are parallel in organization and purpose. The same company owns not only the individual railroad but real estate along the route, a department store, and sometimes hotels located at the main terminal. The company is profitable, even if it loses money on the running of the passenger line, because of the many passengers it carries from outlying areas to the main terminal where the department store is located. Compared to American private railways, this structure has helped to maintain effective and reasonably priced rail transport over the long term. The role of the ministerial elite lay not in managing the system but in devising the system and providing the facilities and encouragement so that private companies could make it work. Now that costs of rail transport are rising, the National Railways is also considering a series of money-making schemes in large terminal buildings to keep down costs.

The Ministry of Transport also oversees tourist and freight information. By 1970 the ministry had linked travel agents to all inns and hotels throughout the country by a single on-line or teleprinter reservation system. A computer system also keeps track of cargo assigned to each freight train throughout the country.

The modernization efforts of the Ministry of Agriculture, Forestry, and Fisheries are constrained by the government's policy of maintaining the small family farms in order to stabilize the rural family, the village, and the political support base of the Liberal Democratic Party. In the late 1950s, when farm technology first enabled the average rural family to farm far more than its own land (averaging about three acres), the government discouraged the consolidation of farms that would have permitted more efficient agriculture. Therefore, many rural men and women who might otherwise have moved to the city remained in the rural areas but began commuting to work in nearby towns and cities. This left farm work to the elderly. In an effort to make small-scale farming attractive and profitable during rapid economic growth, the government used the mechanism of high rice price subsidies, since almost ninety percent of the farm families were engaged in rice growing. The ministry bureaucrats, with the support of Diet members from rural districts, have maintained barriers on agricultural imports. But given this framework of small family farms and artificially high prices, the ministry has assisted in introducing modern fertilizers, hand cultivators, rice transplanters, and insecticides, and in educating farmers about the proper timing of such techniques. The result has been rapid diffusion of modern technology and a rapid rise in productivity per acre. The development and cultivation of new fruits and vegetables and the growth of dairy and beef farming have been rapid and extensive.

In the 1950s the Japanese government gave top priority to economic growth, to the neglect of wages, consumer goods, housing, welfare packages, and pollution control. However, in the 1960s capital for these social overhead expenses began to catch up and in the early 1970s sometimes grew more rapidly than the gross national product, albeit from a lower base. The leaders sometimes neglected these problems until they became intolerable, although one could defend their general strategy of first concentrating on the economic base and then, more recently, attacking these issues with the same gusto and creativity they previously concentrated on issues related to economic growth.

For example, the government leaders were initially slow in dealing with the issue of pollution. They had identified so much with the purposes of growth that initially they were reluctant to consider problems which would slow down growth. Death and disease from mercury poisoning were serious problems recognized by some Ministry of Health and Welfare bureaucrats long before most bureaucrats deigned to act. Local governments were concerned about air pollution in Tokyo, Yokkaichi, and elsewhere before the central government began to give the issue serious attention. By the early 1970s, however, central government bureaucrats mobilized to attack the problem with vigor. Japanese auto companies originally were no more eager than their American counterparts to accept the stiff auto pollution standards demanded by the government, but when Honda announced it was prepared to meet them, its Japanese competitors had no choice but to follow quickly. As a result, Japan has auto emission standards that meet rules as strict as those of the original Muskie Law proposal in the United States. America has yet to achieve these high goals. Similarly, after consultation with appropriate industry leaders, Environment Agency bureaucrats created standards for smoke emissions from newly opened plants that are the most rigid in the world.

One of Japan's most imaginative pollution control plans is built on the principle that requires automobile producers to pay an emission tax and polluters to pay the cost of medical care and compensation to victims. Since the number of pollution victims in a given area is commonly more than public health or court officials can examine individually to determine precisely the source and amount of pollution, bureaucrats worked out a system to determine disaster areas with geographic boundaries. All polluters in the area are required to contribute to a fund to compensate victims certified by local health officials as suffering from a pollution-related disease.

In this way, the Japanese avoid the complex litigation, investigation, and expense required in America when individuals sue insurance companies to provide compensation. As a result, companies are eager to control emission to avoid both monetary payments and adverse publicity. Some Americans concerned with pollution are beginning to urge that America consider similar measures.

When the costs of pollution control are particularly expensive in industries considered basic to the economy, the government helps to arrange low-interest loans to facilitate modernization. To hasten progress in confronting pollution, government bureaucrats in the past have also worked closely with the business community, which has contributed financially to basic research on pollution control and borne the major share of pollution abatement costs.

A 1975 OECD report estimated that Japan was spending about three percent of its GNP on antipollution expenses, several times as much as any other member country, and noted that "anti-pollution investments have been much more important in Japan than elsewhere." The report concluded that "Japan has undoubtedly reversed rising pollution trends for a number of pollutants, particularly in the fields of air pollution and of toxic chemicals." And, despite the higher concentration of industrial production, "By now the air breathed in the main Japanese cities is quite as 'clean' as the air of American, French, British, or German cities," an impressive accomplishment given the highest concentration of industry in the smallest space.

Bureaucrats are concerned with issues as diverse as modernizing fisheries and shipping fleets, redistricting and consolidating geographic administrative units, equalizing standards of living, maintaining social equilibrium, and elevating educational standards throughout the country. Yet the elite corps has remained small in size. Bureaucrats conceive visions, but whenever possible they pass the implementation to the private sector, where concern for profit heightens motivation and increases efficiency. They place key former bureaucrats in high positions in these public corporations and retain budgetary supervision, thus ensuring that they remain responsive to bureaucratic initiatives. They monitor developments and provide nudges when necessary, but their role is more specialized. Like conductors, they know what music they want to hear, they worry about everything it takes to make good music in the end, and they try to work with each player to give his all while staying in tune with the other players. They do not try to be players themselves. In short, the bureaucratic elite neither reign nor rule but conceive, discuss, persuade, encourage. They bring the entire society within their scope of concern, but their genius lies in avoiding managing while creating the conditions for strong private players.

GUARDING THE GUARDIANS

Postwar bureaucrats are no longer above the political fray as sacred servants of the Imperial Way. But their extraordinary talents and contributions have provided them with an aura of authority that insulates them from the crudest of attacks. Big business leaders depend on them and politicians who reach high office are close to them, having succeeded by following the rules of a game that requires close cooperation with the bureaucracy. With elite bureaucrats thus protected from political pressures, how does Japan avoid a problem that has, as Michel Croizier shows, devastated France, the other country with a comparably elite bureaucracy: formation of a disruptive chasm that isolates various strata, dividing the elite bureaucracy and the people?

Japanese bureaucrats do have considerable authority, and they are not above flaunting their status. They may make powerful businessmen wait to see them, and few ordinary citizens would be so brash as to make direct requests of arrogant senior bureaucrats without some help from their local political representative. They can be abrupt when giving explanations of policy, impatient when asked their opinion, aloof when receiving a request. Yet their authority is not sufficient for them to give orders. In their search for information, for example, they depend on the voluntary cooperation of the private sector and they therefore must be more sensitive than French bureaucrats to their views.

The willingness of the private sector to cooperate with bureaucrats derives not so much from the formal authority of the bureaucrats as from the public's belief that the bureaucrat is doing the job properly. This in turn owes much to the activities of the Press Club located in each ministry, usually near the minister's and vice minister's offices. Here more than twenty reporters, one or more from each of the major Japanese papers, news agencies, radio, and television networks work full-time to cover the ministry. They are usually assigned here several years after starting work, and their term is commonly two years. At the ministry, they attend occasional official briefiings and keep track of ministry activities. They have access to major officials almost every week and may have special briefings daily. Through reading ministry reports, interviewing and socializing with officials, and exchanging information in the Press Club, the reporters soon develop a highly detailed understanding of affairs in the ministry. The reporter in the Press Club does not necessarily report everything, for he is constrained by the opinion of his colleagues in the Press Club, the ministry officials, and his editors, who weed out peculiar interpretations. But the editors expect him to report accurately the thinking of the ministry as a decision is being made. Bureaucrats notify reporters as they narrow down their options, and the journalist is able to prepare his readership for the ministry's final decision. In this way the reader follows the reasoning of the bureaucracy, and, as in the community decision on a transport system, he anticipates and understands the final outcome. In addition to articles reporting ministry thinking, the newspaper also publishes editorials concerned with the content, and the editorial writers do not hesitate to criticize bureaucratic decisions that are not in accord with public opinion. Editorials, unlike reporting, often have an antigovernment thrust, for everyone recognizes that some controversy and criticism of the government is necessary to sell newspapers.

Ordinarily the reporter must not publish "leaks" prematurely, but the bureaucrat must also play by the rules and disclose important developments. Japanese readers, more than American readers, expect the newspapers to present detailed information on the thinking of the bureaucracy, and if the bureaucrats clearly neglected the public interest, members of the press are expected to use their intimate knowledge or contacts with nonofficial sources to gain information. The long-term close relationship with officials leads to an undesirable lack of independent by-lined criticism in major newspapers, but reporters are also able to write more informally under a pseudonym in the numerous weeklies without jeopardizing their relationships with ministry officials. The weeklies carry gossipy criticism that bureaucrats can easily dismiss, but they also contain serious criticism not so easily dismissed when bureaucrats clearly depart from the public's perception of national interest.

Most of the public opinion polling in Japan is conducted by the newspapers or by the various ministeries and the prime minister's office. In the case of newspapers, this ensures widespread diffusion of poll results and makes it more difficult for newspaper articles and editorials to veer far from public opinion. The polls conducted under the guidance of the ministries and the prime minister's office survey opinion on major questions relevant to national policy. They provide a more direct input from public opinion to the bureaucracy than any mechanism in the United States and make it more difficult for bureaucrats to veer too far from the polls, the results of which are readily available to the public.

Diet interpellation is another mechanism for guarding the guardians. This gives opposition party members an opportunity to question LDP leaders on legislative matters, but since most legislation is prepared by the bureaucrats, they regard it as an examination of their work. Although Diet members are ordinarily reluctant to appear uninformed and may even consult with acquaintances in the bureaucracy about questions they should ask in public, the interpellation is by no means a sham. Bureaucrats are indeed worried about the fate of their legislation at the hands of the Diet. They complain of the long hours they must spend in the Diet and of the audacity of Diet members who disrupt or threaten to disrupt their well-reasoned plans, but they take the responsibility of appearing in the Diet very seriously. The Finance Ministry officials, for example, are always tense until the Diet has finally approved the annual budget, and as soon as the Diet passes the budget, it is announced on the Finance Ministry loudspeaker, whereupon the employees throughout the ministry break into applause. Opposition parties commonly use Diet interpellation to challenge and embarrass the LDP and the bureaucracy, and bureaucrats must therefore worry not only about their bill's passing but also about possible weak points that will delay passage and leave the bill open to criticism. As a result, even though Diet members may not be well-informed on all legislation, interpellation requires that each bill prepared by the bureaucracy be more or less acceptable to the public and defensible as a rational program for meeting national interests.

Deliberative councils (*shingikai*), composed of well-known private citizens to consider important issues confronting the country, serve as another check on the bureaucracy. They are analogous to presidential commissions or executive-branch advisory commissions in the United States, but they are used much more extensively. Every ministry except the Foreign Ministry has at least one deliberative council, and in most cases several, to deal with everything from current policy issues to broad questions such as government structure, industrial structure, and tax policy. There are over two hundred standing councils and in addition numerous ad hoc deliberative councils to consider special issues. By the time an issue reaches a deliberative council, bureaucrats prepare carefully by analyzing the basic issues, discerning how key groups stand on the issue, and anticipating major lines of criticism. The councils bring together some of the best informed and most interested parties in a particular sphere. Officially, deliberative council members are selected as individuals, but in fact the "individuals" are systematically selected from the major relevant organizations and interest groups. Councils concerned with wages, for example, include representatives of management and labor and also well-known social critics or professors representing the neutral public. These neutral participants in fact constitute the crucial swing-vote in determining the outcome of council deliberations.

The deliberative council officially acts only in an advisory capacity. It makes recommendations to the bureaucracy which in turn presents its proposals to the Cabinet or the Diet. But the conclusions of the deliberative councils are usually not too dissimilar to the views of the bureaucracy, although there is a great deal of variation in the power and independence of the various deliberative councils. Since the bureaucrats preparing the materials for the deliberative council often have in mind a fairly clear notion of the conclusions they would like the council to draw, they may select the kind of data and make the kinds of presentations that would tend to lead to these conclusions. They select the members of the council, who, though of different persuasions, are likely to be cooperative in reaching a conclusion without undue delay. Once the council has had its meetings, it is the bureaucrats who write the council reports. Ordinarily council members do not go over the final drafts of the report with great care, in effect granting the bureaucrats considerable leeway in choosing how to summarize the oral deliberations of the council.

Nonetheless, the deliberative council officials are qualified and respected individuals who would by no means agree with everything the bureaucracy might propose. When several possible solutions are almost equally plausible, the deliberative council is usually given the alternatives to debate. Even if it is easy for the bureaucracy to convince a majority of the council to support its viewpoint, there is always the possibility that another member of the council might take his case to the public. During the debates a council member has an opportunity to express his views on television and in the press, and a persuasive case against the bureaucracy's proposals could be embarrassing.

However cleverly bureaucrats might try to manipulate the process, the public airing ensures that their proposals be defensible when subject to public scrutiny. Even if deliberative council members do little more than choose between options outlined by the bureaucracy, public participation forces the bureaucracy to prepare these conclusions with great care. After the debates of the deliberative council are published, the public is able to understand the logic of the advice offered the bureaucracy. When the bureaucracy then makes its decision, the public has been prepared carefully for the conclusion and has a clear understanding of the reasons behind it; at this point it is not easy for Diet members to raise idiosyncratic objections. The public may have no particular respect for the politician who enunciates the conclusion in a policy speech, but it knows that the conclusion has been carefully prepared by the best minds of the country. For most of the public, the outcome appears not as something a narrow group of bureaucrats decided but something "we Japanese" decided.

CENTRAL DIRECTION AND LOCAL ACTION

Until 1868 the Japanese government was far more decentralized than the United States had been after 1789, but Japanese leaders after 1868 chose a course of centralized coordination and planning as a means to rapid modernization. The American-led Occupation after World War II introduced democratic reforms like the local election of governors, but central direction in guiding local developments, now modified by democratic practices, has continued to be widely accepted.

As in the private sector, much of the actual administration is left to local governments. Compared to America, a high proportion of tax income flows through the central government to the local government. This pattern provides leverage for maintaining high overall standards within national plans and still gives flexibility to the local government. Special legislation in the 1950s has permitted the government to consolidate local communities and to redistrict local administrative boundaries to make them more rational. This has permitted more effective regional and metropolitan planning. It allows the national government to develop consistent, integrated plans for redistributing wealth to poorer areas, for raising standards in education, for standardizing local public transport systems, and for standardizing rules about commerce and industry.

So as to equalize local financial resources and yet give local areas flexibility in choosing their own programs, the national government gives larger equalization grants to poorer local areas. In the United States, because the national government gives out a much higher proportion of funds for specific projects, the local governments try to obtain as much as possible for each project; but in Japan, where the local government receives a general grant which it can use for many purposes, it makes greater efforts to conserve funds in each area and it has more flexibility in seeing that programs are not suddenly started and suspended by central government fiat. This Japanese plan of equalization of local resources was in fact conceived by an American professor, Carl Shoup, and introduced during the Allied Occupation as the most rational plan for providing equalization of resources while encouraging local initiative and economy.

The grand vision for redistributing the population and industrial facilities to less crowded parts of the country was embodied in the 1972 Tanaka Plan for Remodeling the Japanese Archipelago, a plan actually written by MITI bureaucrats. The plan was designed to provide tax and other incentives for redistributing industry and population to less crowded areas to reduce excessive concentration. It included construction of rail, bridge, and road transport in less developed areas to stimulate their economies. The plan was just out when the oil crisis caused the government to lower interest rates to stimulate the economy. As funds became readily available, the Tanaka Plan led to land speculation and contributed to runaway inflation. As originally formulated, therefore, the Tanaka Plan proved disastrous and, with subsequent retrenchment to control inflation, unrealizable. But the basic program for reconcentrating industry and growth in middle-sized cities and backward areas and for providing tax incentives and low-interest loans to encourage this has continued to guide the work of bureaucrats in relevant government ministries like MITI, Finance, Construction, Transport, and the Land Agency.

With the amalgamation and redistricting of local communities, Japan has been able to undertake concerted metropolitan planning that is not possible in the United States. The National Land Agency is still analyzing long-term population and economic trends with a view toward consolidating administrative districts where it is desirable to do so. Japan's metropolitan transport systems can cover a broader geographical area and be integrated into national systems. Japan can distribute industrial, commercial, recreational, and other facilities throughout the metropolitan area according to certain guidelines and principles. It can equalize the tax burden between richer and poorer communities and reduce the differentials of public service between rich and poor suburbs, thus creating a more homogeneous nation.

In addition to administration, most of the actual plans for regional development come from the local community. Various parts of the national bureaucracy must cooperate in order for the local community to realize its potential, but the national government makes its guidelines well known. Although the Japanese government takes much greater initiative in defining the desirable course of local development, local communities are given room for initiative. Local business leaders, political leaders, and bureaucrats can do a great deal to remake their area and, through consultation with national politicians and bureaucrats, receive considerable national help. In short, the national government deals with local areas much as it deals with private businesses. It sets up a league, establishes the rules, provides guidance, and reserves the right to make certain decisions, but the key actors are the local leaders.

The maintenance of a centralized authority permits Japan to avoid the overlapping, entangled, inconsistent, unequal, and sometimes totally inadequate programs maintained by American states in matters of welfare, education, crime control, and the like. The variations among American states require an additional layer of national bureaucracy that tries to minimize or go around these inconsistencies. Japan's clear, forthright steps to centralize leadership in these areas in the latter part of the nineteenth century has permitted smoother planning and more rational administration while reducing excessive bureaucratic overlap. It has not ended local experimentation, and indeed the national government has encouraged it. One wonders whether the United States, in an era of such complex problems requiring such a high level of coordination, is still best served by a pattern of government that places such extensive powers in the hands of the states, a pattern that grew out of premodern agrarian conditions, and whether the entangled web of varying state regulations is optimal for achieving the overall goals of the society.

It requires no great effort to discover instances when Japanese bureaucrats made important errors of judgment. In 1951 the head of the Bank of Japan refused to extend a loan to create the first modern postwar steel plant, arguing that Japan could not hope to compete against America's steel industry. Sony had to postpone for two years its efforts to import transistor technology because government bureaucrats considered the company unable to make good use of the technology. After the first oil shock, bureaucrats overstimulated the economy, causing runaway inflation. Just prior to the first yen revaluation shock, officials confidently predicted yen revaluation would not take place and exchanged yen for billions of dollars. In the 1960s bureaucrats pushed the rapid construction of the Narita International Airport, which then stood idle for a decade because they had vastly underestimated public resistance. This was compounded by delays in constructing local transport facilities and inadequate preparations against terrorists. Jurisdictional disputes between ministries have led to inaction. Yet in balance, the bureaucracy has been remarkably effective in guiding the country.

If one factor stands out in keeping such errors to a minimum and providing relatively rapid self-correcting devices, it is the involvement of all relevant parties in the decision-making process and their thorough commitment to the resulting decisions. In English, this process is sometimes referred to as "decision making by consensus," but this does not adequately describe the Japanese decision-making process. In Japanese the term used is *nemawashi*: root binding. The term originally comes from gardening, where it designates the careful untangling and binding of each of the roots of a tree before it is moved. The Japanese bureaucracy provides vigorous direction on many major issues, continuing over a long period of time, and during this process they are in close touch with all relevant groups to make sure they understand the evolving decisions, that their roots are bound. The press clubs and deliberative councils ensure that wider circles of the interested public are similarly informed of these decisions. The relevant groups are not expected to agree with all decisions made by the bureaucrats. Sometimes a group's interests are not in keeping with the emerging decision, and this group must be made to understand the necessity of the decision and the well-considered impartiality of the decision. If that group is disadvantaged by this decision, then it is understood that they will be given special consideration now or in the future. The long-term continuity in bureaucratic leadership, unimpaired by changes of politicians, ensures the reliability of bureaucrats in carrying through future commitments. The disadvantaged group's roots are thus bound and do not impede the effective moving of the tree. Not all a tree's roots can always be smoothly bound, but a majority is not enough, and a serious effort is made to include as many roots as possible.

An important part of root binding is to give each group ample time to adjust to the emerging decision, to explain the goals of the decision and let them understand the information that leads to this conclusion. If all groups are in order, then the tree can be moved with extraordinary rapidity, but if not all groups are convinced or are not prepared, then the decision is delayed. Some Westerners working with the Japanese bureaucracy have complained that the slowness of the process can be exasperating. Occasionally top Japanese bureaucrats talk enviously of their Western counterparts who can simply give out orders or directives or plans, but when pushed they acknowledge that the Japanese system works better in the long run. The final administrative decision or Diet bill or pronouncement coming from the Japanese bureaucracy is not a tidy, tightly knit, clearly reasoned, lawyer-like brief that might emanate from the White House. It is evasive, indirect, even inconsistent in points, not because Japanese bureaucrats like evasiveness but because they want to maximize the level of cooperation of all relevant groups.

An example of the results of root binding can be seen in what may be the most critical problem for both countries in recent years, the energy shortage. The Carter Administration put forth a brilliantly argued, thoughtful plan for dealing with the problem of energy, but it lacked the consensus and support of relevant groups, and its key parts could not therefore be implemented quickly and vigorously. The Japanese bureaucracy, in contrast, consulted closely even with oil companies, working out in conjunction with leaders of the private sector a series of programs for energy conservation. They increased the cost of gasoline about twice the rate of increase in America, gasoline mileage in new cars expanded rapidly, solar energy units were installed in many homes, and companies developed fuel economy programs.

The result was that Japan basically kept petroleum imports constant despite economic growth, while American oil imports were growing rapidly despite lower economic growth. Large Japanese trees cannot be moved automatically, and in the 1930s, despite cultural homogeneity, they were often moved by intimidating potential opposition. They are helped by homogeneity, but they make the best of it by highlighting a sense of common national purpose, working closely with key groups whose cooperation is needed, and preparing the general public. The public may complain about imperfect plans from arrogant bureaucrats, but in the end it is not "their plan" but "our plan," and the roots stick with the tree.

5

Politics: Higher Interests and Fair Shares

IF THE TERM "DEMOCRACY" is used to signify the expression of diverse interests in the political arena and the capacity of the government to satisfy these interests, it could be argued that Japan is now a more effective democracy than America. The interests of the Japanese are expressed not by specialized groups but by basic multipurposed groups—like villages, towns, firms, professional associations—that are generally better organized and disciplined and more systematic in representing the wishes of their membership than the more ephemeral American special-interest groups. Groups in Japan interact with one another more frequently, so that they are particularly effective aggregating interests—engaging in joint political activity for a broader common purpose. And at all levels in Japan, people make a conscious effort to provide a balanced though not equal "fair share" to all recognized groups in the society. The distribution of fair shares, like the aggregation of interests, is made possible by the solidarity of these multipurpose groups.

GROUP SOLIDARITY

The solidarity of Japanese communities is hardly unique. Traditional New England villages and the villages in Europe from which many American immigrants came also had strong group ties, enabling them to work for common goals and to discipline community members. What is unusual is that the Japanese have been able to retain this sense of community— to keep what George Lodge termed their "communitarian values"—in a time when group consciousness attenuated in many nations.

One could argue that Japan's success in perpetuating a sense of community stems from its late transition from feudalism directly to modern corporate society, without an intervening period of individualism lasting hundreds of years as in Western Europe. But whatever its historical roots, group solidarity remains in Japan because people work at it. Whether in villages, towns, urban neighborhoods, or work places, leaders exert themselves to retain the loyalty of group members by responding to their needs. Children are taught the value of cooperation for everyone's benefit, and, however annoying they may find group pressures, adults remain responsive to group attitudes for they are convinced that everyone gains from restraining egoism.

Even today, a Japanese tends to maintain primary loyalty to one all-embracing group in which he expresses all aspects of his personality, from private and personal to formal and businesslike. Membership is not casually begun or terminated, for mutual obligations are strong and enduring. The American tends to belong to no such basic group but to express different aspects of his personality in the various special-purpose groups to which he belongs. The Japanese may belong to as many groups as his American counterpart, but one primary membership stands out, and the others are clearly secondary. The farmer, for example, may belong primarily to the local agricultural cooperative, and this becomes the basic reference point for him and his family even when he participates in other groups. An employee of a company is known by his affiliation with that company no matter in what groups he participates. This primary identification with the company is reinforced by other groups, for they want members who are trusted by the company. It is further reinforced by national organizations, for they choose to work through the primary local group to distribute their political favors and economic benefits while seeking local bases of support.

Now that young men living on farms earn most of their income in nonagricultural pursuits, commonly commuting to work, the power of the village over the family is no longer as great as it was. Nonetheless, the people in the village not only share a common Shinto shrine and hold common celebrations but often meet in the village recreation hall. They are quick to organize for road improvements and other beautification and modernization projects for their community as a whole, as many villages did in building swimming pools after the 1964 Tokyo Olympics. The local agricultural cooperative is still able to make available less expensive seed, fertilizer, agricultural equipment, insurance, and charter trips than farmers could attain individually. The cooperative may also arrange investments that are more reliable and profitable than individuals could have made on their own. Although the richer people in the village may in fact have more influence in the outcome of these activities than the poorer, they are also obligated to make a much greater financial contribution to the common good, a pattern not unlike that in traditional European and American villages.

In urban and suburban neighborhoods, especially in older, established neighborhoods, but even in new public apartment projects (*danchi*), local residents belong to neighborhood associations. In the university, students commonly have one predominant activity club to which they belong. The club does engage in a specialized activity like skiing or English speaking, but it is far more all-embracing and requires more loyalty and continuity than the typical extracurricular activity on American campuses. Perhaps the nearest analogue is the American fraternity or sorority, but in a Japanese university virtually everyone belongs to such a club. The Japanese activity club is strong on nostalgia and sentimentality, celebrating farewells, taking pictures for commemoration, singing and drinking together. Essentially the same type of primary membership group exists among small shopkeepers on a street of small stores, among employees of larger organizations, and among independent professional groups such as doctors and dentists.

In Japanese villages there is a high degree of family continuity spanning several generations. In urban neighborhoods also family home sites turn over less frequently than in the United States. In large companies, peers who enter the company together remain close throughout their working career and sometimes later as well. This continuity helps to strengthen group opinion, and if this leads to excesses on such superficial matters as how members talk and dress, it does help make members more responsive to one another's opinions.

HIGHER AGGREGATION OF INTERESTS

These multipurpose groups spend a great deal of time talking and thinking about their long-range interests and are therefore much better informed about matters relating to their interests than the more ephemeral interest groups in America. Village leaders, for example, are well-informed about prefectural and national programs for which they might qualify and, when dissatisfied with the response of bureaucrats, take their case to a prefectural assemblyman or Diet member. They will probably have endorsed him and contributed as a group to his campaign funds to ensure a receptive hearing when they visit him with proposals on behalf of their community. Interest in political affairs is high: about seventy percent of voters turn out for local elections, compared to about fifty percent in the United States. The assemblyman or Diet member knows that each village in his constituency is watching his behavior in other villages, and he must therefore develop a strategy of either helping all to a comparable degree or concentrating on certain communities where he has an especially strong following. He may work with a village separately on local issues, but on complicated issues affecting other communities he knows he must side with large groups that have aggregated their interests to form the largest pressure group. This process of combining interests is by no means unique to Japan, but what is unusual is how consistently all villagers in a village vote as a bloc, how much they discuss candidates and issues with each other, and how much time representatives of different villages spend with each other in trying to find common interests that they can jointly pursue at higher levels.

The group to which an individual owes his primary loyalty is the basic building block for aggregating interests. Since this basic group unites people with a common source of income—fellow employees of a company, farmers in a given community, fellow professionals, or fellow shopkeepers—the main interests aggregated tend to be those most affecting members' pocketbooks. This contrasts with America, where special-issue groups dealing with the environment, civil liberties, and abortion, for example—groups that unite people from diverse occupations and diverse communities—are much more important. In Japan the group with income from a certain source may be linked with like groups elsewhere or with diverse groups in the same locality. Local communities can then aggregate their interests in progressively larger geographical areas, and at the national level some associations link many different occupational groupings from many different localities.

Despite Japan's small size, there are three important geographical levels between the nation and the municipality. One is the "large region," of which there are nine. The next level down is the prefecture, of which there are forty-seven, including two urban prefectures (Osaka and Kyoto) and one metropolis (Tokyo). Of the three levels, only the prefecture has corresponding government institutions. The third and lowest level consists of smaller planning areas, many of which more or less correspond to some of the roughly two hundred and fifty feudal fiefs of the Tokugawa period. National Land Agency officials and other bureaucrats have found it fruitful to work with these areas, which are somewhat larger than a municipality, in a variety of area development programs. Since local community consolidation in the 1950s, the only formal governmental level below the prefecture is the municipality.

Corresponding to the nine large regions are nine regional associations of large business enterprises, each of which promotes its respective interests. These associations meet to work out concrete plans for regional development, but they also engage in social activity as well, thereby reinforcing the sense of community, especially among regional leaders. Over the years these leaders have developed a set of informal rules to ensure the success of their associations. For example, so that the head of the association could not use this post to enhance his own company's interests, he should not be from a prominent regional company with competitors of comparable size. Yet he should be an important, successful, and respected person of sufficient age for his personal authority to reinforce his official authority, enabling him to mobilize cooperation when necessary. He thus tends to be a company president or chairman who has already handed over some company responsibilities to younger men, permitting him to devote perhaps half of his time or more to the region as a whole. He tends to be from a company so dominant that the enterprise has no regional rival or from a small but highly respected locally based company so he cannot misuse his position. There is a neat and popular solution to the problem of headship which derives from the post-World War II splitting of the government-owned electric power monopoly into nine private electric power companies, each servicing an area corresponding to one of the nine regions. Since electric power is the major business without competitors in the area, since its scope of interests corresponds precisely to that of the region, and since businessmen want to be on good terms with the power company, the chairman of the electric power company is commonly elected president of the regional businessmen's association. Other important businesses, like metropolitan-area railways, regional banks, and industries with a main office in the region, also play a major role in regional organizations, and vice-presidents of the regional association are chosen systematically to represent major sectors and industrial groups, for they have a prominent role in working toward regional agreements. Local leaders of large national companies with facilities in the region are represented in regional business associations, but because of national interests they cannot be expected to fight vigorously for regional interests; they are therefore rarely chosen even as vice-presidents and have less power in regional associations than the size of their business would otherwise warrant. Young growing companies that have not yet had long years of cooperation with other regional leaders are not given prominence equal to their economic power until they have proven they can work well with others.

Since each of the regions plays a major national role, leaders of their business associations regularly see not only prefectural politicians and Diet members from their region but all leading Tokyo politicians and bureaucrats concerned with major national problems. Their constant contact with national politicians assures that national leaders are alert to local sensitivities and well-informed about weak spots in regional development. Although much of the contact is informal and social in order to develop a relationship of trust, the participants are aware of their respective responsibilities to the region and the nation. In a sense their respective roles make statesmen of the participants because business leaders in this context cannot speak of their individual company's interest. They are selected because of their sense of responsibility to the region as a whole, and they value the personal and social relationships that come from fulfilling regional responsibility. They do not solve big problems in these meetings alone, for interaction occurs at many levels. The Kansai business leaders, for example, ordinarily meet with the prime minister once a month at an exclusive restaurant for informal discussion of Kansai problems. The leaders in these meetings discuss only general issues, leaving to association staff members the problem of working out the details with bureaucrats in Tokyo, which the leaders then approve. Without the agreement and participation of their underlings, however, the top leaders do not have the leeway to make final commitments. Regional business leaders work with regional labor leaders, newspaper and television representatives, and university faculty in similar pursuit of regional interests. Although American regional leaders may occasionally meet informally for similar purposes, in Japan each organization spends more time considering details and working out agreements so that when high-level officials meet, they do so as representatives expressing carefully considered regional plans with a high level of consensus among participating companies and with the understanding of local politicians, newspaper editors, and labor and farm groups as well.

In Tokyo the forty-seven prefectures each maintain a large meeting center (*kaikan*) with many conference rooms and offices and appropriate staff to represent prefectural interests. These prefectural offices are in constant contact with national politicians, bureaucrats, reporters, and businessmen in an effort to monitor all recent developments of interest to the prefecture. They value informal contacts to keep one step ahead of formal announcements and thereby better represent their prefecture. The prefectural representatives are concerned not only with annual budget allowances for schools, hospitals, welfare establishments, and construction projects but with virtually every major project affecting prefectural activity. Representatives of prefectural groups of all kinds constantly visit Tokyo, checking in at their respective prefectural offices and talking to appropriate politicians and bureaucrats in their respective spheres. Many maintain dual residences, one in their home prefecture and one in Tokyo. Because there is a government office in the prefecture, prefectural initiative is more often in the hands of the government than in the case of the large regions, which lack government offices and therefore must rely more on big business associations. Nonetheless, the prefectural Chamber of Commerce looks after prefectural business interests, and their representatives systematically work out priorities for economic development just as government officials do. If anything, there is greater camaraderie and information exchange at the prefectural level than in the large regions.

Some local politicians of particularly great power represent the interests of their constituencies more effectively than others, and stories of major politicians arranging for a train stop to be built in or near their hometown are not without foundation. The project for building a bridge to Shikoku was long-delayed because three effective local politicians were vying for location. But each prefectural government and prefectural business community is well organized to look out for the interests of their locality, and this forces Diet members and bureaucrats to work out even-handed policies for balanced development and to formulate a convincing rationale for selecting certain localities for certain projects. It ensures well-organized prefectural groupings and forces the national government to be sensitive to local problems and to evaluate the overall impact on regional development when considering a particular project. Interested national officials know they can turn to the prefectures for well-considered plans. And this pooling of common interests makes idiosyncratic solutions virtually impossible.

Below the prefectural level the sense of solidarity going back to fiefs of the Tokugawa era sometimes lurks in the background, but the emphasis in contemporary organizations is on present-day economic development. Local business associations parallel to those at higher levels look after the interests of their municipality or other sub-prefectural unit. Although leadership may be less sophisticated than at higher levels, thorough-going organization and careful consultation results in the same approach for evaluating overall interests.

Although associations of functional specialties such as farming, medicine, dentistry, and industry are represented at the regional, prefectural, and lower levels, these sectoral groups are generally branches of national associations, and the strongest representation of each sector tends to be at the national level. Virtually every industrial, professional, and agricultural sector is well organized to represent its special interests. Labor associations work together to create the united front that leads to an annual rise in wages. Agricultural associations, with the Agricultural Cooperative (Nōkyō) in the lead, cooperate to maintain high price supports for rice. Fruit growers of various kinds meet to aggregate their national interests, aware that their individual interests will easily be sacrificed at the national level unless they band together. Indeed, the reason Japanese politicians are reluctant to open Japan to free import of cherries and citrus fruits despite trade imbalances and American pressure is that Japanese farmers are so united that a politician showing flexibility on any agricultural product runs the risk of strong, well-united farm opposition. These special-interest groups make their case strongly to leading politicians and Ministry of Agriculture bureaucrats, who defend them. Medical and dental associations also coordinate their efforts to obtain adequate fees for service, but consumer organizations and insurance companies similarly represent consumer interests, leading to constant bargaining between representatives of the practitioners and consumers.

Virtually all major Japanese firms specialize in a single sector like banking, trading, real estate, department stores, heavy industry, electric appliances, petroleum, and textiles. This pattern—developed partly through bureaucratic guidance —to encourage the expertise and long-range technical development necessary for the most competitive performance is very different, for example, from American conglomerates, which spread over several sectors and leave and enter various industrial sectors with relative ease. Given the specialization of Japanese firms in a given industrial sector, the aggregation of interests can take two directions. One is the organization of all firms from a single industrial sector, which maximizes the cooperation that comes from looking after their common interests in building up their sector. The second is the organization of firms into "groups" consisting of one firm from each sector. A firm in a group has the advantage of special affiliation with companies in different sectors. *Zaibatsu* (literally, "financial clique") groups (like Mitsui, Mitsubishi, and Sumitomo) link firms formerly united under their prewar holding company, and non-*zaibatsu* groups (like Fuji, Sanwa, Daiwa, and Dai-ichi Kangyō) center around large banks.

In addition to these two types of organization, a third type combines virtually all firms of a given size in all sectors: Nikkeiren (Japanese Federation of Employers), for example, deals with labor problems of all large firms, Keidanren (Federation of Economic Organizations) and the eight other regional associations deal with all issues aside from labor confronting big business, and the Chamber of Commerce (composed of all companies) includes all firms but now particularly represents small business.

Depending on the issue and the extent of common interests, trade associations, or ad hoc groups of companies in a sector, look out for a range of interests impossible to represent in the United States, where antitrust laws are more rigid. To make sure that they have entrée when politicians consider issues like tax rates, consolidation and rationalization of firms, industrial and safety standards, and protection against foreign industrial threats, they make regular collective political contributions as a sector. On more detailed issues they deal regularly with the bureaucracy, and major trade associations include staff members who were elite bureaucrats in big ministries, creating smooth relationships with the bureaucracy. The associations discuss virtually every issue considered by MITI in their sphere, for even if MITI eventually resolves the issue, it would not do so without fully understanding the dominant views of the sector. In a declining industry, it is the trade association that helps shape the depression cartel with apportionment of quotas for reduced production. When the United States demands that Japan limit exports to the United States, this association, in cooperation with MITI, apportions quotas for reducing exports, although paradoxically the kind of restraint the United States demands is prohibited in America by antitrust legislation. Similarly, in times of growth, because of the danger of "over-heating" the economy and of creating excess capacity, it is this industrial sector organization that works out with the appropriate MITI branch a fair system for restraining expansion.

Sectoral associations sometimes develop special projects which they administer directly. The banking association, for example, developed the system that permits deposits to be transferred by a centralized computer, operated by the banking association, from any regular commercial bank to any account in any other commercial bank. The steel sector, interested in keeping down the cost of electricity and fuel, takes an active role in securing stable sources of energy for the entire nation and in lobbying within Keidanren and the government to limit the inflationary pressures of electricity and fuel costs. Similarly, the automobile sector seeks to keep down the cost of steel as well as electricity and fuel so it may continue to compete internationally.

After the consolidation of the Nippon Steel Corporation in 1969, counterpressures to check oligopolies, monopolies, and sectoral cooperation grew rapidly. These pressures rose to new heights in 1973 after some companies took advantage of the oil-embargo jitters to corner certain markets and restrict the flow of goods, profiteering from artificially high prices. The Fair Trade Commission, then fueled by popular sentiment, drew on long-standing American trust-busting efforts to fight sectoral cooperation and monopolies. Not long after these oil shocks, Japan passed some antimonopoly legislation, but the stricter provisions advocated by some groups were not enacted, partly because of effective representations by the business community. Most Japanese companies acknowledge that profiteering from cornering markets should be prevented, and many business leaders did condemn the offending companies. Some business leaders undoubtedly cooperated only to escape political pressure for a more virulent antimonopoly law, but the capacity of the business community to restrain such practices by a combination of social pressure and threat of legislation is quite possibly more effective than legislation itself, with all the attendant problems of regulation and litigation.

Although business sector associations are naturally opposed to strong antimonopoly legislation and a trust-busting Fair Trade Commission, they tone down public expressions on this issue to avoid public indignation. MITI officials are, if anything, more open than the business community in opposing the Fair Trade Commission. In part it is a classic jurisdictional dispute, but in part it is because MITI's approach is so directly contrary to that of the Fair Trade Commission. MITI officials believe in the ultimate value of the marketplace, but in the short range they think it advisable to gain the cooperation of companies in a sector in cushioning economic fluctuations, thus reducing disruptions to the specific industries, their employees, and the economy as a whole. They are confident that their administrative guidance with the sanctions at their disposal can contain the dangers of oligopoly. The public supports sectoral cooperation, for they want their companies to avoid the dangers of sudden layoffs and unemployment. Furthermore, both the bureaucrats and the public believe that improvement of safety and pollution standards as well as economic prosperity require sectoral cooperation.

The foreigner is struck with the paradox of extraordinarily competitive relations among firms in a single sector whose leaders nonetheless genuinely enjoy each other's company when working for the sector as a whole. Officials who fight to increase their company's market share can seem totally relaxed in the camaraderie of drinking with counterparts in rival companies. Sector association leaders at times fight almost as arduously and effectively in the interest of the sector as a whole as the individual company leaders fight for the good of their own businesses. Indeed, they cannot understand how Americans can keep their individual companies abreast of modern developments without the kind of cooperation that American antitrust practice forbids.

Cooperation within a *zaibatsu* or non-*zaibatsu* group is even easier than within a sector association, for the companies have many business interests in common and few in competition. The *zaibatsu* groups date back before World War II, when a holding company at the top of the *zaibatsu* had direct control over the range of *zaibatsu*-related companies. In the postwar period, holding companies were outlawed and dispersed by the Occupation, and even after regrouping, the companies are much more independent and group ties weaker than before the war. A non-*zaibatsu* group is organized similarly, although these groups are of more recent origin and are even more loosely structured. The companies in a group are bound together by friendship and regular meetings among top leaders as well as by loans, some mutual stockholding, interlocking directorates, information sharing, division of insurance risks, and, in case of trouble, mutual assistance, but all these kinds of relations may, to a lesser degree, extend across group lines.

Within the group, the bank or the trading company commonly plays a predominant role, for both have maximum contact with other group companies. In new fields like computers, petrochemicals, and atomic energy, other group-affiliated companies help finance the growing company, thereby tying it closely to the group, but the older, well-established company with its own funds enjoys virtual independence. A company in a declining industry may place some personnel in a group-affiliated company in a more prosperous sector. Companies in the group may collect funds jointly for political leaders, making use of these contacts, for example, to get necessary approval for large group projects abroad. The projects are not always undertaken solely at the request of the group; in some cases, Japanese government officials, spotting an overseas opportunity for Japanese companies, encourage the group to work out a program to compete effectively with project proposals from other countries. Sometimes government bureaucrats help arrange low-interest loans (as, for example, through the Export–Import Bank) and necessary insurance to reduce the risk and make the project financially appealing. These projects require complicated cooperative efforts which companies with group affiliation can achieve more effectively and easily than nonrelated companies. The Sumitomo project in Singapore, the Mitsui project in Iran, and the Mitsubishi project in Saudi Arabia are notable examples.

In aggregating interests at the national level, the Chamber of Commerce speaks for small business. By law every company in Japan is a registered member of the Chamber of Commerce. The majority of companies are naturally smaller ones, and as a result the Japanese Chamber of Commerce has come to represent the interests of small- and medium-sized enterprises. At the prefectural level and below, because there are few large company headquarters, the Chamber of Commerce branches commonly serve as the focus for the entire local business community. It is not unlike local American Chamber of Commerce branches, but on the whole the Japanese Chambers of Commerce are better organized and more active and work more closely with government officials in planning the development of their region. This is evident in projects like filling in land along the ocean, reclaiming land, and planning for local industrial sites. Because the total business conducted by small companies cannot compare with that of large businesses, and because their diverse interests are not so easily aggregated and many of them are dependent on large companies, their aggregation of interest is less effective than that of large businesses. Nonetheless, in the spirit of "fair share," an effort is made by government bureaucrats as well as Diet members representing local business interests to provide special programs of financial aid, low-interest loans, insurance, and security for small businesses. Although sizeable numbers of individual small businesses have gone bankrupt in some "recession," large numbers of new firms have started and the small-business sector has remained strong despite the rapid growth and concentration of very large companies.

Keidanren, composed of the seven-hundred-odd largest Japanese companies, is organized to represent big business with a thoroughness without peer in the world. Its role might be compared to that of the National Association of Manufacturers if that association enjoyed the regular and active participation of the very top business leaders working closely with a large professional staff to forge agreements on behalf of big business as a whole. In the mass media Keidanren is termed the "main temple" and its chairman the "prime minister" of the business community. Although there is no other regional association of top businessmen for the Tokyo area, it is really a national organization, and all major corporations in Japan, regardless of location of headquarters, belong. Keidanren occupies a large fourteen-story building in the heart of Japan's Wall Street, Otemachi, and here each day there are dozens of meetings for the leaders of the largest companies to study and discuss issues of interest to their sector or to some substantial part of the business community. On the first floor is the Press Club, with desks for the reporters from major papers and networks who work there full time covering the business community.

In a sense Keidanren also acts as the Foreign Ministry of the Japanese business community, sponsoring meetings with foreign businessmen and sending abroad specialized missions of business leaders to find solutions to trade problems with key countries. When threats of European and American protectionism arise, Keidanren consults broadly in Japan, does the careful root binding with foreign business leaders, and if necessary sends out delegations to conclude the agreements. In dealing with communist countries, especially the Soviet Union, Keidanren organizes joint projects and deals with communist trading companies to assure that state monopolies do not take undue advantage of rivalries among Japanese companies. As for the very largest overseas projects such as those currently underway in Brazil and the Soviet Union, Keidanren itself sponsors the project because it alone has the capacity to represent and work with a wide variety of Japanese firms that cross industrial group lines.

Because it represents numerous and diverse companies with so many different interests, Keidanren cannot express its view on every small matter even if its study groups and committees do discuss every important issue and most minor issues of interest to the business community. It cannot be partial to any single group or any industrial sector, although it can give special attention and aid to needy sectors. Keidanren concentrates on issues of interest to the business community as a whole, and rather than express its views to the outside, it discusses issues in broad national terms, taking, for example, a firm stand in favor of stimulating the economy in opposition to prime ministers like Fukuda who tend to be more concerned about inflation. In this Keidanren represents the predominant view of most businesses. Similarly, it tries to design tax proposals that represent a compromise between the interests of the various companies but still provide encouragement to business as a whole. It only sponsors study missions that will affect many companies in different areas; other study missions are sponsored by groups, sectoral associations, or ad hoc groupings for special purposes.

Keidanren is, of course, criticized in the press for pushing the interests of big business while slighting the interests of small business and the public at large. To be sure, Keidanren officials do pursue the interests of big business and do so vigorously, but the top leaders are themselves convinced that they are moved by broader goals. They achieve fame and wealth in their own company many years before assuming leadership in Keidanren, and once there, they see themselves as playing a grander role as business statesmen, with visions benefiting all Japanese. When these leaders of the business community first began to meet with businessmen from the United States, many confidentially expressed surprise at the extent to which American businessmen thought only of their own company and were ill-prepared to consider business problems from a broader perspective, let alone negotiate agreements on complex issues. Many senior American business leaders have been impressed with the statesmanship of their Japanese counterparts like Keidanren leader Taizō Ishizaka. Many of these senior leaders have not only a broad training in European history and literature, Chinese classics, Japanese history, Marxist and "modern" economics but a bold vision for the future and an overarching philosophy.

Keidanren uses a uniquely Japanese method of collecting political contributions from the business community. Beginning in 1955 when the Liberal Democratic Party was formed, Keidanren has developed and modified a system to assess each of the large industrial sectors for a political contribution. The largest business sectors such as steel, electric power, and banking have been the pacesetters, giving the largest contributions, and the other industrial sectors are assessed proportionately. The automobile sector, for example, which originally gave less than steel, has now grown so substantially that its contribution is roughly the same as that of steel and electric power. Within each industrial sector the major companies are expected to give in proportion to their size and profitability. Keidanren distributes the funds it collects from the big business community primarily to the Liberal Democratic Party through an intermediary citizen's group (long called the National Association), but some is also given to various opposition parties. Political representation from the business community concentrates on the most general issues: that the country maintain a private business economy rather than a socialist one, that the LDP select leaders who can maintain stability, and that governmental policy encourage economic growth and stability.

It tends to favor basic industry necessary for national development. Compared to Japan in the 1930s or present-day America, its efforts are not distorted by a large defense industry strongly protected by one part of the government. The big business community does not expect a precise quid pro quo. It expects only a sympathetic understanding of conditions necessary for general business health.

This large centralized financial contribution tends to tilt the government toward big rather than small business, but it also tilts it toward the interests of the business community as a whole rather than toward the interests of any particular industry or company. If one company or one industrial sector tries to pressure the government in its favor, the government is likely to be cautious in responding because of the considerable support of the rest of the business community. This higher level of aggregation of interests within the business community tends to ensure that the highest level politicians also think in comparably broad terms of the interests of the country rather than of peculiar, sectarian interests. Although big business does not fully speak for farmers and laborers, big business reaches its conclusion only after fully understanding and accommodating to their views, for it realizes that its own success depends on the active cooperation of these groups.

The aggregation of interests is no casual process. It includes an exhaustive discussion of issues by all relevant parties from the outset, so that any conclusion reflects a thorough understanding of the issues. Every single group can turn to several associations in pursuing its interests, but it is constrained by the resulting cooperation. It is too facile to describe the result as a consensus, for everyone's best interests are not necessarily served, but the conclusion is acknowledged as a considered view that represents the best long-term interests of the largest part of the business community. The Japanese believe that the American system—wherein individual contributors pressure individual politicians to their own ends, and some groups are better organized than others—leads to haphazard results that do not necessarily reflect the major interests of the largest number. They perceive America as making political decisions that are inadequately considered, subject to idiosyncracies, and lacking in constancy and breadth of vision. It is not that Japanese politicians have broader visions than their Western counterparts but that the private sector's constant interaction, mutual consultation, and hammering out of common understandings creates a stronger support base for the political leader and the bureaucrat with broad vision to respond to. It makes it infinitely easier for national leaders to respond to the general interest against narrow special interest groups. Dismissing this as Japan, Inc. vastly understates the struggle between different Japanese groups in the course of achieving agreements. In contemporary societies so rent by disruptive centrifugal forces, it also vastly underestimates the value of groups' being sufficiently aware of larger interests to be willing to sacrifice short-range egoistic interests for the long-term general good.

Fair Shares

At the risk of oversimplification, one may say that a fundamental underlying rule of American political life may be characterized as "fair play," contrasted with a basic rule of Japanese political life, "fair share." In America one must follow the rules of the game; if the game is fought fairly, the loser, being a good sport, congratulates the winner and to the winner belong the spoils. In political elections, as in many other spheres, the winner takes the pie. In Japan, aside from sports tournaments, there are rarely such clear-cut contests. Even before the contest is concluded, the Japanese may look at the pie to see if it can be expanded, to see how many ways it can be cut, to see what acceptable rules can be devised for apportioning it. However, they are interested not only in rules but in results, and rules may be changed to accord with a sense of "fair share." After the contest everyone must receive some share. If there is reasonable doubt as to how one contest was decided or if an indivisible pie is given to one party, the disadvantaged party has a standing claim to a larger share of the next pie.

In the elections to the lower house of the Diet, each district selects three to five representatives, almost assuring that some opposition parties and members of rival factions in the LDP will have representation. LDP politicians may scheme to keep their party in the solid majority, but they do not believe it desirable to eliminate opposition. When the largest companies apportion their political contributions, they try to ensure good connections with every political leader who has a reasonable chance of becoming prime minister. To this end they contribute more heavily to the most promising factions of the Liberal Democratic Party but they also give some to all major opposition parties, with the possible exception of the Communist Party, where there is no clear evidence of such gifts. If in fact the Communist Party receives no contributions from such large companies, it is not because companies refuse but because the Communist Party wants to remain independent and can do so from the money it earns from its publications. Similarly, after the Liberal Democratic Party selects the prime minister, he in turn must assemble a cabinet balancing the different LDP factions and ensuring that each is represented. Although opposition party leaders have not yet been included in the cabinet, they are nonetheless consulted to bind their roots before important measures are considered in the Diet. Grandstanding by LDP leaders is carefully resisted. If public rhetoric is dull and almost inarticulate, it is nonetheless carefully worded to minimize the danger of giving offense to anyone, including opposition leaders. Measures that pass the

Diet are, like the rhetoric, often filled with vague generalities which reduce the offensiveness to various groups. Most bills pass the Diet unanimously, supported by opposition parties as well as the LDP.

When the national budget is apportioned, there is an implicit assumption among interest groups that each will in some way receive its fair share. For example, in the case of international expositions, consideration is given to those metropolitan areas deserving modern construction. The first such project—the 1964 Olympics—was naturally located in the capital and the largest metropolitan area, Tokyo. Since the winter Olympics that year had to be hosted in the northern island, there was no choice but to make Sapporo the headquarters, although there were larger metropolitan areas that otherwise should have received their turn first. The next huge project, Banpaku (Expo), was naturally held in the second largest area, the Osaka-Kobe-Kyoto area. Now it is understood that the next time such a large event occurs, it will be in the next largest area, although since the Nagoya and Fukuoka areas are comparable in size, each might be able to present a plausible case. But the loser would then get the next round. Regional location of national construction projects is decided according to the same principles.

In apportioning the annual budget, the Finance Ministry generally allows major recipients, prefectures, and ministries to retain about ninety-five percent of their previous share of the budget without making a special case. Assuming that each unit needs to have considerable security over its own funds to plan effectively for the future, old organizations are rarely surgically removed but merely allowed to wither. The margin of five to ten percent of each ministry's share of the budget is up for reallocation for new projects. In this marginal area, each ministry must compete to develop new and especially promising projects. Thus, although all government branches are assured a sizeable share, there is also the possibility of financing new projects and pressure to rationalize and economize on existing ones. But each ministry is given the freedom to carry on its own retrenchment for the five to ten percent each year, thus avoiding the antagonism between the regulator and the regulated that develops in America when the often poorly informed outsider arbitrarily and hastily chops up programs, creating management problems for those inside.

Income distribution statistics for Japan indicate that the gap between the highest and lowest quintile is among the smallest in the world. The ratio of income of the highest quintile to the lowest quintile in 1970, for example, was 4.3, while in the United States it was 7.1. And, according to recent figures on students entering Tokyo University, the most competitive national university, roughly thirty-five percent came from families whose incomes fall within the top twenty percent, and fourteen percent from families in the bottom twenty percent. The success in income distribution derives not simply from a booming economy with full employment but from conscious policy. In national polls about ninety percent of the Japanese public consider themselves middle class.

As the nation began to recover from World War II, government leaders recognized that capitalists, company white-collar employees, industrial laborers, farmers, and government workers should share in the fruits of economic growth. Since the 1950s there has been an implicit understanding in many circles as to how these different groups would share in the benefits—not through a welfare system but through adjusting wage increases to balance improvements among various segments of the population. Consumer organizations have been weak, but people organize groups to improve their circumstances by raising their income through their place of work. Each spring labor unions compare figures and then formulate their demands for wage increases. Similarly, management associations jointly declare the necessity of limiting wage hikes to avoid ruining the companies. Although representatives of large associations present general and specific arguments to prepare the climate of public opinion, the final decisions are made in individual companies. Companies are not bound by rigidities imposed, for example, by the Swedish system, where national ratios of wages are set for various kinds of work. Although each company retains some flexibility, statisticians who have analyzed wage increases in various companies are able to predict final wage settlements with a high degree of accuracy, using a formula that takes into account productivity increases, cost of living increases, and profitability. This testifies to a widespread consensus among workers and management in the various companies as to what constitutes an equitable share of the profits. Each company knows that to maintain the enthusiasm and support of its workers it must be roughly as generous as other companies of the same kind. The constancy of considerations does not preclude some changes as, for example, when the gap between young and old workers began to narrow in response to the shortage of beginning workers. Over the years, however, as information has spread, the differentials between people with the same level of skill in different industries has declined.

There are differences in public and private sector salary increases in a given year, for government employees tend not to receive such large increases in the years of excellent business as do workers in the private sector, nor such slight increases in the more difficult years. However, over several years the average increase in the two sectors is remarkably close. National and local governments also raise their salaries at about the same rate, with only minor variations. Since government employees watch the wage increases in private industry very closely, the government recognizes that to maintain a devoted work force it must increase salaries at roughly the same pace as private industry.

The same sense of fair share applies to increases in the standard of living of farmers, whose income has also kept up with nonindustrial salaries. Adjustment of rice prices is the single best way to affect farm income because rice is the most staple crop, being produced by about ninety percent of all farmers. Each year the government determines rice price subsidies so as to keep the income of farmers in line with the rising salary of private and government workers, an aim that was codified in 1961 in legislation drafted by the Ministry of Agriculture. In a given year there may be marginal differences of two or three percent between the increase of nonagricultural salaries and the increase in farmers' profits from rice sales. This differential is determined by such factors as the extent of the obligation of LDP leaders to farmers in the most recent election and the sufficiency of the rice supply in meeting demand. If there is a great shortage of rice in a given year, rice subsidies rise slightly more than nonagricultural wages, and, conversely, if there is a surplus of rice, rice subsidies rise slightly less. This minor differential gives the government some leverage for adjusting the rice supply to meet demand.

The balance between government benefits to big business and small business rests on a long-term acceptance of change and modernization which generally favors big business, but an effort is made to provide a fair share to small business until the people dislocated are placed in other lines of work. The government has encouraged the rapid modernization of industry, sometimes requiring the merger of small plants that cannot meet its new standards for modernity of facilities. It has not opposed the transformation of many small industrial plants from independent units to subcontractors of larger plants for it often leads to modernization of the subcontractors.

But in certain light industrial sectors in which small business remains competitive, the government has helped make loans available to the smaller firms. In the retailing sector it has established limits on the construction of new department stores, discount houses, and shopping centers, thus slowing down the impact they have on small retail stores. It is acknowledged that in the long run the share of the market of small private shops will decline, but the government tries to make the process orderly. Bureaucrats argue that small business should get a fair share, and the fair share should decline at a moderate, predictable pace so as to prevent sudden disruption, but they cannot halt the tide of progress.

The balancing act between big business and agriculture rests on the fact that LDP political funds come mostly from big business at the national level and from small business and farmers at the local level. Because of the size of contributions from big business, politicians cannot afford to alienate it in basic policy formation. But the LDP depends on votes as well as funds, and it relies on small businessmen and especially on farmers for those votes. Since farmers in a locality tend toward bloc voting more than the floating urban voters, their interests are strongly represented in the Diet. Because Diet members support the interests of the farmers, the Ministry of Agriculture cannot stray from the interests of the farming community.

Labor unions and their allies in the Socialist, Democratic Socialist, and Communist parties can also create difficulties in delaying and disrupting Diet progress if some effort is not made to accommodate their demands. The implicit sense of what constitutes a fair share takes account of relative power, but there is public sympathy with the underdog and this provides a balance wheel if rewards are in danger of becoming too one-sided. Despite symbolic gestures of vehement disagreement from these opposition parties, in fact there is considerable compromise underlying most Diet action. In large part this is because government leaders and even their business supporters recognize the advisability of granting them a fair share of the rewards of growth to ensure that they too have a stake in the system.

These broad levels of agreement about equitable shares reduce the threat of strikes because special interest groups are unlikely to receive much more than their fair share no matter how much they struggle and leaders are unlikely to give them much less. The system provides security and predictability without removing the flexibility of companies to respond to special problems of economic fluctuation and to special opportunities for investment. Because all other affected groups can be mobilized to prevent one group from getting an undue increase at any one point, inflation control becomes immeasurably easier than in the United States and helps explain why the Japanese economy recovered so quickly from oil-shock inflation and why it has maintained an inflation rate significantly lower than America's in recent years. Japanese homogeneity may make it easier to forge these understandings, but it is the constant effort, mutual awareness, and discussion that make it work, precedures which are not inherently impossible to achieve in other societies.

THREATS OLD AND NEW: OVERCONFORMITY AND CHAOS

From about 1935 to 1945 the information reaching the Japanese public from abroad was for the most part highly restricted and heavily filtered. Only a small percentage of intellectuals, bureaucrats, and people of culture could be considered sophisticated in understanding developments and thinking in the West. At the same time, with the expansion of Japan into Korea, Taiwan, and later into Manchuria and China proper, the military came to have a dominant role in the society. The democracy that had begun to sprout in the Meiji period and had expanded rapidly in form and substance in the 1920s proved fragile under pressure from the military. The average citizen, having grown up in an extremely close-knit society, found no basis for resisting a military dictatorship and a controlled press.

The transition of the average person from a subject to a citizen with an increased awareness of government activity and a greater sense of his rights to be represented in the decision-making process has thus taken place quite recently. Compared to the citizenry of other countries, the Japanese citizen has in fact been relatively passive. The elder generation, trained in the 1930s and 1940s, has not entirely outgrown the experience of docile acquiescence in matters of great import to the nation.

This has led many Japanese intellectuals and Western scholars of Japan to worry about the strong pressure for conformity that could restrict dissent and stifle individualism, perhaps even returning Japan to prewar totalitarian patterns. The fear is not without foundation. In the newspaper world, for example, despite the thoroughness of international news reporting and the coverage of internal Japanese developments, the range of opinion expressed in the three major dailies is narrow, and certain important stories may be suppressed. It is generally accepted that government bureaucrats are extraordinarily honest, but there are occasional instances of bureaucratic indiscretion known to reporters that are not published for fear of tarnishing the image of the bureaucracy. For example, it is widely believed that if the Lockheed scandal had not occurred just after Watergate, when so many Japanese were filled with admiration for America's capacity to root out difficulties at the highest level, the affair would have been quieted much more easily. In late 1972 a long article appeared in *Bungei Shunju*, a well-known literary magazine, detailing the indiscretions of Kakuei Tanaka, then prime minister. However, for several weeks after it appeared this important article was not discussed, directly or indirectly, in any of the major Japanese papers or on television. At that point Tanaka appeared before the Foreign Correspondents Club, which led to many foreign newspaper articles about his indiscretions; only then did Japanese papers feel compelled to write about these problems, which in turn triggered Tanaka's downfall. To be sure, once news of the scandal had appeared in the press, it was no longer possible for newspapers to avoid divulging many of the details, but many are convinced that the press never thoroughly explored all aspects of the story.

It is understood that politicians receive funds from people seeking favors and that they have some obligations to respond to these requests. Although their activity in this regard is not totally unlike the activity of politicians in America and elsewhere, by any standards Japanese politicians and newspaper reporters receive an impressive number of gifts and entertainment from those wishing favors. The distortion of public policy to favor certain vested interest groups on the basis of political contributions is probably not great, but there have been several well-known incidents of such manipulation, all publicized only later, and it is generally assumed that there are more cases known by reporters and key business leaders that are suppressed.

Because of the strength of group ties, people tend to adapt themselves to their group, accepting its viewpoints on specific issues rather than developing individual opinions. Even if a vote is held, the vast majority commonly follow the group position without developing a separate position of their own. At the local level, whether in the village, town, urban work place, or neighborhood, certain leaders tend to set the tone and define the framework in which issues are considered. What passes as village or community consensus therefore may in fact reflect not agreement but the reluctance of many ordinary people to express their views for fear of offending these leaders. At the national level, the power of big business has often stifled dissenting opinion. The sense of community among top leaders tends to exclude those who do not meet their standards— whether size of firm, nature of business, or personal style—and this often makes it difficult for outsiders to get a fair hearing in influential circles.

These pressures for conformity are inextricably linked with the capacity of those groups to maintain their cohesiveness. No one would advocate limiting the variety of views expressed or suppressing stories. It is doubtful, however, that the limits to expression of variant opinion imposed by group cohesiveness still constitute a serious threat to Japanese democracy. The prewar totalitarian state dominated an unsophisticated public that had no choice but to follow blindly a militaristic government because so few of its members had the sophistication to know otherwise or the opportunities to say otherwise. With the explosion of foreign movies and later television shows since World War II, the sophistication of the Japanese public about foreign and domestic affairs has reached a level that precludes a return to prewar ignorance. The experience of the Japanese in forming and voicing their own opinions has grown immeasurably. Similarly, the level of involvement of millions of Japanese in business overseas and the constant electronic contact with the outside renders next to impossible the threat of communication restriction and thought control of the population. One might imagine that even sophisticated people with constant contact with foreigners could somehow be nationally controlled under an extraordinarily powerful military, but the possibility of a strong military appears remote. In addition, the public has grown much more accustomed to free expression of ideas. In short, it is hard to imagine that the control of thought by a totalitarian leadership is a viable threat to Japan.

In the opinion of many thoughtful Japanese leaders, the greatest threat to Japanese-style democracy comes not from the possibility of external aggression or the potential cutoff of raw materials or foreign markets. Nor does it come from committed rightists, Marxists, urban guerrillas, or the Red Army. The real threat, in their view, is the dissipation of group cohesiveness. During the university disputes of 1968-69, faculty and university officials were unable to bargain with the New Left. That group was not well organized, it did not have a defined constituency nor a precise point of view, and there was no means to assure that any agreement would stick. Some citizens' groups are equally ephemeral or nebulous. They protest, prevent construction projects, and disrupt ongoing organizations, but they are not sufficiently organized to represent a constituency nor are they empowered to reach agreements. With the old left, including Socialists, Communists, and even their student affiliates, there is opposition but there is also structure for negotiation. There are arguments and counterarguments, demonstrations and manipulations, but in the end an agreement or at least a modus vivendi with tacit understanding is reached. With unorganized groups there is no way to reach an understanding.

In the view of most Japanese, their style of democracy rests on the ability of groups to retain sufficient power over their members to maintain solidarity and ensure that agreements are honored, since both the higher aggregation of interests and the distribution of fair shares is accomplished through group solidarity. The increase in urbanization, physical mobility, and apartment living rather than independent housing all threaten to weaken group organization. The growing affluence that permits young people to buy motorcycles and cars and to worry less about their sources of income, combined with the new cultural systems, in part imported from abroad, create a new type of modern youth much less susceptible to group organization. In the view of many Japanese leaders, this constitutes the most serious threat to their democracy.

In balance Japan has been more successful than modern Western countries in stemming the tide against egoism and nihilism. There is enough flexibility in the Japanese political scene to allow new loose groupings to form where other established groups do not adequately represent their interests, and most civic leaders try to develop relations with them; but to become effective, new groups must go the way of more structured groups, carefully cooperating with others while defending their own interests. It could be argued that in the complex modern world the dangers of chaos from centrifugal force is a greater threat to most countries than the threat of overly tight control. Japan, which has put great emphasis on cooperation, is in a fortunate position at this juncture in history when coordination of diverse groups is so difficult. Japan's success derives not from a carefully enunciated ideology but from a strong commitment to what George Lodge calls communitarian values and from the determination and imaginative efforts of group participants at all levels to maintain their cohesiveness. Convinced that it is difficult to respond to loosely organized citizens' movements on a national scale, business and government leaders have endeavored to institutionalize relationships with local protesters. They try to identify consumer advocates who can carry on the dialogue while retaining the respect of their fellow protesters. Although this might be criticized as co-opting the movement, businessmen and politicians know that in the end they will have to share a portion of the pie with these new organizations. If necessary, they are even prepared to adapt their own way of operations, for they are eager to absorb new ideas and to make constructive use of the energy of capable young people who might otherwise be alienated.

While political participation continues to expand broadly

and rapidly to include vigorous new groups, leaders are cautious not to make concessions that would weaken the capacity of their organizations to maintain their inegrity. Within organizations, officials insist on retaining the flexibility to reward those who cooperate, even if the short-term reward is approval and honor rather than money or high office. An organization's institutional memory ensures that this short-range symbolic approval will be translated into long-range material benefit. Members know that others will not quickly or easily forget if they should be remiss in responding to group expectations. An individual approaching higher levels with requests is powerless if he does not come with organizational backing, for higher-level politicians and bureaucrats are aware above all of the petitioner's group membership. An individual cannot expect to have a share in the spoils unless he stays with his group, because it is through groups that the fair share is distributed. In short, even in Japan the threat of chaos may be greater than the threat of overconformity, but by Western standards chaos does not seem imminent.

6

The Large Company: Identification and Performance

AFTER TOURING automobile assembly lines in both countries, a visitor observed, "The American factory seems almost like an armed camp. Foremen stand guard to make sure workers do not slack off. Workers grumble at foremen, and foremen are cross with workers. In the Japanese factory, employees seem to work even without the foreman watching. Workers do not appear angry at superiors and actually seem to hope their company succeeds."

Japanese workers' pride in their work and loyalty to their company are reflected in their capacity to produce goods that are not only competitive in price but reliable in quality. Some workers, especially younger workers in small plants, may be alienated from their company, but compared to Americans, they are absent less, strike less, and are willing to work overtime and refrain from using all their allotted vacation time without any immediate monetary benefit. The average Japanese laborer may accomplish no more than a loyal hard-working American counterpart in a comparable factory, but loyalty to the company is typically higher and hard work more common. Many an American businessman, after touring a Japanese company and inspecting figures on time lost from absenteeism and strikes, has expressed the wish that he had such a labor force.

It is tempting to account for the differences by historical tradition, but American workers have become less disciplined in recent decades, albeit with the same Amercan tradition, and modern Japanese employees of large companies are far more loyal than, for example, Japanese textile workers at the turn of the century. It is common to assign American labor problems to our affluence, but discipline has remained strong in affluent Japan. Furthermore, Japanese companies establishing plants in America have achieved with a few years of modified Japanese-style management a level of employee devotion on the average higher than in comparable American plants. Before resorting to an explanation that centers on a semimystical "Oriental spirit," one might consider whether Japanese success bears any relationship to company management and treatment of workers.

THE EMERGENCE OF THE JAPANESE COMPANY SYSTEM

The Japanese company system as we know it today began to emerge only late in the nineteenth century. Craft shops, with paternalistic masters and their apprentices and journeymen, date back centuries, but these "feudalistic" shops are not totally different from the kind of paternalistic shops of Paul Revere's America or preindustrial Europe.

Modern Japanese corporate paternalism drew on the recent feudal past, but it emerged in industries that borrowed modern industrial technology and organization and required a high level of skill. In new industries with lower skill requirements like textiles, no long training was necessary. Here, young, dexterous employees were, if anything, more useful than older experienced ones with less dexterity, and young women were at least as agile as men. Late nineteenth- and early twentieth-century Japanese textile manufacturers, therefore, offered wages based on a piece rate system without significant salary increases for seniority. Wages were so low and factory conditions so unsatisfactory that most workers left before completing two or three years, and in some factories turnover was even more rapid.

Modern industries requiring a high level of skill faced different problems. As Ronald Dore has shown, the resulting late development pattern, unlike other industrialized countries' earlier indigenous development, relied on more concerted planning, training, and investment. In sizeable companies that manufactured steel, machine tools, electric equipment, and the like, companies needed to train both a group of highly skilled laborers and a group of white-collar managerial personnel. Because these skills were not based on experience with indigenous developments, it took considerable time and capital investment to train them. And since these new companies were in basic industries that were well-financed and ultimately backed by the government, the companies were in a position to guarantee long-term employment. They therefore developed a seniority system of wage increases such that the newly trained employees in whom the company invested so heavily would be motivated to remain. The system of seniority and permanent employment was by no means universal in Japanese industry, but it became the predominant pattern in the large-scale modern industrial sector and has since spread to the large commercial organizations as well. As the modern industrial sector expanded, a higher proportion of company employees has gradually been brought into this seniority and permanent employment pattern.

The modern form of the Japanese company has evolved considerably since the early 1900s. In the 1930s and during World War II Japanese companies were brought under increasingly tight government control. During the Allied Occupation, the large *zaibatsu* firms were split up into smaller independent firms, but they gradually recombined into the present-day loosely organized groups after the end of the Occupation. During the 1950s and 1960s under government guidance many smaller firms were consolidated in order to modernize, and new American technology and management were introduced. For a time companies even considered copying the American pattern whereby workers could be dismissed and laid off more easily and hired in midcareer: it might get rid of employees with low performance, reward bold, innovative employees held down by the system, increase flexibility, give employees stifled in one company more options elsewhere, and reduce costs in a declining sector. By the late 1960s, when Japanese businesses started outperforming companies in the West, Japanese management intellectuals were satisfied that their seniority system was preferable to the dominant Western pattern, and they began to articulate a new philosophy of management.

The new philosophy incorporates many concepts from modern Western management and has much in common with large companies of American origin such as IBM, Polaroid, and Kodak. There is attention to basic business strategy, to product life cycles, to market surveys and marketing strategy, to accounting, to econometric models, to modern advertising, to up-to-date information processing. But some basics of the pre-World War II Japanese system remain: long-term perspective, permanent employment, seniority, and company loyalty. In addition, certain features gradually developed have recently been articulated to a higher degree: separation of rank and task, low differentials in pay and status for workers of a given age, "bottoms-up" management, and small-group responsibility.

The Japanese firm is less interested in short-term profits and more concerned with the long run. Executives may disparage their success in planning and forecasting, but they continue their best efforts and, when appropriate, boldly sacrifice profits for several years to build the groundwork for later success. They take care in cultivating good relations with institutions that might potentially be useful. They provide extensive training for personnel in skills that might be needed in the future. They invest in technology at seemingly high prices if it might later pay off. They invest heavily in plant modernization even when present plants meet immediate demands. As products become competitive, they conduct extensive preparatory work to lay a solid grounding for markets.

The company's capacity to think in long-range terms is made possible in part by their relatively greater reliance on bank loans than on the sale of securities to meet their capital requirements. Since stock now accounts for less than one-sixth of a company's capital needs compared to one-half in the United States, stockholders lack power to pressure for showing a profit each year, and banks are as interested in a company's long-range growth as the company itself. When companies are able to pay interest, the banks want to continue to lend them money, for banks are as dependent on quality companies to lend to as companies are dependent on the banks for borrowing. Indeed, when quality companies with their own capital want to cut costs by repaying loans, the banks try to make it attractive to continue borrowing.

Despite their interest in the future, most Japanese companies have not considered it profitable to invest heavily in basic research and development. It has made more sense to purchase foreign technology, for even if costs seemed high at the time of purchase, in retrospect the technology was obtained at bargain prices. The company concentrates research on adapting the technology for large-scale production, sometimes in such a way that it no longer needs to pay royalties on a particular patent. Japanese laws are such that processes, not functions, are patented. Thus, the company can buy technology, make new inventions that meet the same function as the original patent, and end their dependence on foreign technology. Until the 1970s many Western companies sold technology cheaply. Some did so because it was a perishable item likely to become obsolete or to be pirated, but often they were short-sighted in licensing patents—eager for a quick profit, ignorant of the long-term Japanese competitive threat, and unwilling to take the trouble to invest in developing the Japanese market. In recent years, as foreign companies are more clearly aware of the potential value of patents to Japanese mass producers, the prices and terms of technological transfer have become much higher, and the Japanese companies have therefore begun to move selectively into more research and development. Having caught up with much of Western technology, Japanese research is more concentrated in innovative rather than adaptive areas, and in areas with high potential economic payoff. Japan now has about as many people engaged in nonmilitary research as does the United States.

Just as MITI has tried to reorient industrial structure toward industrial sectors that can compete more effectively on world markets in the future, so each individual company tries to concentrate on product lines or segments that are likely to be more profitable in the future and to reduce its activity in declining sectors well before it is no longer profitable to continue.

It is not that Japanese are not interested in profitability, but that they are prepared to defer maximizing immediate profits in order to increase market share. Beginning in the late 1970s when the Japanese growth rate started leveling off, most Japanese companies have been trying even harder to find ways to cut costs to maintain profitability. But they tend to judge their company's success less by annual profit than by the annual changes in the market share their company has compared to other companies in the industrial sector. As the Boston Consulting Group has demonstrated, profitability is closely related to market share, for as firms expand they have more low-priced young labor and more modern plants. Therefore the companies' emphasis on market share has been well-placed.

The company's interest in the long term is also related to the system of permanent employment whereby an ordinary employee remains in the firm from the time he first enters after leaving school until he retires, which in most firms averages about fifty-seven or fifty-eight. The firm is committed to the employee and provides a sense of belonging, personal support, welfare and retirement benefits, and increased salary and rank with age. Barring serious long-term depression, the employee expects that he will never be laid off, and even if the company were to disband or be absorbed by another company, he expects that a new job elsewhere will be arranged. Companies are able to offer this kind of security despite economic fluctuations for several reasons. In times of temporary growth, additional temporary employees may be hired. For example, housewives may be added to the work force with the clear understanding that they will remain only while business needs them. Employees retiring from the company may be offered special short-term assignments in the company, usually at a lower salary than before retirement. Work may be subcontracted to small companies with the understanding that these contracts imply no permanent relationship.

If a large, reliable company should encounter economic difficulty, it will not go out of business because it is backed by banks, and behind the banks are various government institutions. Japanese companies have large debts to banks, but virtually all major companies are considered important for the economy as a whole, and therefore the Bank of Japan, backed by the Finance Ministry, stands behind the city banks that lend to the companies. Every company borrows from a main bank and then from other banks. If the company should be badly in debt and need to be bailed out, the main bank arranges a new management team for the company, often from its own staff, thereby strengthening lines of control over the company, which had previously been essentially autonomous. To the company officials replaced, this is not only a loss of power for them and their followers but a disgrace, something to avoid at all costs. Similarly, even in a declining industry, management and unions consider consolidation and consequent loss of power a last resort, something to fight against as long as possible. Every large company that has collapsed in Japan had resorted to questionable practices and behaved improperly toward its main bank. There is virtually no danger of a reliable major firm collapsing, but this security does not lead companies to relax their determination to perform at a high level.

The Japanese company with a given amount of resources has much greater security than an American firm in making bold efforts to modernize and undertake new activities. In addition to financial backing through banks, the company can be sure that key government ministries are concerned with their success and will help out in unpredictable emergencies in finding land, getting resources, gaining crucial technology. They know the government will be unlikely to undertake antitrust or other legal action that will greatly upset the company's overall capacities. The Japanese company signs fewer contracts and works more with other firms with whom there is a high degree of mutual trust, especially within the same group. They can therefore make more flexible adjustments in case of unpredictable outside forces, greatly reducing legal risks which American companies would have to bear regardless of new circumstances.

A company that encounters economic difficulties has many ways of adjusting without sacrificing the permanent employment system. Usually in addition to monthly salary, the company pays sizeable semiannual bonuses amounting to several months' salary. The size of the bonus depends on company profits, and therefore in times of depression it may be reduced without affecting basic monthly salary. In the spring, when basic monthly salary is determined, salary increases can be reduced or eliminated. The company can request employees to take an immediate vacation with partial rather than full pay or to reduce working hours, or to take minor salary cuts while requesting high officials to take larger salary cuts. If the difficulty is more severe, a company will reduce its entering class or even take in no new employees, adjusting assignments within the company so that jobs that would have been done by new employees will be done by others. Since companies follow long-term trends very closely, in industries that are expected to level off or decline, as for example in family electronics products which are increasingly made in Taiwan and Korea where labor costs are lower, companies will have anticipated the decline and admitted fewer employees in the years preceding the decline. Temporary employees will be released and permanent employees reassigned to their tasks. If the situation is very severe, the products formerly made by subcontractors will be made by regular permanent workers when contracts with subcontractors are terminated. Some individual subcontracting firms may be in trouble, but until now there have been enough new opportunities that few workers still in their prime are unable to find new work. If the recession is so severe that this kind of remedy is not adequate, then the company may move into some product line where it can keep people busy, for it makes sense to the Japanese to employ steadily a devoted work force and to take a small loss in order to provide work opportunities for one's permanent staff. As a further remedy, a company may encourage its workers to retire somewhat earlier by providing special benefits. If all these strategies are insufficient, some employees may be transferred from a company in a declining sector to affiliated companies in growing sectors. In fact, however, the number of cases of permanent employees being transferred to other companies in hard times is small. The system has so many cushions that permanent employees in large companies have ample reason to feel secure. Japanese companies may trim around the edges but they are not about to abandon the system.

Because an employee has job security and knows his salary will rise with seniority, he is willing to accept moderately low wages during his first few years in the company. Also, since retirement age is normally in the late fifties, salary increments can go up fairly rapidly without a company's worrying about having very high-paid elderly employees for many years. Although the system is designed to provide incentives for the young person trained by the company to remain loyal throughout his career and to have a sense of advancement, one of the important side effects is that it creates great pressure on a company to hire young people. Companies are reluctant to hire a midcareer person not only because his sense of loyalty would be questionable but because it is to the company's advantage to employ him during his low-priced younger years. In boom years, school and university graduates usually have had several positions to choose from, and even in relatively depressed years unemployment among young people leaving school is virtually nonexistent, much lower than the general figure for unemployment, which escalated to over two percent in the late 1970s.

The seniority system in the company works much as in the bureaucracy. Although there are pay differentials later in the career based on performance and responsibility, these are small compared to those accounted for by seniority pay. Responsible executives consciously try to keep pay distinctions among those with the same seniority no larger than, and if anything smaller than, what most employees consider appropriate. New employees ordinarily receive precisely the same pay for the first several years in the company; when differentials begin to appear later, they are minor, having more psychological than monetary significance. Equal pay tends to dampen competition and strengthen camaraderie among peers during their early years. If anything, the peer group recognizes that the ablest of their group are not being fully compensated in salary for their contribution, and this tends to dull any envy of peers toward the fastest rising in their group. Even those who rise more rapidly after differentials come into play can be promoted only if they enjoy the respect and approval of their associates; this prevents the growing distinctions from being overly disruptive. In a basic social sense, all those with the same seniority are considered as equals.

Those with higher positions continue to dress like others, often in company uniforms, and peers retain informal terms of address and joking relationships. Top officials receive less salary and fewer stock options than American top executives, and they live more modestly. It is easier to maintain lower pay for Japanese top executives because with loyalty so highly valued, they will not be lured to another company. This self-denial by top executives was designed to keep the devotion of the worker, and it undoubtedly succeeds.

It is understood that no one in a management track will be skipped over in advancement and no one will serve over another who entered the company at an earlier time. The same is true for technical track personnel and for laborers. Japanese executives at times considered increasing incentives for young people by allowing them to rise more rapidly and serve over their elders, but this caused undo strain in personal relations. The embarrassment for a person serving under a younger person is greater than in the United States. A person's official position can only rise until his retirement, and this eliminates any anxiety over the possibility that a worker will be relieved of his job or dropped to a lower position. After the first several years the able person begins to take on positions associated with the elite course inside the company and gradually rises to more important posts. But the differentials among age peers in title as well as pay are slight. A very able person might become section chief a year or two before his peers, or he might become section chief at the same time as his peers but be chief of a more important section.

As with elite bureaucrats, those who come up an elite course within the company have a broad range of experience in all parts of the company. The high official therefore has detailed understanding of issues in all sections as well as close friendships that ensure continuous frank communication. The highest officials just below the level of president have members of their peer group at all other important positions in the company, which makes for unusually effective communication and mutual understanding. It also makes it more difficult for younger men to break into the inner circles if they were to advance more rapidly than others of their age group and requires that they wait until their peer group holds the top positions. This also ensures classmate linkages with other companies and the government bureaucracy, where elite rise in pace, so that contacts with every important institution at every level can be conducted through long-term intimate channels. Managers of a large American corporation commonly have at least as broad a range of experience, and American companies can acquire some know-how by hiring workers with certain skills. However, with more turnover American employees lack the close personal connections within the company and with peers in other key organizations that contribute so much to Japanese company effectiveness.

As in the bureaucracy, only the top handful of officers work beyond normal retirement age, and when one man in an age cohort is chosen president, all his peers resign, usually to assume a high position with a subsidiary or subcontractor. One man therefore stands alone as the senior person concerned with daily affairs in the company, although the chairman of the board, usually the previous president, and board members or consultants, also former chief executives, may carry great weight on major issues or other issues in which they have special interest. It is conventional wisdom in Japan to concentrate the most experienced men at the top, in part because they have mature judgment but also because other senior people do not have to suffer the humiliation of serving under people younger than themselves and will wholeheartedly accept authority from those older who are also competent.

How is it possible for a unit to work effectively when a mediocre senior person is serving above an abler junior person? The answer lies not only in the senior person's lack of worry about being replaced by his junior but in the differentiation between task and title or position. The essential building block of a company is not a man with a particular role assignment and his secretary and assistants, as might be the case in an American company. The essential building block of the organization is the section. A section might have eight or ten people, including the section chief. Within the section there is not as sharp a division of labor as in an American company. To some extent, each person in the same section shares the same overall responsibility and can substitute for another when necessary. The abler younger person knows that he cannot surpass his senior in rank and salary now, but that all concerned informally recognize that he is abler than his superior. He also knows that he will eventually rise higher than his present senior, but that he must cooperate with his present senior for his section to accomplish its tasks and for him to be considered promising. Similarly, the head of the section is held responsible for the successful work of the section. He knows that he needs to take advantage of the talents of the abler person under him, and he therefore eagerly gives him responsible work. He is in no fear of being upstaged by his underling, for they are lumped together when their accomplishments in the section are evaluated. Within the general work of a section, one's assignment to a task at a given time is affected by one's general abilities, skills, and aptitudes more than by one's title within the section. The section is, in a sense, an organic unit composed to match a variety of talents rather than a team with clearly distinct, independent role assignments. The section has a responsibility to perform, and each is expected to help out by dividing up what needs to be done, substituting for someone who is absent, or assisting another when necessary. The assignment is flexible, for the position and tasks are two different systems: the position rises with seniority, but the work depends on the tasks of the unit and the talents and complementarity of the individuals. Work is not determined by a specifically defined position.

When asked to describe a Japanese company, most Japanese managers list as one characteristic the practice of "bottom up" rather than "top down." The lowly section, within its sphere, does not await executive orders but takes the initiatives. It identifies problems, gathers information, consults with relevant parts of the company, calls issues to the attention of higher officials, and draws up documents. Of course the section acts within the context of the wishes of higher officials and is in constant communication with them. Proposals are not usually sent to higher levels until the section has consulted broadly with other sections and has formulated detailed plans. Nowhere in the process is there a fully organized presentation of several options to higher officials, and nowhere is there a neat package of conclusions flowing from higher levels. Good decisions emerge not from brilliant presentations of alternatives but from section people discussing all aspects of the questions over and over with all the most knowledgeable people. Some senior executives in companies play a central role in making decisions, but ordinarily they do so only after appropriate section leaders lay the groundwork through close consultation with other sections and only when lower levels cannot themselves resolve their differences. Section people take great pride in their work because of their initiatives and because they have a chance to develop their leadership and carry great weight within the company on matters relating to their sphere. Consequently, the morale of young workers in their thirties tends to be very high.

For this system to work effectively, leading section personnel need to know and to identify with company purposes to a higher degree than persons in an American firm. They achieve this through long experience and years of discussion with others at all levels. Company aims are not canonized into documents but continue to fluctuate with the changing environment, and therefore section leaders must avoid being locked into a specific list of aims but rather adapt to overall opportunities for the company as a whole. Section leaders are sufficiently tuned to the overall thinking of the company for them to in fact achieve this, and they are given the leeway to act accordingly because higher officials know that section leaders are thoroughly committed to their company, where they will remain until retirement.

With so much authority concentrated at low levels and with so much discussion between levels, how can the company leaders make the bold decisions that have led to Japanese success? First, they operate in a climate of much greater security than the typical American firm. A company receives advice from well-informed bureaucrats, banks, affiliated trading companies, and other companies in its group. It is backed by banks and ultimately the government, which when necessary will assist it in obtaining special resources and facilities and will not pursue it in ways that create uncertainties and costly law suits. Second, because rivals are striving for market share and because the seniority system and bank lending require expansion, it becomes more dangerous to stand pat than to move ahead with bold modernization and innovation. Further, stockholders do not constrain executives with demands for short-term profits. As a result, Japanese companies have consistently been bolder than most of their Western counterparts in modernizing and expanding their capacity.

GROUP SPIRIT AND PERSONAL INCENTIVES

In addition to providing the employee with the economic incentives for long-term loyalty, company officials do their best to reinforce employee identification wth the company. They provide elaborate annual ceremonies for inducting the new employees who enter as a group shortly after the end of the school year. The official training program may be any-where from a few weeks to years, and includes not only useful background information but emotional accounts of company history and purposes. For spiritual and disciplinary training the employee may go on retreats, visit temples, or endure special hardships. To strengthen the bonds of solidarity, the new em-ployee may be housed in company dorms while undergoing training, even if it means being separated from his spouse or parents. But even after the formal training program is over, the young employee continues to be treated as an apprentice for some time. He continues to receive training and super-vision, and he is expected to behave with appropriate deference to his seniors. In American terms it is perhaps like a combina-tion of the behavior of the fraternity pledge, without the hazing, and the young doctor in residency training.

Companies commonly have their own uniforms, badges, songs, and mottos. Each company has a special lore about the spirit of a "Matsushita person" or "Sumitomo person" or "Sanwa person," but to the outside observer the spirit sounds strikingly similar: enthusiastic, loyal, devoted. Company reception halls are available to employees' families for receptions and celebrations. Resort houses in the mountains and on the seacoast can be used by company employees who have put in the appropriate years of loyal service. Dormitories or apartment projects are available to employees of many companies. Unlike America, where mortgages are commonly obtained directly from banks, in Japan a high proportion of mortgages are obtained from the workers' company at subsidized interest rates. The company supplies gifts for many occasions in addition to the large semiannual bonuses. Special discounts of company products are available to employees and their families. Many companies have daily ceremonies—for opening the store, commencing work, or starting physical exercise. Parties large and small bid farewell to the old year, send off employees transferred to another city, welcome them home, congratulate people on promotions or honors, greet visitors, and commemorate retirement. Weekend group trips celebrate the coming of cherry blossoms, fall foliage, or holidays. For family members there are parties, special-interest clubs, courses, lectures, and exhibitions.

In addition to providing gymnasiums and swimming pools, a large company usually has sports teams well-equipped with uniforms and often with showcase facilities. So they can do well in their leagues, many companies recruit talented athletes as company employees, much as American colleges do, and they are given only minor work responsibilities. Outstanding professional sports teams that in the United States would be privately owned and associated with a particular city are in Japan sponsored instead by companies. The very highest officials in the company commonly take off from work to attend important sports contests with their rival companies.

During Prime Minister Tanaka's time companies even tried sponsoring political candidates, but this was abandoned because they had limited appeal, even within the company, and it proved embarrassing for companies to have their candidate lose.

Executives generally want their employees to spend a certain amount of off-duty hours together, preferably under company sponsorship. One company, troubled that too many young employees had their own cars and sufficiently high salary to go off on their own rather than use company facilities, surveyed employee interests and, finding that bowling was then the current rage, provided very attractive uniforms, bowling balls, and other equipment. It also bought a regular block of time for workers at the most luxurious nearby bowling alley. By ensuring that more leisure time was under company auspices, the company reinforced group solidarity.

Loyalty in a large company is a many-layered overlapping labyrinth. Employees have layers of loyalty to the group with which the company is affiliated, to the particular factory or store, to the section, and to the immediate work group. Younger employees who are in a given specialty or career line may also enjoy a special link with senior sponsors in the same career line. Even with the immediate work group, one kind of group spirit thrives when the superior is absent, another when he is present. Part or all of the peer group assembles to commemorate earlier times and gossip about current events. Informal socializing, celebrations, and farewell or welcome-home parties occur at all of these levels.

At times a senior's concern about younger colleagues borders on what Westerners would consider "mothering," for Japanese of both sexes accept personal solicitousness that in the United States would ordinarily be considered unmasculine for men to give or receive. To avoid embarrassing an individual in public, criticism is commonly expressed in private in the spirit of a superior siding with a junior to help with a problem certain to cause him trouble.

With so much security and warmth, how does the system ensure high performance? In initially hiring employees, the company aims to be as merciless as entrance examinations in selecting people of quality. In preparation for selecting among employees of a peer group for more responsible positions, key line officers spend an enormous amount of time informally evaluating the performance of juniors, for decisions about personnel are considered too important to be left to personnel specialists. Employees are generally reassigned every two or three years, and each person knows that the quality of his over-all performance is being evaluated to determine his next assignment. Those who rise to the top are chosen because in addition to high innate ability they have the capacity to see the big picture, to analyze problems clearly, to convey poise and confidence, to inspire support from fellow employees in all parts of the company, and to form successful relationships with top-level people in other companies and in the government.

The Japanese company makes it clear that its substantial benefits to employees are not guaranteed. Benefits are not distributed automatically by contractual agreement to anyone simply because he is a company member or because he falls into a certain category of age, status, and length of service, for leaders believe flexibility of rewards is needed as a critical leverage to maintain discipline. Bonuses, sick leave, and use of company facilities are offered to the hard worker, but signs of disapproval to the dilatory cause doubts about how superiors will respond when they come with their next request.

For motivating the worker, superiors rarely need to talk directly about benefits. Since employees have such long-term personal relationships with each other, small systematic differentiations of treatment by superiors have great psychological significance. Those who receive subtle hints that they are likely to rise eventually to the top positions are tremendously motivated because there is sufficient continuity and predictability to ensure that the hints can be translated into reality. When peers become overly solicitous to see if they can be of help, the worker knows that others consider his performance below par, and he may be devastated. He will rise by seniority alone, but to be at the bottom of his age group is extremely embarrassing and to be at the bottom and disliked for not trying as well is something to be avoided at all costs. But unlike students at the Harvard Business School and members of the United States State Department, for example, those at the bottom of the Japanese peer group do not need to worry that they may become castoffs as long as they exert themselves; the threat of banishment is often implicit but rarely used.

The most important single criterion for assessing quality for regular term promotions is the capacity to work well with others. The person who rises more rapidly is not the one with the original ideas but the one who can cooperate with others in finding a conclusion satisfactory to everyone. Personal achievement cannot be separated from the capacity to work effectively in groups. Eventually the reward for performance and effort include salary and position, but the proximate reward which foretells the eventual success in salary and position is the esteem of colleagues. In an American company without a strong group spirit and without expectations of permanent employment, an employee might come to feel that the only significant reward is salary and position, which in his view ought to be finely tuned to match performance. In the Japanese view, this custom, like tipping which they still avoid, cheapens the sense of service and contributes to contentiousness. In a Japanese company with strong group spirit and a long time frame, the really significant reward, the thing an employee strives for, is the esteem of his colleagues.

THE COMPANY MAN: HARD WORK AND SELF-ESTEEM

Earlier generations of Western social scientists like Durkheim and Parsons thought that occupational specialty could provide the means for integrating the individual in modern society. However, the pace of modern technological and organizational change renders occupation specialty training too rapidly outdated to provide a stable source of life-long identification and basic social integration for the society. No structure in the West compares with the Japanese firm in its capacity to introduce rapid change and to provide identification for a substantial portion of the population. The young American employee hired as a specialist is not interested in learning as broad a range of things about the company as the young Japanese employee, who is more of a generalist. A Japanese employee who knows he will be kept and retrained in midcareer is less likely to worry about innovation and resist technological change. Featherbedding and the reluctance of American workers to be flexible in performing various jobs in a company are problems for American industry not only because workers are afraid of losing their jobs but because they want to protect their skill level. The Japanese worker concerned about the long-range future of his company eagerly seeks technological change and, because his status and future is less related to a special skill level, he is more willing to perform miscellaneous tasks and to assist fellow workers in different tasks as the need arises. The employer gets fuller and more flexible use of employees, and employees find the varied work less monotonous than their American counterparts who stick to the same work.

Like paternalistic craft structures in premodern America, Europe, and Japan, the large modern Japanese company is committed to the whole individual, not simply to the task-related part of the individual. Alfred Sloan once boasted that General Motors continued to pay dividends to stockholders right through the depression even though it had to lay off workers. A Japanese business leader would never say such a thing and, if he did anything remotely resembling it, he would try to hide it, for valuing profits above his employees would destroy his relationship with his workers. The primary commitment of a Japanese firm is not to its stockholders but to its employees.

Japanese workers reciprocate this commitment, for they prefer a company that is not simply "dry," cool, and calculated, but "wet" with human emotion. The American employee with specific assignments and responsibilities and strictly calculated pay per hour is not inclined to work beyond stated time or to do extra personal things for his colleagues, but a Japanese employee is. Every five years, beginning in 1953, there have been public opinion polls in Japan asking if people would prefer to work for someone who made specific assignments and provided help within the confines of the work or someone who expected extras beyond specific assignments but was prepared to offer personal help beyond the regular rules. The Japanese public, by a substantial majority, consistently prefers the supervisor who has personal relations going beyond the work requirements. Americans overwhelmingly prefer the opposite.

Even without company-sponsored activities, employees find time in the evenings or on weekends to have good times with one another without work in front of them. They often socialize on the way home from work. In many companies with a five- or five-and-a-half-day week some employees at almost all levels come in on Saturday and stay later to play mahjong, *go*, *shoji*, or to go drinking. Even among more "modern" employees who, like Americans, want to spend weekend time with families, couples often spend their time with other couples connected with the same company. Socializing is partly for sheer fun, but many consciously try to have good times together to make it easier to work together during the week. Because employees know they have to have each other's goodwill until retirement, they are not as likely as Americans to become righteously indignant with each other. They look for ways to subdue tensions and rivalries and reinforce camaraderie. Inner feelings of competition, anxiety, and annoyance may be at least as strong as in American companies since relationships are so close and since escaping difficult problems by leaving the company is not ordinarily a realistic option. Informal sociability is not only an end in itself but a way to contain these potentially disruptive tendencies.

The success of Japanese companies in avoiding disruptive labor unrest must be understood in the context of long-run individual identification with the company, but it has been reinforced by company handling of labor unions. After World War II, when the Allied Occupation ordered a rapid expansion of labor unions, Japanese company executives moved quickly to make employees members of labor unions. Labor unions were thus born not from virulent struggles led by bitter union leaders but from the initiative of company leaders. Nonetheless, the labor movement, at first protected by the Allied Occupation, became a powerful and sometimes violent political force. Management moved to encourage faithful employees to take part in union activities with the hope of moderating the potentially devastating strikes. They encouraged white-collar employees to join the same company union as the blue-collar employees and provided rooms and other facilities for union activities. These same white-collar employees, after serving their stint in labor unions, then returned to their managerial career line without loss of seniority. When unions became too militant, companies sometimes used questionable tactics to break the union and sponsored a second union that was more sympathetic with company goals. Management realized that simply co-opting unions could not be successful, and they eagerly sought feedback from unions to find opportunities for meeting worker complaints in order to create better working relations and a more satisfied labor force. Japanese unions are organized by the enterprise, and national craft unions tend to be weak. Nonetheless, unions do energetically represent the interests of the workers in pushing for benefits. Otherwise, union leaders would lose the support of workers. Unions also play a role in aggregating worker opinion on issues directly affecting them as part of the root-binding process in the firm. Though very worried about the danger of unions in the late 1940s, management has come to regard their unions as friends in helping stabilize the company. To avoid an excessive adversary relationship and create a proper climate, management finds time to socialize with union leaders without waiting for disputes that engender an atmosphere of controversy.

Because Japan is a rapidly modernizing country, with a dual economy of a modern and less modern sector, workers in larger companies are elite, with better training, more security, and better working conditions than workers in small companies that are less modern. Employees in large companies therefore have felt privileged to be there. Furthermore, since companies were mostly formed by managers rather than independent owners, workers have no rich capitalist class above them but only a managerial class whose style of life is not so different from their own. Japanese executives feel that not only American company owners but managerial staff have given themselves too many emoluments compared to what they gave the workers. This modest differential between managers and workers of a given age tends to reinforce the worker's sense of identification with the firm.

In some areas unions have engaged in long disruptive strikes, but in all such cases workers were not afraid of company losses through strikes. Local government employees, public school teachers, national and private railway workers, workers in government monopolies like tobacco, and, in the early postwar period, mine workers have fought militantly, but they all share a common characteristic: they are convinced that disruptions will not endanger the future of their organization. Government employees know that taxes can be used to raise their wages and improve their conditions regardless of the effectiveness and efficiency of their government unit. Private railway workers know that company income is determined by the rate structure, which can be adjusted if wages are increased. And in the early postwar period, when coal was the main source of energy and the government provided necessary subsidies to private coal companies, workers were not afraid that militant struggle would weaken the competitiveness of their company. In the late 1950s, when coal companies were going out of business because of the decline of available resources, miners struck because they knew they wanted the best possible settlement, backed by government support for a declining industry. In ordinary companies, where workers identify with the long-run interests of the company, strikes have been virtually unknown once the Occupation ended and the economy returned to normal in the early 1950s.

With growing affluence and full employment in the late 1960s, many young Japanese became confident of their ability to earn a living even if they should leave their present company, and this attitude threatened company discipline. Many worried managers therefore fought harder than ever to maintain company solidarity. At the height of rapid growth, when unemployment was less than one percent and many company employees could have found work elsewhere, they still remained in their company. Since the oil shock of 1973, with renewed fears of a depression and increased unemployment, workers have felt especially dependent on their company and discipline has improved further. Although the Japanese standard of living is now on a par with that of the most advanced countries in the world, affluence has not ended hard work.

Even in the public sector there have been few debilitating strikes in recent years. Strikes in the public sector are officially illegal, and when some unions tested this legality in 1976, the strike was stopped before the announced termination date by public opinion and not the law. Employees from private companies who worked hard and accepted what they considered reasonable salary raises would not tolerate the government providing more favorable conditions for striking workers in the public sector. Newspapers that initially had taken a somewhat favorable attitude toward strikers changed quickly with the vehemence of public reaction. They began reporting, for example, that children of striking workers were ridiculed by classmates for what their parents were doing to the general public. It would not be politically feasible for workers in the public sector to use their capacity to stop the operation of public facilities to raise salaries higher than their counterparts in the private sector. It is not simply that the majority of Japanese workers are basically satisfied because their interests are being served, but that the workers in the private sector who do not strike because of devotion to their company exert public pressure strong enough to contain strikers in the public sector.

Perhaps more important than the success of companies in mobilizing workers for production and avoiding disabling strikes is the impact the system has on the self-esteem of the individual. The American who is fired or laid off as soon as the company's financial statement is in the red and who must go on unemployment insurance finds it hard to maintain great self-respect for his capacity to work. The worker who knows he will then be out of work understandably might demand more salary now, but in so doing he begins to measure his contribution and even his own worth solely in monetary terms. Even a high American official who is dropped or demoted because his division is unprofitable or who is hastily removed when dissatisfaction rises about company performance cannot help but have doubts about himself as well as his company. Unless caught in a horrendous well-publicized scandal, no Japanese official would be comparably disgraced by his company, and even if an official were caught in such an extreme case, other company officials find a way to cushion the blow if he has indeed performed well for the company. Officials who must be demoted to take responsibility for a public problem are often given substitute rewards and honor within the company so that they may not feel especially distraught. Success and failure come from group effort and are never laid on the shoulders of a single person. At worst, if an official performed badly, his term would be brought to a close slightly more rapidly or he might not be promoted to the next post quite as readily. Former officials do not need to be discredited by new officials and generally remain on good terms with their successors. Japanese workers who feel they do more than is required and feel they are appreciated by fellow workers enjoy a greater sense of individual worth than do those who merely get by with the minimal effort, a more common American pattern.

In short, the large Japanese company, an institutional structure that originated not in traditional Japan but in the mid-twentieth century, has developed a very effective modern corporatism well adapted to the needs of the latter part of the twentieth century. It has not eliminated problems. There are bad managers as well as good ones, and workers feel unhappiness with boring assignments, anxiety over personal difficulties, disappointment at not being more appreciated. But by international standards the large modern Japanese corporation is a highly successful institution. It is successful not because of any mystical group loyalty embedded in the character of the Japanese race but because it provides a sense of belonging and a sense of pride to workers, who believe their future is best served by the success of their company. The pride and stability that so many Japanese have because a family member works in a large company helps stabilize the political process and set a tone for the society at large.

7

Basic Education:
Quality and Equality

AMERICAN REPORTERS in Tokyo have expressed envy of their Japanese counterparts for the sophistication of the reading public and the resources of the major newspapers. Crocker Snow, former *Boston Globe* correspondent in Tokyo, observed that the Japanese reporter can assume that the typical reader of the three major dailies (combined circulation, about sixteen million) is better informed about international affairs than the reader of America's east coast elite dailies. News commentators on Japanese national commercial television can assume that the audience has sufficient scientific understanding to use various chemical formulas when discussing pollution, nuclear plants, or other scientific questions. As Richard Halloran, former Tokyo correspondent of the *New York Times*, acknowledges, because a large Japanese newspaper "can smother a story with more manpower than any ten American papers," these large dailies are able to carry detailed information about international developments that compares with Americans' elite papers. They have more analysis of their own government's planning and policy options than even the *Washington Post* carries about the American government. These newspapers are highly competitive commercial operations, and they include such thorough coverage because the general public has sufficient knowledge and interest.

Beyond such subjective impressions, it is difficult to find a meaningful quantitative measure to compare the educational level of the adult population of different countries. Probably the most meaningful cross-national comparisons can be made in fields like mathematics and natural science, where cultural and historical factors play a relatively smaller role than social science and humanities. Where data is available for such cross-national comparisons, no country outperformed Japan overall. Nathan Glazer points out that on the 1964 twelve-nation achievement tests in mathematics for thirteen-year-olds, Japan scored second to Israel. However, these were selected samples, and when adjusted to estimate the average in the age group, Japan ranked third, although the first and second place countries edged Japan by only an insignificant amount. When adjusted to estimate the top three or four percent of the entire age group, Japan was first both for mathematics majors in the preuniversity group and, by an even larger margin, for non-university majors.

In the 1970 international science test given to ten-and fourteen-year-olds in nineteen countries, Japanese youth performed comparably well. Among ten-year-olds, the Japanese were first in the subtests for earth sciences, chemistry, and biology. Although they ranked fourth in information, they ended overall in first place because they were first in understanding, in application, and in higher mental processes. Fourteen-year-old Japanese scored second to their Hungarian counterparts in biology but first in physics, chemistry, and practical science. Although they ranked only second in information, they were also first overall because of their test results in understanding, application, and higher processes. These findings are not unrelated to the fact that Japanese middle schools have science labs, and ninety-three percent of the science teachers were trained in science at universities, a record unrivaled in other countries. In grand total score America ranked fifteenth of nineteen countries.

Only a handful of American children, even among those living in Japan, have ventured to attend regular Japanese schools, whereas thousands of Japanese children have attended American schools. It is commonly understood that those Japanese who attend elementary and junior high school in comfortable American suburbs will be a year or two behind their grade level in mathematics and the natural sciences when they return to Japan. The same is true even for the physical education skills stressed in Japanese schools, to say nothing of Japanese and Chinese history.

Lest it be assumed that music and artistic skills in Japan are neglected, William K. Cummings, who has done the most thorough cross-cultural study of Japanese and American elementary education, comments as follows from his observations of music classes in Japanese schools: "By the sixth grade, most students are able to switch readily between at least three different instruments. The first time I saw this level of achievement, I could not believe my eyes. But after the fifth primary school, I had to recognize that it was widespread. While the members of the orchestras and bands in American primary schools achieve this level, most of the remaining students are musically illiterate. Comparisons in art are nearly as dramatic." When a foreign television producer's delegation observed Japan's NHK television concerts, they were surprised how little time is spent by the television staff in rehearsing for the program until it was explained that producers, cameramen, and other support staff all used the same musical scores for cues, reflecting a capacity of everyone to read music that could not be assumed in an American television studio.

Some of the differences might be accounted for simply by the fact that the Japanese attend school about one-third more than Americans, for 240 days a year compared to 180 days a year in America; and, as Cummings notes, attendance rates in primary and junior high school are much higher in Japan.

What is perhaps even more remarkable than the high quality of Japanese education is that such an insignificant percentage of Japanese do not achieve a high standard of literacy. Whereas the United States Army must reject a sizeable proportion of applicants because of illiteracy, the inability to read and write is virtually absent in Japan. Although precise cross-cultural comparisons are almost impossible, illiteracy has been estimated by some to be as high as twenty percent in the United States, but in Japan illiteracy rates are generally estimated to be below one percent.

The Japanese drive to extend formal education has been as vigorous as their efforts to increase their GNP. In 1955 only about one-half of Japanese youth entered high school and less than ten percent postsecondary institutions. By the late 1970s over ninety percent of both Japanese girls and boys were completing high school, compared to approximately eighty percent of all American youth. Virtually all Japanese who enter a school complete it. In 1975, for example, ninety-seven percent of those entering high school completed it, compared with seventy-nine percent in America. At the postsecondary level in Japan, approximately the same number of males and females enter colleges, but females more commonly complete two-year courses and males more commonly four-year courses. Although approximately thirty-five to forty percent of college-aged youth were attending a university both in the United States and Japan, because of sizeable numbers of American drop-outs Japanese more often complete their training. Almost forty percent of Japanese males in their mid-twenties have completed four-year colleges compared to about twenty percent of Americans (although the American figure rises to about thirty percent by the late twenties). Very few Japanese attend graduate school. However, the desire for higher education in Japan is greater than enrollment figures suggest, for university openings are still not adequate to meet the demand. In America virtually any high school graduate can find a college or university to attend, but in Japan there are roughly three openings for four applicants. Even after students have completed their schooling, an extraordinarily high number continue taking a variety of correspondence courses and special study programs in their place of work, whether or not they are required to do so by their company. A very high percentage of the Japanese continue to read serious books and to master new bodies of knowledge.

Japanese education is not without major problems. Universities have an important function in certifying students, but faculty devotion to teaching and to students is limited, student preparations are far less than prior to the entrance examination, analytic rigor in the classroom is lacking, and attendance is poor. University expenditures per student are unreasonably low, and the level and variety of advanced research are highly limited. The Japanese student in his essays is more likely to follow guidelines than to develop his originality. Entrance examinations to high schools or universities can be so competitive as to cause students to restrict their intellectual breadth, eliminate extracurricular activities, neglect their social development, and, in case of failure, become psychologically depressed.

Americans are not about to import these problems, which show deep failures in Japanese education. Yet the maintenance of high motivation for learning, the uniformly high quality of the nine years of compulsory education, and the wide scope of educational television in Japan are remarkable achievements worthy of emulation.

Japanese Successes: Basic Education

THE DRIVE TO LEARN: EXAMINATIONS
AND GROUP RESPONSIBILITY

Japanese are not satisfied just to attend school more hours per day and more days per year than Americans. Over half of Japanese youth at some time attend supplementary schools (*juku*) during their elementary or secondary school years. Supplementary schools come in all shapes and sizes, but the vast majority are to improve the students' chances of passing an entrance examination to a slightly more desirable high school and college. Most students have a good idea af what institution they might qualify to enter by entrance examinations if they prepare thoroughly for one or two years. Yet after entrance examinations are over, about eighteen percent of the men and a somewhat smaller percent of the women who fail to pass an examination to their desired institution remain for one year or more as *ronin* (masterless samurai), without institutional affiliation, preparing for another try at entrance examinations.

The pressure surrounding entrance examinations derives from the fact that they are the exclusive means for determining admission to institutions of higher learning and for obtaining that all-important first position. In fact, the American student who attends a good university and receives a good first job is likely to be significantly more successful than one who does not, but there is somehow an American hope that one will have many opportunities to move throughout one's career. In Japan the widely acknowledged importance of the university attended for determining later success concentrates life-long career ambitions on the entrance examinations.

The entrance examinations measure acquired knowledge on the assumption, widely accepted, that success depends not on innate ability, IQ, or general aptitude but on the capacity to use innate ability for disciplined study. It is acknowledged that native ability may affect the capacity of an individual to absorb information, but in the Japanese view there is only one way to alter the result: study. Those who spend a year or more going through special cram courses in order to enter what they consider an acceptable institution are not criticized for plodding but are praised for perseverance.

Entrance examinations are much maligned for causing excessive tension, rote memorization, and one-sided intellectual development, and for eliminating extracurricular activities and destroying the joy of youth of preexamination students. Horror stories of examination preparation receive ample publicity, although extreme cases are in fact small in number. There are suicides over exam failures but these have declined since the late 1960s, and the overall Japanese suicide rate is not high by European standards. Educators have urged and undertaken a variety of reforms to reduce examination fever, albeit without appreciable success, for the desire to achieve through entrance examinations remains unabashed.

No one defends extreme cases of "examination hell," and if the system were imported to America, it would probably not be carried to such extravagant lengths. It should be noted, however, that entrance examinations have a great deal of logic in their favor. They are highly predictable so that schools, students, and their parents know what to prepare for. The teacher's authority in judging a student's record is negligible, since grades or written recommendations are unimportant for college admission. It is unmistakably clear to students that their future depends on meritocratic performance as measured by entrance examinations. Motivation comes from the inside, and the student, mindful of his responsibilities to parents and school and concerned about his future, wants to learn so that he may be prepared for the entrance examination. As shown by the questionnaire returns accompanying the science achievement tests in nineteen countries, Japanese children enjoy school more than students in other countries. The teacher becomes an ally who is trying to assist the student in facing the examination. The Japanese teacher has a broader sense of responsibility for helping the student outside classroom hours and is typically available in school many days during summer recess.

The motivation for achievement through examinations is increased by the tight-knit membership of a variety of groups. Families are, in a sense, competing with other families, and the child's success in examinations is seen as directly reflecting on a family's success. As Thomas Rohlen has shown, the small, intact family does much better in preparing the child for entrance examinations than the large family, the broken family, or the family with one parent deceased, for the intact family exerts itself, sending the child to supplementary classes, assisting him at home, and arranging family life to ensure the sanctity of study. Parents, and especially mothers, take a great interest in how well the school prepares their student for the examination. Through the junior high school level it is unrealistic for most parents to send their children to schools other than their local public school; therefore parents take an active role in local school activities, supporting teachers of excellence and school administrators who try to maintain quality education.

Furthermore, there is intense competition between schools to place their students well. Just as villages compete to erect the best most modern buildings, so schools strive to get a higher share of their graduates admitted to the best schools at the next higher level. Since teachers are responsible for their students' personal and motivational life as well as for classroom behavior, they feel responsible for the success rate of their students.

The system thus reinforces the key actors—students, teachers, and parents—in their identification with the student preparing for the examinations. Given the tendency to relax that comes with affluence, schools in Japan, as in other modern countries, face the danger of lax standards. From his interviews in various Japanese schools, Rohlen concludes that having the entrance examination system in the background is necessary to maintain discipline and high standards.

Compared to examinations that would certify high school graduation—an idea now being considered in America—entrance examinations have clear advantages. With certification examinations, it is unlikely that many students, teachers, and parents would be positively motivated since only those close to the margin of failure would be at all concerned. On the other hand, entrance examinations make sense to the Japanese because they are not simply arbitrary evaluations by authorities but a legitimate demand by educational institutions that those who enter meet a certain standard. Most of the ninety percent of the age group who wish to enter high school and the fifty percent who wish to go on for higher education are highly motivated to prepare for entrance examinations to be able to enter an institution of their choice. Once a student enters an institution, examinations do not end, but he does not need to worry about being terminated for academic failure, and this allows the student to develop a feeling of belonging in a mutually supportive group environment.

By the time the Japanese student enters a good high school or good university, he has internalized attitudes about hard work. He may not have enjoyed the pressure of examination hell, but he has learned discipline as well as mastered a body of knowledge. For all the excesses of the entrance examination system, the desire to succeed on them maintains group solidarity and the motivation to study. In entrance examinations a student's competition is not with a small circle of intimate friends but with thousands of unknowns who want to enter the same institution. The strong attachment of the student to his peer group in school, to his family, to his teachers, and they to him, greatly reinforces the motivation to study. All want the student to succeed. In later life, it is again in large part the individual's attachment to the work group and his long-term time perspective that makes him want to master materials that might someday prove useful to him, his work group, and the company at large. As a result of the examination system the nation acquires a large reservoir of well-trained people with a substantial core of common culture, people who are curious, teachable, disciplined, and sensitive to humanistic and civic concerns. Despite complaints, no one has moved to weaken entrance examinations, for no one has yet devised a better system to maintain motivation, hard work, and family and school solidarity.

UNIFORM NATIONAL STANDARDS

Until the end of World War II, the Japanese Ministry of Education wrote the textbooks for each subject in each grade. After the war a new set of guidelines was established by the Allied Occupation to provide a more democratic orientation for compulsory education. Compulsory education in Japan is measured not by age but by completing the ninth grade, although in fact virtually all students complete it at age fifteen. Some of the guidelines for course content were influenced by American educators from states like California and New York which had similar statewide guidelines. After the Occupation, the Japanese Ministry of Education kept the democratic thrust but prepared even more detailed, book-length guidelines for the essentials of the curriculum (*gakushū shidō yōryō*, officially translated as "Course of Study") of all elementary, lower secondary, and upper secondary schools in the country.

In the elementary schools the Course of Study includes Japanese language, social studies, arithmetic, science, music, arts, handicrafts, homemaking, and physical education. In junior high school it covers Japanese language, social studies, mathematics, science, music, fine arts, health, physical education, industrial arts, homemaking, and foreign language. The curriculum is quite comprehensive by American standards, including political and moral issues, physical training, the arts, vocational information, and world affairs as well as basic academic subject matter. In preparing the Course of Study, twenty of the nation's leading educators for each subject weighed various alternatives to determine the nature of skills that students should be expected to acquire. In addition to setting overall objectives and listing for their subject specific topics to be covered, they provided suggestions for teaching methods. The Course of Study was first completed in 1958, and the revisions were made in 1968 and 1978. (The 1968 volumes have been translated into English). Other specialized handbooks provide suggestions for the use of audiovisual and other materials.

For example, goals for the second grade student include the following: "To listen with delight to a story or juvenile tale; to hear a story, considering the sequence of the matters involved; to convey a message without missing its vital point; to speak to all of the audience with a clear voice; to speak, considering the sequence of the matters involved; to speak in response to the content of the other party's statement."

A common practice for developing confidence in speaking positively in front of a class begins by asking students simply to call out "present" in a loud, firm voice, then at a later time to go on speaking loudly and clearly on small matters they are certain to know the answer to, and then move on to slightly more complicated matters.

The objectives for the study of geography for lower secondary schools are:

(i) Through studies of various regions of Japan and the world, to have the pupils seek foundations for geographical views and considerations, take cognizance of our country from a broad viewpoint and understand the importance of making advanced and rational use of the land, thereby cultivating an attitude of endeavoring to develop the country.

(ii) To have them realize that there are both regional peculiarities and common features in every geographical phenomenon, consider the geographical conditions accountable for them, and establish foundations for proper understanding of each region and the peoples' lives.

(iii) To have them understand that there are various types of regional groupings, large and small, in Japan and the world, which are mutually interdependent, and think about the role of Japan in international society, thereby deepening their realization as a member of the nation and the world.

(iv) To have them understand that the relations of human beings with nature and social conditions have been undergoing ceaseless changes due to human activities and that each region has also been transforming correspondingly. And, to have them understand the importance of the proper development and preservation of nature.

(v) To foster the ability necessary for proper consideration of geographical phenomena through direct contact; the proper handling of maps and charts, the writing of reports, etc.

Some examples of the topics to be covered in lower secondary history are as follows:

(v) Emergence of "Buke" (warriors' class) Government
Through studies of the administration of the Kamakura Shogunate, life of warriors, culture during the Kamakura period, invasion by the Mongolians, and so forth, the teacher should have the pupils understand how the Kamakura Shogunate came into existence and how the "Buke" (warriors' class) government replaced the "Kuge" (court nobles) government.

(a) Formation of Europe

Referring to Greek Culture and Roman Culture, the teacher should have the pupils understand that these, coupled with Christian Culture, formed the basis of the European world in later years.

(b) Contact with the Islamic World

The teacher should have pupils understand the outline of contacts between the European world and the Islamic world, while referring to the natural features and advancement of the Islamic world.

(c) European peoples' overseas expansion

Referring to the Renaissance and Reformation, the teacher should have the pupils understand that the Europeans had been expanding overseas since new sea routes were discovered. In addition, the pupils should be led to take note of the expansion of the Netherlands and Britain in later years as well.

(xvi) Development of Modern Japan

Through studies of international relations and Japan's external policy, development of Japan's modern industries and social changes, formation of modern culture, revision of unequal treaties, etc., the teacher should have the pupils understand that, since the early Meiji years, this country had, amidst complicated international relations, established her national structure on the basis of political, social, economic, and cultural developments, gradually elevated her international position and grew up as a modern state. And also, the pupils should be led to realize that many problems emanated from the posture of overtaking other powerful nations rapidly.

Similarly detailed outlines are provided for other topics in history and all other subjects.

The number and location of vocational courses are determined by and adjusted to estimates of manpower needs. In certain fishing communities near Sendai, for example, modern courses on fishing techniques are offered that are not paralleled by courses in any American fishing communities, and it is not surprising that the skill levels and technology of American fishing communities have fallen far behind those of Japanese fishing communities. Vocational training suffers from many of the same problems as in the United States, in that it tends to attract the less diligent, the less motivated, and less able students. However, the Course of Study provides detailed quality guidelines for home economics, agriculture, industrial science, business, fishing, and nursing.

As in many European countries, textbooks are published by private companies and approved by boards of leading educational specialists chosen by the Ministry of Education. In fact, usually there are only four or five approved textbooks on a given subject for a given grade. Although they are generally bland by American standards, in order to be approved the books must be well written, must be filled with the best scholarly information available, and must cover all the topics in the Course of Study. The price of textbooks is very low, but the market is large and the leading textbook publishers compete keenly to develop high-quality books. In a sense, textbook publishers in a given field, competing first for Ministry of Education approval and then for sales to local schools, are like manufacturing companies in an industrial sector competing first for MITI approval and then for successful markets. Only a small number of publishers have the resources to meet the very high standards involved.

Textbook certification in social sciences raises difficult questions of judgment. Until 1945 the single textbook approved for each subject had strong nationalistic biases. Since then leftist intellectuals who are concerned about the concentration of power in government hands have worried that the Ministry of Education might favor conservative texts, and traditionalists have worried that traditional moral training is inadequate. In fact, textbooks generally avoid controversy by presenting objective information or, where opinion was sharply divided, by offering several differing views with some context for each of the views. In one difficult case, a textbook written by a famous historian Ienaga Saburo was judged by other historians to be overly one-sided, and when Ienaga refused to include alternative positions in the textbook the Ministry did not approve it, arguing that in such controversial matters Ienaga's views could be presented but that other views should also be presented. William K. Cummings, who was originally skeptical of the claims of textbook objectivity, concluded after his study that although there are debatable cases concerning certification of controversial texts, as a whole social science textbooks "presented a remarkably open-minded, even a progressive picture of Japanese society . . . The social studies texts enabled the students to reflect on their own social situation."

The success since World War II in maintaining fair-minded social science texts rests on the balance of political forces and the independent professional ethos of educators and Ministry of Education officials. Whatever pressures educators might feel from a conservative government are balanced by the pressures from the leftist Teachers' Union, and this balance of power helps ensure that educators have the independence to maintain quality and objectivity.

When an American state or a European country or Japan sets educational standards, there is a risk that the approval of textbooks may lead to political bias. It is not easy to maintain high national standards without some such risks, but given the balance of political forces in North America, contemporary Western Europe, and postwar Japan, and the exposure of youth to a wide variety of ideas through television and other media, the danger of narrow thought control as in prewar Japan and prewar Germany seems small. If anything, in the United States, which has no national standards and no standards in many states, the danger is that teachers might provide incomplete training or that, having so little supervision, they might impose personal biases. In Japan every parent can be assured that his child will be presented the knowledge and well-considered ideas of the best educators, that noncertified textbooks are widely sold, and that television (with average viewing time comparable to that in the United States) will provide his child with considerable diversity.

The Course of Study plays an important part in the curriculum of education majors in the university and of teacher-qualifying examinations in each prefecture. The seven-to-ten-day prefectural training program commonly given new teachers is financed by the Ministry of Education and draws heavily on the Course of Study. After a teacher has about five years of experience, and again after ten years, he undergoes similar programs to update his knowledge. Finally, if a teacher is to be promoted to a higher administrative position such as Dean of Studies (*kyōtō*), he is given another round of orientation and upgrading. Ministry of Education officials are not necessarily satisfied with the typical teacher's level of awareness of the Course of Study, but these training sessions undoubtedly help assure that teachers have a clear idea of the goals of education.

In addition to the periodic training of teachers, every ten years when a new version of the Course of Study is issued, special programs introduce them to the teachers. The Ministry of Education first invites leading educators from each prefecture to national centers for two days of discussion. These leaders then carry the program back to their prefecture for two days of similar discussion with local school leaders, and the final round of meetings occurs at the local school level.

Thomas Rohlen, who has perhaps conducted more detailed study of Japanese educational practices at the secondary level than any other American, has concluded that the supervision of teachers by colleagues at the local level is more important than national guidelines in maintaining standards. In their beginning years teachers are not embarrassed to seek guidance from more experienced teachers about how best to respond to various classroom situations in order to keep the students positively motivated and to ensure that they all clearly understand the material. Their frequent informal study meetings after school provide, in effect, an ongoing supervision and mutual support system that greatly raises the quality of teaching.

Although the teachers must cover certain topics and tend to follow the advice of their seniors, they do have flexibility in the particular ways in which they teach the material. American teachers are given more encouragement to be creative in the classroom, but it is questionable whether most teachers' colleges train students adequately in subject content to create their own materials and whether the typical teacher in fact has the energy to engage in original preparations, given classroom discipline problems and the typical teaching and paper-grading load. Cummings observes that the Japanese teacher seems more secure in knowing what he is expected to cover, whereas the American teacher is often uncertain about what is expected of him because of experimentation and innovation.

From 1961 to 1964 students throughout the country were given achievement tests so that Ministry of Education officials could know how each local school throughout the country performed. Objections from the Teachers' Union over the possible use of such tests in hiring and discharging was sufficiently strong for the Ministry of Education to discontinue comprehensive national testing, but sample testing was continued in order to determine general performance level. Even if the national sampling service does not test a local school, the number of graduates of that school who pass examinations to the select schools at the next higher level is known, and it is therefore possible to have a judgment on the success of each school in inculcating the basic skills. Higher level educational administrators can thus provide special help to schools that fall below standards. In the United States there is no federal agency that sets standards or even attempts to define what all students of a given age should know. To be sure, some American states set standards for students to graduate, but in general there is a less complete system for assuring that students are given adequate training to meet these standards. Americans are now concerned about the decline in the quality of preparation in primary or secondary schools, but no national data is ever collected in such a way as to tell how well a given school is training its students.

It is impressive how well schools throughout Japan ensure that virtually every pupil achieves minimal standards. No student is failed, and all students of the same age proceed together up through grade nine. The threat of failure or of being held back is considered neither desirable nor necessary to encourage students to maintain minimal performance standards. Approximately ninety-five percent of lower secondary students attend public institutions. There is no tracking, and all students are expected to acquire the basic materials of that grade. Some teachers have complained that this system slows down the more talented students and that some of the poorer students still do not catch on to many things in the class. However, the assumption that everyone can and will get through puts pressure on the teachers and the poorer students. Americans are much more prepared to accept that some students are unteachable and to give up on difficult students. Japanese teachers exert themselves to see that every student in the class has achieved a certain level before the end of the school year. They mobilize other students and parents to work with students with difficulties, for they are responsible not just for presenting the material and giving the students an opportunity to learn but for making sure that they do learn.

To assure that every school has the financial resources to provide a minimal level of compulsory education, the Japanese government provides subsidies to poorer prefectures and isolated school districts. A good part of the educational budget is met by the prefectures and some by the local community, but the national budget constitutes about one-fourth of the budget for the nine years of compulsory education. In a relatively wealthy prefecture like Tokyo, about eighteen percent of the public funds for the elementary school budget comes from the national budget, but in a poor prefecture like Aomori about thirty-three percent of the elementary school budget comes from the national government. Within a prefecture an effort is made to supply equal facilities for all pupils, and therefore in isolated rural areas with a smaller number of students the expenses per pupil are actually greater than in the metropolitan areas. As a result, there is much more uniformity in school facilities and expenses between school districts than in the United States. In most American states, where major costs of education are still met by local taxes, rich suburban schools can sometimes spend twice as much per pupil as poorer suburbs or urban areas. Furthermore, in America dollars spent per pupil in the poorest states are substantially lower than that in the richest states despite special programs of federal aid.

Even in Japan there are some differences in salary and teacher qualifications between localities, but they are modest. Special subsidies and salary incentives attract teachers to remote communities, and the resulting shortage of teachers in the urban areas forces cities to reduce the large differences in qualifications to a much smaller level than those between school districts in the United States. Certification of teachers is by prefecture, but general qualifications are closely monitored by the Ministry of Education, which does not allow the disparity of standards between prefectures to become very large. Cummings' analysis of cross-national science achievement data suggests that less than one percent of test score results in Japan is explainable by urban–rural differences.

In the United States, because there are no national standards and because of much greater variation in courses, it is more difficult to determine overall quality of training, although Educational Testing Service examinations and Stanford Achievement Tests do provide measures of performance in scores on such tests. At best, American average scores, as measured by international tests in mathematics and science, are well below Japan's, and the range of scores is also much wider. In short, the schools of America do not come as close in providing equality of training.

The uniformly high quality of training provides Japan with an unexcelled supply of generally competent labor power prepared for company life and receptive to learning more specialized skills at the workplace. If anything, the high level of education has overtrained students for their jobs and has created shortages of blue-collar workers. However, the Japanese do not share the disdain for physical labor found in some countries. Japanese schools, for example, use fewer cleaning personnel than America, and because teachers and all students share the "dirty" cleaning work in the schools, students learn to take physical labor for granted, not as something to be done only by those at the bottom of the social scale. Japanese students also learn the value of saving, as every pupil in every elementary school saves a few yen each week over several years to finance the sixth grade school trip (ordinarily to Tokyo for non-Tokyo residents).

Japanese schools, like the Japanese home, also teach self-discipline. They teach it at a general level in ethics and society courses, in an exemplary way in accounts of great men in reading classes, and in a practical way through the handling of classroom situations. All students are expected to be courteous and considerate to their teachers and to other students.

Expected standards of behavior are high, but explicit punishments are used less than quiet but clear expression of disapproval. Students, in their regular group sessions for self-reflection, are expected to talk about their inadequacies, as when they are insufficiently considerate of each other and of the school. On matters considered to be serious, like smoking cigarettes, teachers are likely to visit the student's family or to call the parents in to the school to discuss the seriousness of the problem, pointing out the importance of not having black marks on a student's record and their desire for the student to be the kind of person who could get a good job later. The school thus prepares the student for the work organization and the community, for they also rely less on regulation than on inner discipline and sensitivity to others.

Much of a student's study time, outside as well as inside the regular classroom, is spent in group study. Through group projects, group trips, classroom organization, and above all through close-knit activity clubs with membership lasting several years the student is not only allowed to enjoy group life but taught to be sensitive to his peers and to restrain personal egoism. Indeed, student organizations themselves play a major role in advising a student about ways to gain the respect of his peers. This prepares the student for life in a modern organization, where he is expected to develop a long-range commitment to work peers and to be considerate of them.

Not only does this high uniform standard of training strengthen social cohesion and provide a labor force with superior training, but it also eases the problems of spatial mobility. In the United States, which has great variation from one school district to another, a child who is transferred to a new school when his parents move may have great difficulty adjusting to the academic level of various subjects. At best, many of the things the child has learned are not in step with the curriculum in other schools. The mobile child in a highly mobile society such as the United States is therefore caught in confusions, disruptions, and inefficiencies. In Japan, movement to different offices of the same firm is frequent even if interfirm mobility is not. But Japan's standardization of curriculum makes spatial mobility of pupils a much less serious problem than in countries with more heterogeneous school systems, although preparation for entrance examinations makes it difficult to transfer schools at high school age.

Some Americans believe that certain disadvantaged groups should be allowed to receive certification even if they have not met the same standards as others and that certain minority youth should be allowed to attend bilingual schools. The Japanese approach would be different. They would not allow a school in a second language but would provide supplementary courses until minority students entered the regular track. Japanese traveling to French Canada, Belgium, New York, and other areas with dual cultures are surprised that minority groups are required to know so little of the dominant national language and culture. In their view, it is ultimately damaging to minority groups not to provide and require the same high level of training as that of the majority, for without it minority groups would have lower standards of performance and would not be able to compete effectively in the marketplace, and regulations could not entirely overcome market forces. The Japanese problem with Koreans, *burakumin* (descendants of outcasts), and other minorities is admittedly much smaller in size than the American problem with minority groups, but their approach is fundamentally different: they have more confidence in the necessity of training the entire population to meet a high level of educational standards.

It is often said that the Japanese population is highly homogeneous, and by contrast to the American population, which came from many more diverse sources, this is certainly true. But Japan in the mid-nineteenth century was more a collection of diverse fiefs than a single culturally unified nation. Japan has become a homogeneous country not only because of the new national media like radio and television but also because there is a common core of culture transmitted to virtually the entire population. The Japanese encourage diversity in culture, art, cuisine, and style of life, but it is to be in addition to a very substantial common core. This core reduces the danger that cleavages will disrupt the social fabric and increases the chance that the populace will work together against crime and disorder and pull together when the national interest requires it. Japanese homogeneity did not result from tradition alone, for up until shortly before World War II regional accents in certain parts of the country were mutually unintelligible and regional variations in culture substantial. Homogeneity was created and is maintained by social policy, and educational policy is one of the pillars of this social policy.

Homogeneity results in a high common base of general knowledge, so that education can proceed to even higher levels, whereas in America, which has not pushed so hard for a homogeneous cultural base, a teacher must spend more time helping students of diverse backgrounds catch up to a lower basic level. In Japan standardized opportunities and uncompromising uniform standards of performance make it more difficult for students to explain their poor performance as being caused by extraneous factors; the burden of performance is theirs. In turn, it becomes infinitely easier for work organizations to later demand the same high standards of performance as that required in the schools.

TELEVISION FOR EDUCATION

Educational television in Japan has existed only since 1959, but by 1977 its national network broadcast some fifty-two hours a week of educational and cultural programs. Each week it transmits ninety-six programs to schools, from 9:00 to 12:15 and 1:00 to 3:15, Monday through Friday, and from 9:00 to 12:00 on Saturday. As of early 1976, programs were used by more than 10,000 of Japan's 13,000 kindergartens, over 23,000 of Japan's 24,600 primary schools, and 4,700 of Japan's 10,700 junior high schools. Schools decide whether and how much to use these various programs, which are designed to supplement regular classes.

There are special courses for students with various disabilities and for those who need supplementary work to keep up with their grade level, but there are also regular programs for the public. In contrast to programs offered by America's Public Broadcasting System, which are often, in effect, high-level entertainment, the programs transmitted to Japanese schools are basically informative, primarily including illustrated lectures for the general public. Although there is an effort to make these programs appealing, they are selected not on the basis of popularity but on the basis of meeting educational needs and conveying informative content.

The two channels of national public television (NHK and NHK Educational Television) are financed through a user tax, a small fee paid by every household that has a television set. These funds enable NHK to have complete autonomy, for the Diet and other politicians have no control over how the funds are to be used. The Diet cannot even propose rates but only approve rates proposed by NHK.

Along with the television programs, NHK Educational Television makes available special textbooks. Ordinarily textbooks sell only twenty to thirty thousand copies, although the text to accompany *Sesame Street* (offered to increase the English abilities of small children) sells about forty thousand copies and the largest selling basic English textbook sells about five hundred thousand copies per year.

There is a continuous program of research and consultation with schools to build up new and better programs. Every August and September the educational television station carries out investigations into selected sample schools in each prefecture. Then in November there is a meeting of the high-level Central Consultative Conference (*Chūō jimon iinkai*), ordinarily composed of four leading scholars, four broadcasting specialists (one each specializing in kindergarten, elementary school, junior high school, and senior high school), and four people from the Ministry of Education. They meet throughout November and December to make final plans for the next academic year, which begins in April.

There is a separate committee, the Program Development Committee (*bangumi kaihatsu iinkai*), that engages in testing every August and September to assist in planning the development of completely new programs. The committee is a part of NHK and consists of a team of around ten people with the varied skills required for planning a new program. It takes about two years to develop a program. Each year, in addition to the survey data collected for annual programs, there are special meetings with teachers in the various prefectures to hear their opinions about desirable programs for meeting the needs of various schools. There are eight such three-day meetings annually, with eastern and western Japan having separate meetings to discuss kindergarten, elementary, middle school, and high school programs. These eight meetings draw together actual users of the programs, teachers who have a sense of how effective they are with students and how they could be more useful.

As in the national educational system in general, the budget for educational television is concentrated overwhelmingly on the years of compulsory education. Quality is maintained not only by the outside evaluation but by the high quality of the people planning and developing programs. There are approximately 125 academic specialists working in the schools division of NHK who were trained in various departments of universities. Winning a job in NHK is a highly competitive exercise. There is a special three-month training program within NHK for all beginning employees. Although the staff draws heavily on academic experts and others especially skilled in writing, they have found that to communicate well in television they must rely on their own staff to write the final program and to handle production.

The result is a high-quality national service readily and easily available without charge to local schools. Programs draw on the best information available to scholars, presented in such a way as to fit in with the course of study for compulsory education. In educational television, as in many fields, national planning has made possible a quality program far ahead of anything the United States with its greater resources is even seriously considering.

8

Welfare: Security without Entitlement

IN 1955 the average Japanese life expectancy was sixty-five years for males,
sixty-seven years for females. One might have expected that
in the 1960s and early 1970s, with frantic economic development and environmental pollution, health would suffer. Since
1962 companies with fifty employees or more give annual
physical examinations to all employees. With the exception of
small rises in 1966, 1973, and 1974, the rate of illnesses observed through these examinations has gone down annually.
By 1977, when Japanese longevity surpassed Sweden's to become first in the world, life expectancy was 72.7 for males,
77.9 for females.

In the 1950s as urban areas grew rapidly and expenditures on social benefits lagged behind economic development,
one might have expected alienated city dwellers. Sewage facilities and park areas still rank behind those of other advanced
countries. Although from 1970 to 1975 Japan had more than
eighty percent as many new housing starts as the United States
(about 8.6 million, compared to 10.5 million) with only fifty
percent as much population, the average Japanese still has
only about two-thirds as much housing space as his American
counterpart. Yet large urban districts with defaced personal

and public property and accompanying degradation and alienation, found so frequently in large American cities, are virtually absent in Japan.

Since pension and old-age security payments are just
catching up with modern Western countries, one might have
thought that Japanese old people would have been discouraged
and forlorn. There are discouraged old people in Japan, and
suicide rates rise with old age as in other countries, but as
Erdman Palmore finds in his comparative study of aging in
the United States and Japan, Japanese old people are more
active than their American counterparts, and, based on large
sample surveys of different age groups, their sense of satisfaction does not decline with age as in America.

In the 1960s as Japanese production was catching up with
world levels, politicians began to talk of the need for more
expenditures on social benefits to balance economic growth.
Fashionable speakers replaced the term "gross national product" with "net national welfare" in order to show they were
not narrow economic animals but were concerned with the
quality of life. More funds began to flow into the welfare
sector.

However, by the mid-1970s government and business
leaders, at first quietly and then increasingly in indirect public
comments, began expressing a new consensus. The essence of
the consensus is that the welfare state, with "high welfare and
high state burden" as found in England, Sweden, and the
United States, is undesirable. By emphasizing the tax burden,
Japanese leaders have achieved a measure of public support,
but because opposing welfare lacks popular appeal, the new
consensus has not been sloganized and enshrined with a fully-
developed rationale. Nor has it necessarily carried the day
with the Diet, which has voted and established more welfare
than bureaucrats and business leaders consider desirable. Yet
the basic rationale for the new consensus is understood by all

in leadership positions and in muted form ("in a period of low growth, with a heavily strained budget, funds are not available") occasionally appears in the public media. These leaders prefer to keep funds flowing into the productive sectors of the economy, to encourage the working place and the family to share welfare burdens, and to supplement private welfare with state funds only when it is essential to do so.

MINIMAL STATE WELFARE

The Japanese lag in welfare expenditures is not necessarily permanent, but the new consensus has already slowed down the rate of increase and it is tailoring the welfare program in a certain direction. In part the long-range strategy of Japanese leaders after World War II was to concentrate first on industrial growth, next on wages and consumption, then on welfare expenses. By 1973 only twenty percent of public expenditure in Japan went to social benefits, compared to twenty-six percent in Great Britain, twenty-eight percent in the United States, and substantially more in all other Western European nations. As welfare expenditures increased, they were concentrated in health (in the early 1960s) and pensions (in the early 1970s) while other areas were virtually neglected.

In the health field the percentage of the GNP spent for medical expenditure grew rapidly for several years after national health care was established and then remained fairly steady except for 1973 to 1975, when it grew to keep pace with inflation, while the GNP remained steady. Overall, the percentage of GNP devoted to health care increased from 2.6 percent in 1961 to 4.3 percent in 1975; while the GNP multiplied by seven times in the period, health expenditures multiplied by twelve times. Japanese expenses on health care, including the ratio of doctors, nurses, hospitals, and hospital beds to the population, now compares favorably with the Western European average. In the Japanese system the patient chooses his private doctor, pays a set fee for service determined by the national plan, with the patient assuming thirty percent of the costs, the rest provided by the national plan. People over seventy have all their medical care provided by the national plan. Because fees for visits are low, doctors encourage patients to come frequently, and a Japanese citizen visits the doctor more often than citizens in other countries. Although brief visits are not necessarily desirable and may be motivated largely by monetary concerns, in balance it gives more opportunity for doctors to diagnose problems, to catch illnesses early. Japanese doctors also make a substantial income from drugs, and Japanese patients consume more drugs than patients in other countries; the merits of this system are now being debated and alternatives are being considered. Government payments for a hospital bed are low, forcing hospitals to cut costs, and the period of hospitalization is much longer in Japan than in other modern countries of North America and Western Europe. In general, Japan has also raised medical costs very rapidly, and their internship and residency training has at times exploited the trainee without providing the well-developed supervision and didactic education about clinical work provided in American teaching hospitals. Yet the system of private physicians, low standard fees for doctors' visits and hospital service, and patient responsibility for as much as thirty percent of health care provides more frequent doctor visits for all elements of the population than the American delivery system.

Following heightened attention to the problems of the elderly in the late 1960s, annuity and pension payments began to increase very rapidly. There are two major pension plans covering about ninety percent of Japanese pensions: those for former company employees (*kōsei nenkin*) and those for unattached independent citizens (*kokumin nenkin*), further divided between contributory payments (for those young enough to be part of recent payment plans) and noncontributory (those for the very old and infirm unable to pay their own way). In 1971, 1,200,000 former company employees received 176 billion yen (almost 1 billion dollars) in pension payments, but by 1976, 2,400,000 received 950 billion yen (over 5 billion dollars). For noncontributory national pensions, the 165 billion yen (less than 1 billion dollars) paid to 4,400,000 people in 1973 increased up to 706 billion yen (almost 4 billion dollars) paid to 5,100,000 by 1976. For contributory national payments it increased from 50 billion yen (less that 300 million dollars) paid to 750,000 people in 1973 to 563 billion yen (almost 3 billion dollars) paid to 3,000,000 people in 1976. As a whole, the Ministry of Finance has been careful to assure that funds are available in pension funds before rapidy increasing payments, although political pressures have forced them to increase payments more rapidly than they would prefer. Except for the national payment scheme, the government ordinarily contributes up to twenty-five percent, but most of the funds come from reserves. Reserves totaled 14 trillion yen (about 80 billion dollars) in 1975 and are deposited in the Ministry of Finance for public investment.

Aside from health and old age, welfare payments are still minute by American standards. Unemployment insurance is low because of the low unemployment rate; companies find it cheaper to set aside their own funds and pay for disguised unemployment when necessary than to support a very large bureaucratic system of unemployment insurance that is then paid out to workers laid off or fired. Even when workers are unemployed, the length of time for which they receive unemployment compensation is generally shorter than in Western countries. By law, all workers under thirty and all workers with less than one year of employment cannot receive more than ninety days of unemployment insurance payments, and ordinarily they receive considerably less.

Japan has fewer categories of aid programs than the United States. It has a general program of "livelihood protection subsidies" (*seikatsu hogo*) that covers a range of expenses from enough food to avoid starvation, to medical aid (to cover the thirty percent of private expenses that individual citizens cannot afford), to miscellaneous costs such as the modest compulsory education fees. These payments can be much smaller, partly because Japan has so few broken homes and aid for dependent children is therefore a minor expense. In 1975, for example, there were 1,400,000 mother and children households in Japan, compared to 7,200,000 in the United States. Amounts paid are adjusted to need, but in any case they are not sufficient to live on comfortably. Before the period of rapid growth, as many as 1,600,000 people were receiving a livelihood protection subsidy, but with the very rapid economic growth, the number of people receiving such a subsidy declined by the mid-1970s to 1,300,000. In 1975, even after rapid increases, the livelihood protection subsidies for the average recipient household was 67,000 yen (about 350 dollars); the total disbursements for the entire country were 685 billion yen (about 3.5 billion dollars), over two-thirds of which went for medical care. Aside from health care and old-age pensions, people do not have a sense of entitlement about welfare, there is a sense of stigma about accepting it, and it is given out very sparingly. The family (including relatives beyond the nuclear family) and the workplace are expected to bear a much bigger responsibility and to put aside funds to provide for their own security.

GROUP WELFARE

Historically, the Japanese government did not establish a single comprehensive welfare scheme for everyone, but progressively developed special schemes for various occupational categories. It basically followed the Bismarckian model of the government's encouraging private organizations to set up welfare programs and keeping to a minimum the direct involvement of the state. Early in the twentieth century, plans were devised to provide for government employees, seamen, and minors; other plans gradually included employees in all large companies. After World War II these were expanded to include laborers, farmers, and eventually all self-employed. Just as the government holds to the principle that polluters should bear the costs of polluting, so it has generally accepted the principle that companies should be responsible for all the welfare costs of their employees. These programs did not necessarily stem from the most benevolent motives; many of the original programs concentrated on productive workers with the purpose of keeping a healthy working population, but the programs have since been extended to the nonworking population.

Since the employer in all lines of work is responsible for welfare, the employee knows he will be better looked after if he remains loyal to his company or his government branch. When the economy is very vigorous the individual can find other opportunities, but nonetheless the system tends to reinforce the tie between the individual and his place of work.

In the health system, for example, there is a program of health care for employees of large companies (*kenkō hoken*), employees of small- and middle-sized companies (*kanshō hoken*), public and quasi-public employees (*kyōsai kumiai*), day laborers, ship crew members, and all citizens who are not affiliated with one of the above (*kokumin kenkō hoken*). These programs cover, respectively, about twenty-five, twenty-five, ten, and forty percent of the population. Corresponding to these are pension systems for those working at large companies (*kōsei nenkin*), for public and quasi-public employees (*kyōsai kumiai*), and for nonaffiliated citizens (*kokumin nenkin*).

The scheme of providing welfare through separate occupational groupings rather than through a single system is quietly but enthusiastically supported by big-businessmen. According to a recent survey, large companies provided twice as many benefits as they were required to provide by law. Businessmen oppose the government's assuming heavy welfare burdens, for they want to pay less in taxes and to avoid the large governmental administrative overhead required for a large public welfare system. Perhaps even more important, they want to maintain the advantage that large companies enjoy over small companies, for if a potential employee is offered an equivalent salary at a large and a small company, other things being equal, he will take the large company because it can provide more security over the long run. This broader sense of security strengthens the identification of the worker with his company. Big-businessmen prefer to offer the benefits because the system reinforces the loyalty of the worker.

Although it is difficult to compare welfare benefits in a Japanese and an American company because the categories are so different, Japanese companies concentrate their benefits in areas that will keep the employee attached to the company over a long period of time. Benefits in the United States include substantial paid sick leave, vacation time, and coffee breaks—benefits rarely provided by Japanese companies in comparable amounts. In contrast, some seven percent of the Japanese population live in housing supplied by employers. An additional fifty percent—almost as much of the population as in the United States—own the dwellings where they live, and over half of the money that company employees borrow to buy housing is lent by employers. In 1975 the average interest rate for money borrowed from employers was three to four percent, compared to nine to ten percent for private loans in general. Even small companies unable to buy housing often lease housing and rent it to their employees below cost.

Large companies often have their own medical facilities, including hospitals and recuperation homes; these provide a much higher level of service than facilities supported by the national health plan. Since company retirement age is usually between fifty-five and sixty, most employees need a second job after retirement, and a company ordinarily assists a faithful employee in finding this post-retirement work. Many benefits provided by the company for longtime employees, such as the use of company mountain and seaside cottages and entertainment halls, are not easily calculated in value. Entertainment allowances are generous, but it is not easy to distinguish what portion should be considered company needs and what portion employee welfare. However difficult to calculate, as Robert Immerman, longtime American labor attaché in Tokyo, has noted, it is clear that the total Japanese company welfare package is larger than the American.

The Japanese company avoids tight contractual arrangements with employees and unions, leaving considerable discretion to company executives. The company tries to keep abreast of worker desires and offer more services than seem minimally necessary to meet union demands. By avoiding contractual agreements, company officials retain the leverage to give more rewards to those who have been faithful and hardworking. Especially in allocating company loans, assisting with postretirement employment, and allowing the use of special company recreation sites, company officials enjoy considerable leeway, conveying the message that perquisites are not automatic and that loyalty will be rewarded.

The Japanese government's intention to maintain strong ties between the individual and his company is perhaps most clearly revealed in the new program developed for depressed industries. As part of the Japanese employment maintenance program initiated in January 1975, if an employer in a depressed industry does not lay off employees, the government will compensate for half the pay of idle employees, or two-thirds of the pay in small- and medium-sized firms. From January 1975 to April 1977, 69,414 business establishments received such subsidies for some 3,500,000 idle workers for a total of 29,000,000 man-days. Executives of companies in depressed industries are the first to point out that in fact these payments by the government are still totally inadequate, but their very existence is a creative way to maintain social stability and the attachment of the company to the individual employee, something missing in America, where an unneeded employee in a depressed industry is furloughed or fired and paid unemployment compensation.

Although it is difficult to match the security of the large companies, independent professionals and small businesses respectively form groups not only to make payments for mandatory welfare benefits but to provide additional collective security to their members. Their associations commonly offer collective insurance through private companies, and large organizations often create their own independent welfare funds.

With the decline of the growth rate, one might have expected that people in small businesses would suffer greatly. The smaller firms in affected industries indeed suffered many bankruptcies, but the overall number of workers in them remained remarkably steady through the early 1970s and actually increased in 1976 and 1977. Since many large companies anticipated the decline in growth rate, they greatly reduced the number of incoming employees. One result was that, with fewer employees, companies were less able to respond to certain short-range opportunities, and many opportunities fell to smaller companies. As Hiroshi Wagatsuma and George De Vos found in their study of the small business sector, small businesses have been surprisingly adaptable and their psychological profiles are remarkably similar to more successful upper-middle-class people. Individual companies occasionally fail, but the same people keep forming new companies, drawing on others from small companies that are also going out of business. The same pattern is true not only for artisans and small manufacturers but also for service establishments like restaurants and bars, where the number of workers has continued to increase faster than the very modest population increases.

The Agricultural Cooperative, a very powerful organization to which every farm household belongs, has in effect an extensive program of security benefits for its members. Farmers make mandatory government welfare payments through the Cooperative, and the Cooperative buys and invests on a broad scale, providing greater security for investment than the farmers could hope to attain individually. By 1970 the association had five trillion yen in savings (almost thirty billion dollars) for the five million rural households and a few non-farm depositors. By 1976 total savings reached fourteen trillion yen (almost eighty billion dollars), or almost three million yen (almost sixteen thousand dollars) per household. In a 1976 survey of farm households, it was found that the average farm household deposited about eight hundred thousand yen (about forty-five hundred dollars) more than it withdrew from savings each year. The retired farmer is thus able to enjoy a higher income as a result of this saving and investment than he would merely by mandatory social security alone.

The family farm also provides a form of social security. The typical farm is small (two or three acres) as a result of the land reform policy of the Allied Occupation and the accompanying legislation discouraging reconcentration. By the mid-1960s, with increased mechanization, much less labor power was required on the farm. Young farmers therefore go out to work in towns and cities, in a variety of industries. With good transport facilities and automobiles, most of them are now able to commute to work from their homes. Even if they are retired from urban employment at age fifty or fifty-five, they can return to farm work, earning enough to cover food and other expenses for the household until well into old age. This is the dominant pattern for the five million rural households in Japan, one that provides old-age security and a sense of pride and activity for the elders in almost twenty percent of the nation's family households.

In the urban areas the small retail store, often owned by the elderly, also provides an equivalent to a welfare security system, for while it is not economically efficient, it is protected by government rules about the penetration of large stores and is supported by neighborhood shoppers, who appreciate convenience. It provides an opportunity for widows, divorcees, and workers retired from small- and medium-sized enterprises, for it requires almost no capital investment. As of 1978 Japan had 1.61 million retail outlets and the number was continuing to rise, while the United States had 1.55 million and the number was continuing to fall.

Families, rural and urban, have expected to provide funds for themselves in their old age, although it is likely that the very rapid increase in pension payments in the early 1970s will have an impact, lessening family financial responsibility. In 1973 Japanese saved twenty percent of disposable personal income, compared to Americans, who saved eight percent. Survey research data collected during the last several years show increased savings since the mid-1970s. In households where heads are approaching retirement, savings rates have increased beyond the national household average. These surveys show that a higher proportion of savings are now being set aside for retirement than in previous years when a higher percentage of families reported they were saving for household purchases, housing, and the education of their children. In Japan the family has been clearly responsible for the education of its children, and families put aside money for that purpose. In the United States, where there is less clarity about whether the family, the government, or private institutions are responsible for the education of the student, there is virtually no family saving for educational purposes.

Japanese family members also assume a much larger share of the responsibility for caring for the sick than American family members. Hospitals not only encourage family members to help out but often supply mats or cots and cooking facilities at the hospital, providing quality personal care without great financial burden.

The Japanese family still accepts a large responsibility in caring for the aged. In 1953 eighty-one percent of the Japanese over sixty-five were living with their children, and in 1974 this had declined only to seventy-five percent. As John C. and Ruth Campbell have noted, less than two percent of Japanese over sixty-five were in nursing homes and other institutions, compared to almost six percent in the United States. Palmore notes that in 1973, seventy-nine percent of Japanese couples over sixty-five live with one of their children, compared to between fourteen and eighteen percent in Denmark, the United States, and Great Britain. Among Japanese widowers, eighty-two percent over sixty-five live with children, and of widows, eighty-four percent. Only about ten percent of Japanese over sixty-five are not living with a spouse or child. The pattern of elders living with their children does impose a burden on the young couple, especially upon the young housewife, and this is a cost that needs to be considered in this system. The advantage for the elderly is quite clear. Even in old age the Japanese continue to be active, to maintain strong social ties to their families, and to engage in work and hobbies. Although the percentage of working men over sixty-five has declined slightly since the 1960s, in 1973, while forty-eight percent of Japanese were employed compared to forty percent of Americans, forty-seven percent of the Japanese men over sixty-five were still in the labor force, compared to about fifteen percent in North America and the west European countries. In 1976 forty-three percent of Japanese men and fifteen percent of Japanese women over sixty-five were still working. Palmore concludes that the relatively high satisfaction of the elderly is related to a high activity level and to their involvement in family affairs. The low pension payments until recently have made this a necessity, but in general Japanese individuals in the household are taught to be more aware of the needs of others and have therefore adapted more easily to three-generation households and to young couples living near elders than in comparable American families.

The Japanese employment system operates to give more encouragement to youth. Middle-age people save for old age because when unemployment comes the burden will fall more heavily on them. In 1977, although the growth rate in Japan had slowed considerably, there were still roughly two openings for each young applicant entering the market because of the permanent employment system, whereby companies are motivated to hire inexpensive young workers. Compared to the United States, where unemployment is especially high among the young, the Japanese system reduces alienation and pessimism at this crucial stage of life when attitudes toward work are in their most formative stage.

There are many in Japan, including the leaders of the Japanese Medical Association, who would argue that the system of having different welfare schemes for different companies and other groups of the population is a feudalistic holdover that should be rationalized by having a more unified standardized national welfare program for everyone. Clearly, the greatest disadvantage of the system is that the unattached individual does not receive as complete a coverage of various benefits as those attached to the largest companies. The large company's health and pension funds thrive and grow while government sponsored funds for self-employed individuals are in chronic deficit. Certain groups in Japan suffer from these disparities to an extent that many civic-minded Japanese consider undesirable and that the vast majority of Americans would consider undesirable. Minority groups like Koreans (perhaps numbering six hundred thousand) and the descendants of outcasts (perhaps numbering two million) often have much more difficulty finding employment in middle age and have much less adequate welfare provisions. Widows and divorcées not only receive inadequate coverage from protection plans, but even those who wish to enter the labor force are handicapped because they have not accumulated seniority and thus receive far less pay than other workers of their age. Those from small industries who seek new jobs at middle age have very little chance for sharing attractive living conditions.

No benevolent-minded person in Japan or the United States would find the extent of these differentials attractive. Despite ups and downs, the long-term trend for the Japanese welfare programs of the Social Insurance Agency has been to gradually fill the gaps in groups which were inadequately covered. For example, one gap filled in 1973 was the provision for free medical care for all people seventy and older. One could argue, however, that the injustices should be dealt with by reducing the differentials between groups without sacrificing the system of company and group responsibility. Large company funds could be taxed and some of the proceeds given to support those who are unattached. Large companies could be required to bear a larger portion of their former employees' old age expenses. Special programs could be made available for training and employing women heads of households. Since 1976 monthly bonuses have been given to companies for employing widows or women with disabled husbands, and these bonuses could be increased. One could argue that the strength of the company, the professional associations, the village, and the family is a precious commodity in the postindustrial age with its centrifugal tendencies and that a welfare system which reinforces these ties should not be casually cast aside as a feudal remnant.

MINIMAL BUREAUCRACY, MAXIMUM IMPACT

In the health and welfare fields, as in other fields, the Japanese bureaucracy is highly centralized. It has broad scope but tries to play a minimal role in direct administration. Compared to the United States, which has confusing and overlapping national and state jurisdictions with many inconsistencies, Japan has simpler, more consistent national plans. Although the varying programs for different groups is not without administrative problems, services are nonetheless standardized throughout the country. With less duplication, Japan is able to streamline its welfare bureaucracy.

Just as the economic bureaucracy accepts a broad responsibility for promoting the economic health of the nation, so the national health bureaucracy accepts a broad responsibility for looking after the health of the populace. As in other fields, bureaucrats take more initiative than their counterparts in the United States. For example, they make far more frequent inspections of restaurants, hospitals, and other institutions to see that they observe standards of nutrition and cleanliness. They take a more active role in health examinations for youth, providing dental and medical checkups for all school children. They make more use of schools and neighborhoods for giving vaccinations and injections of all types, and therefore the Japanese population is better protected against such diseases than people in the United States.

In improving nutrition and in trying to prevent damage from charcoal, gas fumes, and the like, the Japanese government takes an aggressive role in using the mass media. NHK and National Education Television give detailed advice to mothers about nutrition and the health of their children. Mothers are also called in to the public schools and lectured on child care.

In the United States politicians are at the mercy of welfare pressure groups, and the result has been that fees and payments for certain welfare programs have risen astronomically, sometimes at the expense of a coherent, equitable plan. In Japan the bureaucracy, which has a greater measure of power relative to politicians, is somewhat better able to resist special pressures and to provide a sound fiscal base, although it is by no means immune from pressure groups, as John C. Campbell has shown in his analysis of Diet decisions to raise welfare payments prior to crucial elections.

In the case of livelihood maintenance subsidies, the Japanese government relies less on professional welfare workers and more on some 160,000 officially designated volunteers to make home visits. These volunteers, respected senior people in the local neighborhood or village, make recommendations about need for the 1,300,000 people who receive maintenance subsidies. These volunteers consider it an honor to be called on to talk with and visit needy people in their local community. Since advice and suggestions are not standardized, the program suffers from the lack of professional judgment, and it was therefore attacked by the Allied Occupation and is still criticized by some Japanese professional socialworkers. The advantage of the system is that senior people in the community respected for maturity and personal judgment take an interest in family situations, giving advice about how to achieve greater frugality, how to resolve personal difficulties, and how to cope with employment problems. Because they live nearby and visit people in their homes, the volunteers understand the local situation and tend to bring to bear the more enlightened side of community opinion. Over the years the Japanese have built up a roster of such people, one in each neighborhood or local community, who take an interest in the neighborhood and help look after people with problems. This informal system not only mobilizes local community support but reduces the demands on a welfare budget that has a very small paid staff by American standards. In 1976 the United States Department of Health, Education and Welfare had 155,100 employees; Japanese Ministries of Education and of Health and Welfare had 11,200.

REDISTRIBUTION AND WELL-BEING
WITHOUT DEPENDENCE

One of the tenets of the Japanese approach to welfare in the broad sense is that there should be economic employment opportunities for everyone and that those who work and exert themselves for their organizations should be appropriately looked after. The government's policy of distributing wealth throughout the society is not based on public welfare but on fine calibrations of wages, taxes, budget redistribution to poorer prefectures, and subsidized rice price paid to farmers. People are not entitled to anything but the barest essentials unless they contribute to their groups. As a result, there is no sizeable group that feels indignant out of a sense of entitlement or self-deprecatory out of a sense of inadequate achievement. Nor is there the deep social cleavage between taxpayers who object to supporting those who work less and the recipients who object to the inadequacy of their payments, their uncertainty, and the spirit in which they are given.

In the view of Japanese businessmen, the ordinary worker in England, Sweden, or the United States has lost the drive for work. The differential between the low-paid worker and the welfare recipient is too small to retain a strong commitment to the organization. Despite the growth of welfare payments, bureaucrats in various ministries strive to maintain this differential. Bureaucrats in the Finance Ministry, for example, take care to ensure that the effect of tax policy is to encourage people to save, to accept responsibility for others in the company and the family. Even when Japan's growth far surpassed other countries and unemployment was virtually nonexistent, the Japanese employee sought workplaces that provided security and he exerted himself for his company, for public welfare was not a real alternative for a comfortable life.

In the West in preindustrial times when communities were small, charity, elicited by generosity and appreciated by the recipient, was a humane way of ensuring minimal living standards. In the complex modern world, however, where groups have grown in size and formality, charity, however benevolent in its origins, has been transformed into a government-sponsored system impersonally operated, leading to a sense of entitlement. The recipient has less appreciation for what is received than annoyance at what is not received. The resulting cycle of frustration, lack of motivation for work, unattractiveness to employer, and self-depreciation has disastrous consequences to the social fabric of many Western nations. The Japanese are reluctant to sing the praises of their modest public welfare system, but Japanese who travel to American cities are invariably struck by the run-down nature of American slums, the lack of respect for public property, and the general degradation of American cities. As paradoxical as it may be to Americans, the Japanese, with a poorly financed welfare system aside from health and pensions, have managed much better than we to avoid the despair that underlies this degradation.

Ample employment opportunities help maintain high morale, a sense of purpose, self-respect, and group effort; the opportunity to work more than compensates for the inadequate welfare payments. How well the system would work if the Japanese economy were to decline precipitously is speculative, but with the vigor of the national efforts, this may not be tested in the foreseeable future. In short, the Japanese have been able to provide for the well-being of their population without requiring many except the very old and infirm to become economically dependent on the state, and they have done it in such a way as to reinforce their communitarian ideals.

9

Crime Control: Enforcement and Public Support

I T HAS BECOME almost conventional wisdom that crime rises in modern industrial countries. This is true for all countries of North America and Western Europe. William Clifford, one-time head of the United Nation's Crime Prevention and Criminal Justice Programs, recalls that in 1969 when international specialists began to notice Japan's falling crime rate, the trend was hardly believed. They confidently predicted that with continued urbanization Japanese rates would begin to soar. In fact, crime rates continued to decline for the next several years and then stabilized. From 1946 to 1973 crime in Japan declined by roughly one-half. Not only are crime rates now lower than during the immediate postwar period, but they are lower than during the early Meiji period, to say nothing of the sixteenth century prior to the establishment of Tokugawa rule, when feudal states engaged in violent warfare.

David Bayley, a political scientist who conducted an excellent study of Japanese police, concludes that Japanese crime reporting is more complete than American, so that when comparisons are made with the American crime rate, the Japanese rate is understated. Using 1973 reports for both countries, he relates that in the United States four times as many serious crimes were recorded per person (8,638,400 in all) as Japanese crimes of all sorts (1,191,549). There were approximately four-and-a-half times as many murders per person in the United States, five times as many rapes, and 105 times as many robberies. Despite the fact that drug offenders are pursued with more vigor in Japan, in 1973 only five hundred were arrested, six percent of whom were on hard drugs; in America, with twice the population, 629,000 were arrested, twenty percent of whom were on hard drugs. The Japanese are also much more successful in apprehending offenders. In the United States the average rate of clearance of reported crimes through arrest in 1974 was twenty-two percent. In Japan in 1974 the overall clearance rate through arrest was sixty-nine percent and it averaged even higher for serious crimes: seventy-seven percent for robbery, eighty-three percent for rape, ninety-three percent for graft, ninety-seven percent for embezzlement, ninety-six percent for murder, ninety-three percent for bodily injury, and eighty-six percent for arson.

Japanese policemen are in much less danger than their American counterparts. The rate of on-duty policemen killed is approximately sixteen times higher in the United States. In the four years from 1969 to 1973, 16 on-duty policemen in Japan were killed, while in one year, 1973, 127 on-duty American policemen were killed.

Why have the Japanese police recently been so successful in controlling crime? Part of the answer lies in the readiness of citizens to call police (throughout the nation there is a single number to call police which everyone knows), the speed of response to calls, and the thoroughness of pursuit. In 1976 the average time it took police to respond to a call throughout the country was three minutes and twenty-three seconds. America has no national statistics on response time, and notification of police is often slow. Japanese police are distributed in some 5,800 mini police stations (_kōban_) in the cities, each commonly serving a population of about ten thousand, and some ten thousand residential mini police stations (*chūzaisho*) in the countryside, each serving an average of about five thousand people. Given Japan's crowding, an area covered by a mini police station is of small geographical size.

Second, Japanese police have great advantages in pursuing complaints. Police in mini stations are in close touch with the local community and know about household composition and household valuables. Residents acknowledge the need for police to ask questions in order to gather information and are prepared to be cooperative. When polled as to how they would advise a relative who commits a crime, the Japanese respond overwhelmingly that they would tell the relative to turn himself in to the police. In the United States the suspect is advised that he has the right to seek counsel and not to cooperate in giving information to the police. Japanese find it puzzling that American suspects are not urged to help the police find out about the crime. In Japan the suspect knows that it is prudent to assist the policemen in gathering information. Nor are Japanese offenders likely to receive leniency because they are considered to have psychological difficulties or to be victims of society or because an able lawyer pursues legal technicalities. Japanese punishments are generally mild (in 1974 less than 38,000 Japanese were in jail), but Japanese officials are relentless and systematic in pursuing all cases. If they show leniency, it is because the suspect is especially cooperative. Japanese officials are also not troubled by jurisdictional disputes between regions and local communities as in the United States. Japanese police are attached to the forty-seven prefectural-level governments and enjoy cooperative relations and overall coordination provided by the National Police Agency. Suspects cannot escape to other jurisdictions, nor do local officials hesitate to transfer suspects from one prefecture to another, even in minor cases.

Third, because there are far fewer crimes with almost as many policemen per population, the Japanese police are able to assign larger numbers of policemen to a single case and to pursue the data in all directions until the problem is solved.

Two other factors, police professionalism and public cooperation, are even more important in explaining Japanese success in controlling crime.

PROFESSIONALISM

Policemen in Japan come more from rural areas than American police, but they tend to have comparable social standing. Despite general full employment and the modest lifestyle of policemen, there have always been, as with other permanent government jobs, at least several applicants for each opening on the Japanese police force. The examinations are not as intellectually demanding as tests administered for entrance to the best universities, but they are taken very seriously by candidates and the educational background of the police compares favorably with the population as a whole. Applicants know that police work is a demanding task and that if they are successful they will be expected to maintain strict discipline. Because there are so many candidates per position, prefectural police officials processing applications know they can require high standards of personal commitment as well as general ability. The officials undertake detailed investigation of the applicant's background and personal connections, rejecting those with antisocial tendencies and those who are judged not to be stable, cooperative, and disciplined.

Rules about police behavior are overly strict by American standards. When a policeman is in uniform he cannot smoke or eat outside the police station. A policeman is expected to be unfailingly courteous to the public, remaining cool even if verbally abused, yet unbending in carrying out his responsibilities.

Bayley found that Japanese police are also better disciplined than American police. In 1973, of the 182,000 policemen in Japan, only 524 were dismissed for misbehavior, about half the number dismissed in New York City alone. There is a Human Rights Bureau of the Japanese Ministry of Justice where the public may complain about policemen without fear of retaliation, but in all of Japan there were 123 complaints made during an entire year. The good relationship between the public and the police did not exist in all periods of Japanese history. In the 1930s and early 1940s Japanese police were known for their haughtiness, sometimes even brutality, and the public kept their distance without complaining. Since World War II, police sensitivity to the public has improved, and the public has become more positive in its attitudes toward police. When Japanese senior police officials are asked to identify the most troublesome problems of police behavior, they now mention off-duty traffic accidents, drunkenness, and indiscretions with women; there were virtually no disciplinary problems on duty.

The National Police Agency, with roughly two thousand police officers and six thousand civilians, sets standards for prefectural police concerning appropriate behavior, salary range, force size, and organizational structure. As in other parts of the national bureaucracy, about fifteen officials are admitted each year into an elite career track in the agency. This corps of elite officials plans overall policy and guides the administrative handling of all major issues, including the standards to be maintained by the prefectural police. Elite officials are rotated between the central office and the prefectural offices, and at any one time several elite officials are assigned to each prefectural police headquarters. They thereby ensure high local standards and coordination between the prefectures and the central government. Also, high officials are aware that in many countries police desiring information feel it necessary to compromise themselves with local gangs and shady businesses. The constant rotation of senior officials from the national headquarters to the prefectures and comparable rotation of prefectural officers to localities within the prefecture make it more difficult for gangs and illegitimate enterprises to maintain the special relationships with particular people that lead to local police corruption.

The National Police Agency also supervises the training of prefectural police. As Bayley notes, whereas policemen in the United States typically receive about eight weeks' training, in Japan the training program is for one year. In addition to supervising the training program for the prefectures, the National Police Agency itself trains all higher officials in the prefectures and provides various programs for specialized personnel. Patrolmen constitute roughly sixty-eight percent of the Japanese police force; in the United States they commonly make up over seventy-five percent, with considerable local variation. The larger proportion of higher positions in Japan permits more opportunity for advancement and more supervision of patrolmen by higher officials. As in other walks of life, there is an expectation that the younger policemen will be nurtured and trained by their seniors. Bayley concludes that there is much more in-service training and stricter supervision of policemen in Japan than in the United States. Supervisors in the Japanese police are considered responsible for the behavior of their subordinates, even to the extent that they may receive criticism and punishment for mistakes committed by their subordinates whether or not the supervisors were specifically responsible for the errors. As in other spheres of Japanese life, the small group has a high esprit and generates internal discipline over its own members, helping prevent police corruption. Social activities, team sports, and informal recreation greatly strengthen the bonds between fellow policemen. This helps discipline flow naturally from bonds of loyalty rather than from outside authority arbitrarily imposed.

One group, the riot police (*kidōtai*), receives further specialized training. Tokyo, being the center of government and possessing a high portion of the university students, employs over half of the ten thousand riot police. To handle large demonstrations and other mass activities, they have developed elaborate tactical plans with shields, helmets, masks, and staves, as well as electronic equipment. Compared to the United States, which relies on various state-run National Guards or units of several different local police forces, both of which are unprepared and uncoordinated for handling riots, the Japanese riot police are much better trained, better coordinated, better protected from personal danger, and less prone to use force. Japanese student leaders visiting the United States in the late 1960s were surprised at how unprepared American students were in helmets, poles, and electronic communication equipment, because they assumed American police were as well prepared as the Japanese.

In the United States it is assumed that policemen might act without adequate regard for the rights of the suspect, and judges therefore constrain police action. In Japan the police are expected to have inner discipline so that courts rarely challenge police decisions and the police do not feel on the defensive. American police have at times abused their authority, but it is a vicious cycle. Constantly hemmed in by regulations and overrulings by the court, they have less opportunity to develop group pride and self-discipline. Japanese police, like high-level bureaucrats or section people in the company, have a great deal of professional pride and confidence in their own work, and they enjoy the respect of their superiors.

As in other administrative spheres, the police are permitted flexibility in handling problems as long as the result conforms to overall goals. Determinations of justice are made less on the basis of technical legal grounds or skillful legal argument than on an overall assessment of whether a person has done something fundamentally wrong and whether he is likely to engage in such misbehavior in the future. In the Japanese view, truth is not best arrived at by adversary relations wherein lawyers try to be as clever as possible in bending the law to favor one side. They are convinced that flexibility avoids contentiousness, reduces the chances of loopholes interfering with justice, and increases the likelihood of finding a sanction that is effective. The notion that a defendant could legally consult lawyers and refuse to talk to the authorities is unthinkable. Authorities may be relentless in their questioning, but in their view truth is arrived at through an open process of information gathering. Japan has about ten thousand lawyers, compared to about three hundred forty thousand in the United States.

The Japanese also do not draw such a sharp line between nonlegal and legal sanctions. They may use quiet warnings or mobilize friends, neighbors, and others to express public disapproval as well as impose fines and imprisonment. They systematically make an effort to assess the attitude of the defendant and his sincerity and determination to avoid future trouble.

In short, policemen are given considerable discretion. The ordinary patrolman handles only the immediate contact and questioning; for further investigation, even in minor misdemeanors, specialists are sent out from the twelve hundred or so police stations that are above the mini police station to gather information and determine the disposition of the case. The scope for discretion is large, but the basic logic for determining how to handle particular cases is clear. In general, what Americans define as crimes without victims are dealt with in a very permissive way unless the acts disturb or endanger others.

In the evening in downtown bar areas it is common to see groups of two or more drunks holding each other up, staggering along and singing happily. The Japanese police, like the public, are more amused by than morally critical of such behavior. They readily assist the large number of drunks who inhabit entertainment quarters each evening in gathering up belongings, avoiding injury, and finding transportation home. If a drunk should hit another person, the police rush to restrain him. And if he should attempt to drive his own vehicle, the Japanese police will be extraordinarily severe. Similarly, gambling is ordinarily considered acceptable. The *pachinko* parlors (which use a kind of pinball machine) with their nonmonetary prizes are so widespread that at one point there was a *pachinko* machine for approximately every twenty-eight people in Japan. Moreover, there is legalized betting, particularly in government-run horse racing, bicycle racing, and boat racing. Police even tolerate the involvement of gangs in this betting and in *pachinko* parlors. Homosexuality has never had the moral disapproval that it has in the United States and has never been treated as a vice. Prostitution began to be regulated only during the Allied Occupation and these regulations have been retained, but the post-Occupation prohibition is not against payment for sexual services but against public solicitation, ownership of a house of prostitution, or management of a group of prostitutes. As long as there is no huge public scene, prostitutes and their customers are allowed to go their way. Local policemen do not chastise a prostitute on their beat as long as she is quiet and discreet.

Many Japanese gangs (*yakuza*) at times engage in illegal activity, but they are often composed of highly disciplined members who identify with conservative nationalistic goals, engage in public activity including publishing magazines, and maintain, by American standards, shockingly open, cordial relations with the police. The police, by constant open interaction with these gangs, implicitly allow certain activities not considered dangerous to public order, but they move quickly to curb activities that go beyond.

The one exception to permissive handling of victimless crimes concerns traffic in dangerous drugs. For a while in the 1960s police condoned glue sniffing as it spread among certain avant-garde groups of young people, but they have always been very severe in controlling the growth, manufacture, importation, and use of narcotic drugs. Because of their tight control over the availability of narcotics, they have never arrested more than three thousand persons for use of hard drugs in any single year.

In dealing with automobile traffic Japanese police are decisive and unyielding. First of all, cars are required to be in much better condition than in most states of America. If one were to drive a car in a bad state of repair, he would be stopped quickly by the police. Procedures for obtaining a driver's license are so severe that license seekers commonly pay as much as fifteen hundred dollars for drivers' training programs. Japanese drivers stop more quickly when the traffic light changes to avoid fines. Although the Japanese are given a five- or ten-mile leeway over the speed limit, police are much more systematic in tracking down people going more than ten miles above the speed limit than in America, and one therefore rarely sees cars going too fast. Using loudspeakers, they behave with confidence and authority at major intersections. When accidents occur, in addition to handling the emergency situation by diverting traffic, caring for the injured, and arranging for the removal of damaged vehicles, the police also take a larger role in investigating causes of accidents than in the United States. Very quickly, measurements are taken, facts are ascertained, and the basic determinations of responsibility are made. Decisions as to who should pay for damages are handed down fairly soon, often at the scene of the accident, and generally both parties are expected to share in the expense, although the party most at fault pays more. The result is that traffic accidents and their consequences are much less likely to result in court cases, cars are repaired more quickly and at a reasonable rate, few large fees are paid to lawyers, and high insurance payments are avoided.

Although the Japanese policeman is given considerable discretion, with detailed supervisory training of some years he, like the teacher, tends to behave as a firm and confident professional who knows the proper way to deal with a particular problem. This in turn reflects a high degree of group consensus about desirable behavior. He is not prone to argue and can be virtually impervious to argument. He aims to be polite but he is rigid, for he has the confidence that his entire organization is prepared to support him as long as he is acting correctly within his jurisdiction.

MAINTENANCE OF PUBLIC COOPERATION

Why does the public cooperate with the police? In the first place, they respect the quality of the police, their professionalism, and their devotion to duty. It is not because the Japanese consider the policeman to be of high social standing but because they recognize his authority and competence within his sphere. Police do not take these attitudes for granted. They exert themselves to maintain the cooperative attitude of the public. In dealing with a suspect or an ordinary citizen individually, a policeman is polite and businesslike. He is self-confident and so he does not need to flaunt his authority. He tries to avoid making comments that might provoke anger. As Bayley notes, a policeman is taught to ask questions indirectly, and, unless pursuing an especially important case, he is unlikely to coerce a person to supply information. The policeman has implicit authority, but he makes every effort to behave as the eagle in the Japanese proverb who hides its claws.

The local neighborhood mini police station has several policemen assigned to neighborhood duty. The local policeman is commonly called the *omawarisan*, the one who makes his rounds. Aside from manning the station to be of assistance to neighborhood people, each policeman makes frequent rounds in his respective neighborhood. Because he often meets local residents on his rounds, he tends to develop friendly personal relationships. He usually travels by foot or by bicycle, scarcely distinguishable in attitude and type of dress from the local postman. The mini police station is also responsible for local household registration, and this aids a policeman in knowing his neighborhood. Each household in Japan is expected to register all residents with the local police station, and policemen visit each home semiannually to note any changes in a household. In addition, he gathers information about ownership and the ordinary location of cars and other valuable property. He notes the daily patterns of coming and going. Because the local policeman is generally the best informed person about the neighborhood, he is sought by outsiders who wish to ask directions about how to find a particular house or shop. He aims to be helpful in giving first aid, assisting children across streets, finding lost items, and providing informal neighborhood news. He posts neighborhood announcements on the bulletin board outside the mini police station.

This kind of friendly service to the local community builds a basis for relationships that makes people in the neighborhood feel confident about approaching a policeman when they have seen suspicious people or suspicious activities. A crime prevention association is organized as part of every village (*burakukai*) or neighborhood (*chōnai kai*) to ensure that certain local people specifically have the responsibility of assisting the police. With this background of knowledge and these neighborhood connections, a policeman is in a good position to notice unusual behavior when asked to do so by local people.

When a policeman is pursuing a suspect, he can count on networks of local relationships. The police can thus get information with greater rapidity from broader circles than if they had to rely on new contacts in each case. Since neighborhoods tend to be better organized than in America, the whole effort is much easier. Higher-level police officials may be rotated every two or three years, but low-ranking policemen are commonly assigned to the same location for a longer period of time to cultivate contacts with the community. Even if individual policemen are rotated, local people nonetheless trust the policeman at the mini station, for his behavior is highly predictable.

Police are lenient to those who are cooperative in giving information and who show respect to the police, for this is considered necessary to get the job done. Bayley found that whereas an American suspect is more likely to protest his innocence and argue with the police, the Japanese suspect is more likely to be compliant and cooperate in supplying information and submitting to search. This is not simply a holdover of prewar attitudes when police could bully the frightened public; it reflects a greater tolerance of surveillance and general social control than in America, where individuals are likely to be more assertive about their rights. The attitude is nourished by Japanese police, who are likely to apply longer and less pleasant questioning to those who proclaim their rights, defend their behavior, and criticize the police than those who are more cooperative.

Part of the public's cooperativeness stems from its general deference toward government agencies. The Japanese are more prepared to cooperate with authorities than Americans, whose widespread alienation and tradition of righteous indignation toward authorities cause them to sympathize more with persons committing crimes against the government and big business. In the late 1960s tens of thousands of Japanese protested against the government, and many remain sympathetic with criticism of the establishment, but probably no more than a few hundred radicals remain committed to physically attacking the basic institutions of society, and the public overwhelmingly unites against anyone who challenges those in authority. Toward anyone who departs significantly from his expected role, the Japanese automatically respond with visible disapproval, whether by gesture, subtle comments, or very strong, even if indirect, criticism. Just as the public is less willing to understand and excuse lateness, sloppiness, and laziness than the American public, so is it less patient with the transgressor and more willing to cooperate with the police in maintaining the public order they so firmly believe in.

The low level of alienation in Japanese society is related to the widespread pride of individuals in their work and workplace. In Japan, as elsewhere, it has been noted that transient populations have much higher crime levels than stable local communities. For example, Japanese government researchers who conducted an intensive study of crime in Kashima found that while many unattached construction workers were present, crime rates were very high. Once these transients were replaced by a more stable population, the crime rate went down precipitously. Because Japan is a relatively stable society with strong group membership, people have a commitment to their own group and to the maintenance of order that unites them firmly against threats to order. Similar attitudes may be found in many small American communities but are unfortunately weaker in large urban areas where cohesiveness has declined.

In virtually all of Japan, as in much of America, there is a feeling that people do have a chance to succeed if they apply themselves. Society values merit and work, not manipulation of the system. The Japanese feel that their efforts will be rewarded, that their compliance to norms will result in gains to themselves and their families. Given sufficient stability and group cohesiveness, the one who attempts to manipulate the group is unlikely to gain, whereas in disorganized societies there is more room for manipulation and the group has more difficulty maintaining control over deviants. Although some American ethnic enclaves may have internal social cohesion, many American urban areas have so little cohesion and such a high level of alienation toward the wider society that deviants are less subject to the informal bonds of social control.

Because an individual in Japan is identified as a member of a group, the group is affected by the reputation of a deviant and therefore exerts considerable pressure on a potential deviant to live up to standards. The Japanese family, for example, is judged to be much more responsible for an individual's behavior than in America, and no sharp line is drawn between parental responsibility for minors and adults. When members of the Red Army, a small militant radical group of the 1970s, committed crimes, they caused families enormous embarrassment, and at least one parent of such a youth committed suicide. When university demonstrations were so much in vogue in the late 1960s, it was not uncommon for humiliated parents to plead with their children not to participate. Television graphically relayed scenes where mothers were searching out their demonstrating children, even those of college age and beyond, pulling them away from the crowd. Any crime that involves a company member, especially if publicized, is an extraordinary embarrassment to the company. When the story of Marubeni's involvement in the Lockheed scandal broke, popular weeklies featured articles on the humiliated young people who had just become Marubeni employees. A school principal and a school teacher are considered so responsible for the behavior of children under them that they may be asked to resign or at least to apologize publicly when a child under their charge gets in trouble with the police. The effect is not only to create greater group pressure on the deviant, but to inhibit him by emphasizing the potential shame he will bring to his group by misbehaving. A potential deviant may even be isolated and expelled from the group if he has blatantly violated group norms against the advice and urging of his fellow members.

Police make use of their areas of discretion in such a way as to maintain public support. They tend to be slow in arresting people when there is not a high level of support for their behavior. If anything, they err on the side of not being as severe as most of the public wishes. The calculations of the police can be seen most clearly in their handling of student riots. The police consciously hold off in responding to provocations until the public mood turns into anger at police inaction and into demands for immediate steps. At that point the police move in. They thus keep the public firmly behind them in their activity and avoid stepping beyond bounds set by public opinion. When students occupy buildings, or the Red Army takes over villas, or Japanese terrorists hold international hostages, the Japanese police tend to be patient, maintaining psychological pressure around the clock for days to encourage mass resisters to give in voluntarily and in order to avoid direct violent confrontations that might create or increase sympathy for potential martyrs. They could have cleared the Narita Airport field early in the 1970s but hesitated because of widespread popular support for the demonstrators.

The essence of the strategy of riot police is to minimize the danger of injury, gain the support of the public, and reduce the threat posed by the resisters. The Japanese police are ordinarily quite permissive to demonstrators, and indeed there are far more public political demonstrations in Tokyo than in Washington, D.C. However, it is only when there is a danger of violence or when the group is occupying a place to which the public needs access, such as train stations, airports, or public buildings, that the police feel called upon to take control.

When they do so, they amass overwhelming force. In 1978, for example, when gasoline was first taken to the Narita Airport over the protest of resisters, over six thousand riot police took charge of protecting the oil from the danger of intruders. They failed to prevent damage to the control tower, but thousands of well-trained, courteous riot police prevented any incidents in the first months of the airport's operation despite a group of highly skilled opponents determined to cause trouble. In dealing with massive student demonstrations and clearing an area, the riot police generally used huge shields, slowly pushing back the demonstrators blocking an area. Thus, the police have little worry of being hit by flying objects and do not need to respond precipitously out of fear. They systematically move those blocking public access. Rather than individually shout and yell at rioters or demonstrators to make themselves heard, the police use large public amplifiers, explaining what they are doing in a calm but firm voice.

Because gun control is very tight, because police are well-trained in hand-to-hand combat, because they amass overwhelming numbers when demonstrators assemble, and because they can count on public support, the police are less likely to attack a suspect out of fear. Because they feel quite confident, they can be firm and definite without needing to fight with or overwhelm a suspect. The policeman is so certain that a suspect who has done wrong will be punished by the arm of the law that he can even behave sympathetically to the unfortunate violator.

The Japanese police themselves may detain a person up to twenty-three days for investigation without a court order, but they are cautious about doing so without substantial reason. Having ample time to interrogate subjects, Japanese police do not have to act in haste, although they do make every effort to conclude investigations quickly.

Japanese police also make every effort to be mild in their

punishment. In the United States in 1973 about forty-five percent of those who were convicted were sent to prison, about forty-one percent were allowed out on probation, and about six percent more were fined. In Japan, by contrast, about ninety-five percent of those who were found guilty were fined and less than five percent were sent to prison. In 1972 approximately forty thousand Japanese were in correctional institutions, compared to approximately three hundred and forty thousand Americans. Former Japanese prisoners are, of course, under the surveillance of the local police in the neighborhood to which they return, even without being on probation. Since the local community cooperates in observing any strange behavior and the police know the location of the former prisoner, they can promptly handle any problems that may arise.

If one commits a serious crime in Japan, one is almost certain to be caught, but the punishment is likely to be relatively mild. In the United States the proportion of wrongdoers apprehended is low, but the person who is tried and found guilty is treated much more harshly. As a result the American public harbors doubts about the justice of the criminal system, and the potential wrongdoer has a much greater chance of escaping detection or, through technicalities or use of skilled lawyers, avoiding punishment. In Japan, less public dissatisfaction is generated against the system because most offenders are punished, and punishment is not so severe as to be judged unfair.

As Donald Klein, comparative political scientist, has said, the Japanese handling of crime "demolishes some firmly held theories that enshroud America with veils of pessimism. It's simply untrue that massively populated cities are sure-fire breeding grounds for crime and public disobedience. Japan's history is equally if not more violent . . . Violence is also part and parcel of Japanese television." Yet now, violence in Japan is extremely rare.

As paradoxical as it may seem, Japan is more successful in controlling crime in the highly populated areas than in other areas. William Clifford attributes the differences to underlying philosophy: "Crowding people into cities under a banner of absolute privacy and maximum individual liberty as a right regardless of the interests of others . . . makes crime difficult to control . . . Japan has kept the citizens within social boundaries, group allegiance and community constraints . . . As crime grows across the world and the city dwellers skulk in fear at night in their homes that have truly become protected castles of guards, guard dogs, security services, special alarms and double locks, they may wonder whether Japan has not, for the time being at least, found a happy medium of tolerance with control."

PART THREE
American Response

IO

Lessons: Can a Western Nation Learn from the East?

INTRODUCING BASIC CHANGE is never easy. But to expect Americans, who are accustomed to thinking of their nation as number one, to acknowledge that in many areas its supremacy has been lost to an Asian nation and to learn from that nation is to ask a good deal. Americans are peculiarly receptive to any explanation of Japan's economic performance which avoids acknowledging Japan's superior competitiveness. It is easier to accept such explanations as Japan's industrial plants were devastated by a world war, and it could therefore build modern facilities; Japan copied Western technology; Japanese companies undersell American ones because they dump goods (sell below costs in foreign markets and at lower prices than in domestic markets); Japanese companies succeed because they are subsidized and protected by their government; Japanese workers receive low salaries; Japanese companies exporting to the United States violate antitrust and customs regulations.

It is more comfortable to overlook Japan's continued modernization decades after rebuilding from World War II, its effective organization, its genius in adapting technology, its patience in marketing, its disciplined work force. It is more comfortable not to ask how its businessmen could remain so zealous in selling goods to America if they were basically selling below cost. It is disquieting to admit that the Japanese have beaten us in economic competition because of their superior planning, organization, and effort. To the extent that our government and business enterprises have begun to study their Japanese counterparts, it is often only to gather information that might prove charges of dumping or antitrust violation. One wonders at our lack of interest in profiting from Japanese successes.

THE COSTS OF INADEQUATE RESPONSE

The American response to the Japanese challenge is perhaps best illustrated by our abortive efforts to develop a foreign trade policy and an industrial restructuring policy. In 1971 when America was acutely worried about its trade imbalance with Japan, the White House trade representative, Peter Peterson, began to develop the outlines of such a policy. With the first dollar devaluation, the sense of urgency disappeared, and key American officials stopped worrying about an overall trade policy. In 1977 Americans faced the same crisis and again began thinking about the desirability of a comprehensive trade policy. Lacking continuous study and consultations, new officials had to start almost from scratch and without the broad public and business understanding necessary to achieve success. Unprepared, the situation became an emergency, as we had little choice but to allow the value of the dollar to decline in 1978 to about fifty percent of its 1971 value while government officials tried to find short-range palliatives to stem the tide of growing protectionism. They hoped that traditional market forces would operate: that as the terms of trade changed and American goods became cheaper, Japanese goods would become more expensive, the market would find its level, and trade would become better balanced. This policy, based on conventional but extremely narrow economic considerations, brought some temporary relief, but it failed for three important reasons. In the first place, because Japan is so dependent on imports of raw materials, the cost of these imports constitutes about three-fourths of the eventual price of steel and Japanese manufactured goods like cars; when the value of the dollar goes down, Japanese buy raw materials much more cheaply, and therefore the change in Japanese export prices is minor. Japan is now able to buy oil, lumber, and other American resources so cheaply that it could easily disturb the American domestic market in a number of products and create new inflationary pressures. Labor-intensive Japanese companies heavily dependent on exports suffer with dollar revaluation, but companies buying materials from abroad prosper. The Japanese government helps ease the readjustment for those industries that suffer; for example, electric power rates were lowered in 1978 since the cost of energy resources had gone down. The second reason this policy does not work is that the Japanese find new ways to respond to the challenge by cutting costs, while the American companies, temporarily protected because of improved export prices, do not feel the pressure to improve and fall further behind their Japanese counterparts. Third, Japanese goods with a superior reputation for quality continue to sell even if prices are raised. If the Japanese, formally or informally, face quotas in the number of items of a particular product they are allowed to sell, they move into the higher quality market, thus increasing the dollar value of exports to America while continuing to observe the quotas—and without contributing to the correction in the trade balance that Americans had hoped for.

Each round of temporary relief from the fall in the value of the dollar distracts attention from basic problems in governmental organization, economic policy, and company modernization. Appraising American policy toward Japan, William L. Givens, business consultant and former Japanese specialist in the State Department, concluded, "Like protectionism, the floating exchange rate is the opiate of the inefficient producer and the crutch of ineffective government."

The deterioration of America's competitiveness will have a far greater impact on our national life than we have thus far contemplated. As American industries fall behind, television factories must retrench, watch plants move elsewhere, and steel plants close down, with fewer jobs for American workers. Although Japanese takeover and modernization of some American plants like television factories will ease some of the burden, Japanese and other foreign investment replaces only a small percentage of the American industries that do not remain competitive. With increased Japanese profitability and continued trade imbalances, Japanese companies in America will draw heavily on Japanese banks and capital rather than American, thus reducing América's profits and increasing Japanese ownership of property and companies in the United States. The continued growth of Japanese industries and investment in this country may ease the unemployment problem, but it is questionable how far this process will continue before it arouses nativist resistance against foreign control.

As Japanese companies gain larger shares of international markets from American companies, American companies become less profitable. As the Boston Consulting Group has shown, a company with a large market share is able to sell enough to make considerable profit, to keep up research expenses, and to modernize facilities. But American companies with declining market shares will not make enough profit to finance continued research and modernization, and they will lose even more of the market, caught in a vicious circle.

As American companies become less profitable, America's government income is affected. Because profitability is down, governments must raise taxes to support the level of services to which people are accustomed, making it even more difficult for

companies to reinvest for modernization and creating understandable resistance if not a revolt of individual taxpayers.
Local governments are caught in a political bind and must cut
services, raise taxes, or both.

The decreasing tax base is already having an effect on
American aid abroad. Even where we have made economic
and military commitments, the recipient countries, watching
the weakness of the American economy, naturally wonder
about America's capacity to meet its commitments. Pessimistic
foreign leaders may yet prove more accurate in their assess-
ments than American offiicals who are endeavoring to provide
reassurance about the reliability of American friendship.

Not only foreign aid but our basic stance toward developing countries is affected by the weakness of our economy. In
1978, for example, the United States asked some European
countries not to pass on steel industry know-how to developing countries since the world's market in steel was satiated.
Japan is not entirely open to imports from competitive third
world countries, but its stronger and more flexible economy
allows it to concentrate on higher quality steel, an area where
it could still remain competitive, and to pass on to developing
countries the technology for basic steel plants they so greatly
desire. The American stance deprives the developing countries
of the means to raise their industrial skills and can only lead
to greater conflicts between the developed and the developing
countries regardles of our humanitarian intentions.

With serious trade imbalances, the United States is becoming increasingly protectionist not only toward Japan but
toward Korea, Taiwan, Hong Kong, Singapore, and other
rapidly developing countries. Whether the Japanese and Koreans use voluntary restraints or America uses formal measures,
the effects of protectionism are the same: even more directly
than the falling value of the American dollar, it preserves the
inefficient producer unable to meet international competitive

standards, and it requires the addition of sizeable bureaucratic machinery. At best, it can never be entirely effective, for there are many ways of going around barriers in such a porous society as America.

Superior foreign competitiveness creates an increasingly defensive mood in the United States. American company officials, straining to meet foreign competition, cut corners in quality and treat employees less generously, while labor unions, afraid of increasing financial stringencies, become more determined to maintain their benefits and to block modernization that might reduce jobs. Government workers, worried about the declining tax base, try first to guarantee their own security and income levels. Lack of competitiveness and increasing protectionism affect American self-confidence, contributing to internal divisiveness and discouragement about many of our difficult domestic problems.

The impact of all these trends would be serious enough if they were anticipated and dealt with in an orderly fashion. However, Congress, suddenly confronted with a shortage of funds, slashes aid or military assistance to countries that have grown to depend on it. National and state administrators impulsively cut budgets when confronted with tax shortages or taxpayer revolts. In declining industries decisions based on legal criteria like bankruptcy, dumping, and anti-trust lead to abrupt closing of plants, allowing insufficient time for planning the relocation of workers. By the time legal procedures in a dumping case are completed, for example, it may be too late for the injured party to regain a competitive position. When such stringencies create a sense of emergency, political pressures force trade negotiators to visit Japan to demand immediate action in dealing with trade imbalances that in fact require long-term solutions. Foreign nations, like American workers suddenly confronted with decisions affecting their lives, are becoming understandably annoyed and less willing to cooperate with America at a time when our declining hegemony requires greater international cooperation.

It is tempting for Americans, having achieved affluence, to feel they no longer need to worry about economic competitiveness and should turn their attention to problems connected with the quality of life. Yet in an era of international economic interdependency, it is not possible to ignore a nation's international competitive position, as England discovered a while ago. America's problems at a national level are rather like those of a family that purchases a new home to relax and enjoy life, only to find that it is unable to make the mortgage payments and to afford the repairs needed to keep the house in order as prices rise faster than income.

If all countries had governments that devoted little attention to international competition, many of America's problems would be less severe. But other countries have developed a system to achieve superior performance, and America cannot effectively respond to the challenge with the old system, no matter how much we devalue the dollar and no matter how many protectionist barriers we erect.

A NEW BASIC MODEL

Any country's practices are deeply rooted in its traditions and cannot easily be transplanted, as all developing nations, including Japan, have found in bringing Western patterns to their countries. Even if America borrows fewer ideas and institutions from Japan than Japan borrowed from us, it is unlikely that the process can be controlled easily by planning, and it may well require many years to define problems, discuss approaches, prepare people to undertake appropriate studies, carry out research, and evaluate conclusions. There is every reason to believe that despite our best efforts at sorting, sifting, and choosing, new practices will turn out to require more adjustments than originally anticipated. Given these caveats, if America wanted not only to profit from individual lessons in various spheres but to develop an integrated program for profiting from Japan's experience, what would be its most critical features? The following features should certainly be included:

An industrial and trade policy. In the past America's economic philosophy has been to preserve the free operation of the market place, and it may be that market forces could eventually correct imbalances and adjust for the rapid decline of American industries that are being lost to other countries. However, the world can no longer tolerate the human, social, and political consequences of waiting for these market forces to reach a new equilibrium.

Rather than escape from the market place into state socialism, Japan accepts the ultimate value of market forces, but aims to hasten institutional adjustment to long-term trends while easing the human readjustments necessitated by changing economic forces. Japan provides key research and financial resources to assist key developments in the national interest when private sources are inadequate. Japan has been a pioneer in the development of such an industrial and trade policy, and many European countries have rapidly been following suit. The United States government—despite all its resources and reserves—can no longer afford not to give more positive guidance through a trade and industrial policy if our country is to continue to provide world leadership and an optimal quality of life for its own citizens.

We should make an effort to distinguish those industries in America that can be competitive on the world market and to support them through tax policy, monetary policy, antitrust policy, and administrative cooperation. We should make an effort to provide temporary cushions for those industries such as textiles that cannot remain competitive. We should not wait for legal action to show that damage has been done to declining industries but should guide them in reducing their capacity gradually while personnel are being retrained and relocated. In our trade negotiations, instead of spending our political capital on the defense of small, dying industries, we should defend the large, strong industries that can be effective in the future. We should create enough awareness of these overall problems in business and labor circles and provide them with a steadier, more predictable government policy. We need an on-going program, supported by careful research on the role of various American industries in the future. We should be bolder in assisting third world countries to develop their own industry, working toward an international division of labor in light of each nation's comparative advantages. We should reduce the number of regulations and regulatory agencies that operate independently of these overall goals.

A small core of permanent high-level bureaucrats. The capacity to provide long-range direction to society requires a continuity of leadership at high levels, a leadership that has the power and responsibility to oversee specific areas of activity whether they are in foreign policy, finance, energy, environment, transportation, or regional planning. Great issues require long time horizons and great continuity before solutions are found; it is not possible to pursue long-term policies when all key personnel change every two to four years. The issues are so complex that bright, noncareer outsiders who are brought in by changing political leaders cannot match a small core of highly able, dedicated professionals in respective spheres who have been given the best possible training, have been exposed to the most progressive thinking of private and governmental groups in America and abroad, and have been seasoned as junior officials working on problems they will face as they acquire greater responsibilities.

The American bureaucracy as now constituted is simply too large and unwieldly, and its talent too uneven, to provide a high degree of coordination and direction in such basic fields. The White House staff is too prone to influence on the basis of short-range political considerations. Many people with great potential are not given the kinds of training, broad experience, and responsibility they need to play a central role in shaping these policies. Bureaucrats responsible for the health of organizations under them have no power over government regulatory agencies that may be operating at cross purposes. In short, there is no substitute for a select group of highly trained professionals, small enough in number to have effective communication with each other, who are not burdened down with the details of management and administration and can work effectively as a unit to give overall guidance in specific areas.

In the beginning, to start the core group of leading specialists, some of the ablest midcareer bureaucrats and non-bureaucrat specialists prepared to make a long-term commitment would have to be recruited. But a system should be established for recruiting and training a small number of the ablest young people of their generation. Along with extensive training and experience, they should be given broad responsibilities and monetary incentives to remain in these positions until they retire from this service at a moderately young age. They should be given enough leeway to develop and guide the implementation of long-range programs in their respective spheres. White House aides in these respective fields should be restricted to members of this group, and the group should be encouraged to maintain liaison with Congress and private leaders to gain the level of understanding required to make policies effective.

A communitarian vision. In bygone days of more genuinely free enterprise, the model of the independent trader or businessman, like that of the cowboy, was not only appealing but appropriate. As George Lodge has noted from his study, business leaders now recognize that this model is no longer appropriate in an era when large organizations confront complex problems, but they nevertheless lament the passing of our individualistic past. Americans at large seem to share the same predilections, for charismatic critics of organizations are cheered while hard-working executives who exert themselves to hold organizations together are criticized. Organizational leaders are constrained by an enormous number of regulations and excessive red tape, and yet we wonder why they cannot make their organizations function more effectively. We clamor to protect the academic freedom of intellectuals, the free enterprise of business, the rights to confidentiality of lawyers, physicians, journalists, and clergymen, the rights of the accused, the privacy of the individual citizen. These are all values worth preserving, but they need to be balanced with equal concern for public responsibility, the interests of the group or society at large. In the guise of pursuing freedoms, we have supported egoism and self-interest and have damaged group or common interests. We are often more concerned with the rights of the deviant than the rights of the responsible citizen. Thus crime control, high educational standards, and effective organizations have been difficult to achieve, for they require that groups have the leverage to give moral approval to the member who restrains his self-assertion and is sensitive to the needs of others.

The Japanese have been on the forefront of making large organizations something people enjoy. Americans tend to think of the organization as an imposition, as an outside force restraining the free individual. Japanese from an early age are taught the values of group life. They learn to make school life and the life of work organizations more pleasurable. Japanese are uncompromising in requiring individual performance, but they can then take this performance for granted and concentrate on camaraderie, games, ceremonies, parties, and celebrations. Employees come in to their workplace on vacation and weekends in large part because they enjoy the camaraderie.

In contrast, while Americans acknowledge the need for large organizations, we have yet to tame them; the communitarian values so essential for successful group living which we once treasured in our villages and towns have not been revitalized in modern cities and complex organizations.

At the organizational level, we need to give more flexibility to universities, companies, and government offices: responsible people in these organizations are now more often concerned with satisfying scores of special regulations or avoiding lawsuits than with accomplishing the overall purpose of their organization. To achieve the purpose for which regulations were created, Americans would do well to follow the Japanese model and rely on moral suasion, on creating a consensus of concerned people who can exert their positive influence. The use of specialized regulatory agencies not responsible for the overall health of the organizations they supervise leads to legalistic rigidities and adversary relationships, thus weakening the force of the moral community. Without this moral force, regulations cannot fully accomplish their original purpose. At all levels, from the individual to the highest government offices, we must restrain the use of adversary relations if we are to avoid the divisiveness that makes cooperation for mutual benefit untenable.

Aggregation of interests. Complex problems of international trade negotiations, energy policy, pollution control, and readjustment of declining industries now require high levels of cooperation between companies within a given industrial sector and between the companies and the American government. Antitrust legislation should be adjusted to encourage this cooperation, and flexible administrative rather than rigid legal procedures should be found for dealing with the dangers of monopoly and oligopoly not in the public interest. The legal risks of working together now encourage companies to make individual arrangements with the bureaucracy and politicians, thus weighting down the government with special concessions, and it makes it impossible for any group to represent common purposes against a single well-organized group not acting in the interests of the majority. Branches of government in various sectors should welcome the cooperation of independent companies under them and should work with these associations on issues of overall public interest.

Aggregation of interests works well when representatives of different groups meet frequently without immediate business in order to build up friendship and trust which become invaluable at the time of difficult negotiations. The representatives must not only have the trust of their own members but must also know thoroughly the interests and inclinations of their constituents. This in turn requires frequent meetings of persons in the same group, sufficient discussion and "root binding" so that there is a consensus which can be represented in higher level discussions. American labor leaders and management seldom see each other except in confrontational situations, but in Japan the frequent informal social gatherings between them creates a better basis for understanding and reduces the mutual antagonism. When various groups send representatives to negotiate, they do not use attorneys but "go-betweens," intermediaries who are known for their capacity to gain the trust and confidence of all groups because of their personal reputation and social position. They are often chosen by one group for their special connections with the group to be negotiated with or at least for their capacity to relate to people in that group. American mediators are often more skilled at articulating a position, but the Japanese have developed the ability to be sensitive to the wishes of the other parties and to win their trust. Americans may more easily win an argument, but the Japanese more easily win an agreement. Japanese make full use of informal consultations and social occasions at the golf course and the geisha house to create the kind of mood where people can achieve agreements. Without importing geisha houses, Americans have ample social mechanisms that should be used to create and maintain trust between key groups so that, when necessary, important matters can be negotiated under optimal conditions.

COSTS AND DANGERS

Some of the most serious problems likely to be encountered in importing Japanese patterns are the following:

Smothering individual rights, individuality, and creativity. At the national level the United States has many safeguards, legal and customary, to protect the rights of the individual and the private group. Japanese people, private organizations, and local governments are more at the mercy of central government bureaucrats and politicians because the traditional attitude of *kanson minpi* (respecting the bureaucrats and looking down on the citizenry) has not entirely disappeared. Firms that do not cooperate with central government officials encounter greater difficulties in dealing with bureaucrats than those that cooperate, and firms that are punished for noncooperation have no real appeal. The leaders of the Japanese Teacher's Union have been frightened of granting power to educational officials to establish merit ratings because they fear this could be used as an excuse to fire teachers with deviant political views; and indeed it was used in this way in 1949–1950.

In Japan the deviant in a group can be isolated, ridiculed, ignored, and banished (*mura hachibu*) from the group as in the traditional village. It is difficult for a deviant to stand against a group or for a creative misfit to gain the support he would gain in America. Those who do not conform to narrow guidelines are criticized and pressured until they fall within those guidelines.

In Japanese schools there is almost no flexibility in the

curriculum during the years of compulsory education that could encourage the development of creative imagination. One should not underestimate Japanese capacity to engage in original research, especially in projects requiring group co-operation; indeed, this capacity has begun to increase. Yet in basic research that relies on individual creativity, the Japanese achievements lag behind those in other fields.

Ignoring the variant, the opposition, and the little man. Although Japanese do make an effort to give all recognized groups a fair share, in fact Koreans and small numbers of Chinese and Westerners, even second and third generation, are not treated as full citizens. *Burakumin*, descendants of the outcasts from the Tokugawa period, are citizens, but most desirable employers and potential marital partners take great pains to avoid taking them in legally and socially. While one cannot exclude the possibility that the growing awareness of these injustices will lead to progress as it has toward blacks in the United States, Japanese are less willing to absorb foreign-ers than European countries and America.

Although opposition groups are given some shares, their shares are distinctly smaller. Opposition parties, labor unions, consumers' groups, and radicals are often ignored or given conspicuously less prestigious positions. They may be excluded from private meetings and treated as outsiders by those in the dominant power positions. There are even gradations within the accepted group, and members of the newly rising group, like the newcomer to a village or club, are treated as con-spicuously less than equal by old revered members.

The elite bureaucrats who are so busy solving the larger problems of economic development and local regional con-struction often ride roughshod over opposition, as they did over the protesting farmers at Narita Airport before the public became aroused. Because of the intimate contacts within the inner circle, those aspiring groups that are left out, such as student protest groups, some consumer groups, and local anti-pollution groups, feel a kind of social exclusion absent in a less cohesive society like America. Over a long time frame, new groups are admitted to inner circles and able individuals from protest groups are absorbed into the networks of friendly relations, but there is a real danger that bureaucrats with a firm power base might become insensitive to popular pressures. The problem may be more severe in France, but it is not absent in Japan and it is a problem that could prove divisive within America if a powerful professional elite were created, especially given widespread antielitist sentiment.

Condemning the misfit. Because there are few opportunities for individuals to change their place of work, one who does not get into a place of work that he or his family considered desirable suffers from an enormous sense of failure. By extension, the student who does not enter a desired high school or university may be equally miserable. Suicide rates are high among Japanese youth, and those who are discouraged by not making the proper organization may be more depressed than their American counterparts, who will have a variety of later options open to them.

Japanese who enter a place of work are not totally devoid of opportunities if they were to leave, but given the difficulty of obtaining a secure position with comparable benefits, most have little real option but to endure. Those who might be able to start a new life under different surroundings find that it is too late to make that kind of change. Those not valued highly by their peers or superiors have no place to turn. They therefore remain in the same organization, without particular satisfaction until they retire and go elsewhere.

The unhappy wife is often subject to the same fate. Officially, there is no problem in getting a divorce, and the procedures are not difficult. However, the weight of social pressure is on the wife to make adjustments to avoid divorce.

Courts may require the husband to divide property with his wife upon divorce, but there is no alimony. After years without employment, the divorcée or widow has difficulty making a satisfactory entry into the labor market. This forces the wife who is unhappy with her marriage into making the best of it. The system causes great economic and social hardship on the unfortunate widow or on the unhappy wife of modest means who proceeds to get a divorce.

Stimulating excessive nationalism. In an effort to stimulate internal cooperation and consensus, Japanese leaders have a way of publicizing international developments so that Japan is seen to be the victim of foreign pressure. One often seeks in vain for articles in the Japanese press that fully give the foreign side of the disputes.

Whether officially violating the General Agreement on Tariffs and Trade (GATT) or not, Japanese bureaucrats use a variety of ways to support Japanese products that are not competitive on the international market. When foreign cars were more competitive, the Japanese required that foreign cars off the assembly line had to be inspected in Japan before they could be sold there. It was not enough to send a model of the car, although it is safe to assume that Japanese automobile manufacturers had close working relationships with the necessary officials. By the time foreign cars arrived in Japan, the new model was so far along in production that it was extraordinarily expensive to make adjustments, and Japanese inspectors could find problems as small as location of mirrors or door handles. It thus was difficult for the foreign car maker, subject to such tactics and sometimes delays as well, to enter economically into the Japanese market. Japanese public corporations, although not officially part of the government, generally do not buy any foreign-made materials, even if they are cheaper and superior. The Japanese Telephone and Telegraph, for example, refuses to buy foreign computers whether or not they are superior, as a spur to the domestic computer industry. When a foreign kidney dialysis machine began to take over the market because it was able to do in several hours what it took Japanese-made machines fourteen hours to do, the Japanese health service changed its rules to pay for use of dialysis machines on the basis of length of time machines were used, so that Japanese health facilities again began to buy Japanese products, subjecting patients to fourteen hours of time for what could have been done in several hours. When foreign pleasure boats began to penetrate the Japanese market, the inspector was granted the power to drop them from several meters high and then subject them to lengthy examinations, the expenses to be borne by the foreign company. Japanese pleasure boat makers simply submitted a model for approval and did not need to endure such testing. When an American soft drink maker began to expand its share of the Japanese market beyond what Japanese officials considered proper, it was required to use no artificial sweeteners while Japanese competitors could still use artificial sweeteners. When an American company wished to erect a caustic soda plant in Japan that was far superior to Japanese competitors, it was given one delay after another for well over a year. Because foreign drug manufacturers are often such superior competitors in Japan, when a Japanese company develops a new product, competitors are not allowed to enter the market for three years, thus effectively keeping out many foreign firms. If a foreign firm develops a new product, it may have such a right for only one year.

Some such practices are finally terminated after several years of foreign protest, but Japanese officials use bureaucratic haze to create delays, without full explanation of reasons or standards, thus further discouraging the foreign competitor and giving Japanese competitors a chance to catch up. Not all foreign complaints prove to be justified, but many such practices continue, though virtually unreported in any Japanese medium despite foreign objections. The problems of the foreign firm are generally known only in a narrow circle of officials and business leaders responsible for such policies.

Japanese children who study abroad and learn foreign languages are given virtually no recognition for their achievements. Even Japanese children who have studied abroad and become fluent in English may be required by their teachers in Japan to go through various archaic exercises to prepare for English entrance examinations rather than encouraged to continue to develop their natural fluency. Japanese employees who serve abroad for a very long period of time have virtually no chance to rise to the very top positions in their firms, for they are considered a bit too *gaijin kusai* (contaminated by foreignness). Employees with foreign experience who do rise may first have to prove their superior loyalty to Japan even if it means rejecting part of the foreign experience.

The major universities in Japan are national universities, and since foreigners cannot be regular government employees, no foreigners are allowed to become full professors in Japanese universities. This is beginning to change, but the number of foreign faculty is unlikely to grow substantially. In most Japanese companies virtually no foreigners are allowed to enter the regular managerial career route even if they can handle the language.

Foreigners are generally excluded from Japanese press clubs and from briefings of the press by Japanese officials, except at special press centers for foreigners, even if they are competent to speak Japanese.

In international economic aid and in international organizations Japan has generally exerted itself in matters of immediate national interest. Although generally taking a responsible and cooperative role in developing an international order, the Japanese have taken little initiative in matters beyond their own narrow self-interest.

Although foreigners are generally treated with courtesy and kindness, Japanese groups rarely accept them in their inner councils. Many large organizations have "managers of foreigners," people skilled in English and foreign ways, who mediate between foreigners and regular line officers. Foreigners may be taken as true friends by many Japanese individuals, but with some notable exceptions most Japanese organizations treat foreigners as honored guests outside the inner circle.

Becoming immobilized. One of the most troubling problems within and between Japanese groups is the deadlock brought about when one important partner refuses to go along. It is generally not considered proper to force a decision on an unwilling party. Narita Airport was long delayed partly because of the deadlock between the bureaucracy and the protesters. Universities are unable to progress because the Ministry of Education and faculties at the various universities are deadlocked over how much government control to permit if there are to be greater government expenditures. Because it is sometimes so difficult to resolve internal problems by means of consensus, a sense of outside pressure must sometimes be used. At other times when groups remain divided it may be that no one has the authority to resolve the dispute since everyone's views must be considered and no one wants to push through something when one group does not agree.

The Japanese have achieved success at a considerable price, the price of strong pressure toward conformity and consensus, sometimes at the expense of the deviant, the opposition, the little man, the outsider. These are excesses that Americans who may wish to copy Japanese patterns will have to consider seriously and devise ways to avoid. At the same time, it may be suggested that America is in little danger of going to Japanese extremes in any of these spheres. America's problem is rather that American groups do not have enough power to maintain their own standards, that they do not have the confidence to carry out the will of the majority against the egoistic deviant. It may be suggested that America needs all the help it can get in moving toward group cooperation.

CAN THE JAPANESE MODEL SURVIVE SUCCESS?

Before Americans begin studying the Japanese model, they need to consider the question raised by many Japanese and some foreigners as well, whether the Japanese model of the last twenty years will remain effective, even in Japan. The Japanese model, so the argument goes, was appropriate to a period of very rapid growth when Japan had many comparative advantages and a receptive international economic and political climate. It worked when there was a high internal consensus about growth, but this consensus is now drawing to a close. Ordinary citizens are now more interested in social benefits than economic growth, and the new generation of youth reared in affluence have very little interest in economic growth at all.

The pessimists note that growth has already slowed down. During rapid expansion the banks had high leverage over firms, and banks were in turn dependent on the government to help provide financing for new investment. Now companies have accumulated more capital and will undertake less new investment. They therefore have less need for the banks and the government and are more prepared to go on their own. The domestic market was lively when one product after another was introduced into Japan, but now Japan is satiated with all the basic electrical and other equipment, so the market is limited only to replacement of old goods. Many Japanese goods have already begun to saturate other world markets, which will no longer be able to absorb products from rapid expansion of Japanese industry. Manufacturers are fully aware of these trends and no amount of government encouragement can make them continue their rate of investment in modern facilities.

Korea, Taiwan, and other countries with lower labor costs and new plants sometimes more modern than Japan's will be able to undersell Japan on world markets in a broad range of products, enjoying the comparative advantage that Japan once did. Japan will therefore give up many of its labor-intensive industries to those countries, and the high technology sector where America still has strength and the service sector toward which Japan is moving do not provide the same growth opportunities that Japan enjoyed during its heyday as a heavy manufacturer.

The Japanese system, as seen by such critics, is in jeopardy as the growth rate declines. Companies are heavily indebted to banks, but when growth was high they could easily repay loans. When they were expanding rapidly, they could hire many young employees at low wages. Now that growth rates have declined, companies have trouble repaying loans and, with permanent employment, they are stuck with a highly paid older work force. With less expansion, they often do not have enough work for everyone, and disguised unemployment is rising rapidly. Firms are so strained maintaining the permanent employment system that the whole system is beginning to crack. The population over sixty-five has doubled in the last twenty-five years and is expected to double again in the next twenty-five years when the proportion of old people will reach European levels. The nation will be confronted with a smaller work force and a larger welfare bill, increasing companies' tax burden, reducing the growth rate, and creating a vicious cycle.

In the past, younger workers, workers in small and medium enterprises, temporary workers in large enterprises, women and other underprivileged groups could be kept under control by the government and big business establishment because they stood to gain some benefits from rapid growth. In difficult times these groups will be the first to be sacrificed. During rapid growth the large number of rural youth who entered the urban industrial work force were willing to endure low wages and difficult woking conditions because it was an improvement over earlier rural conditions, but now that the rural-to-urban transition has been essentially completed, expectations are higher, there are fewer opportunities for rising, and consequently people in lower positions are less easily satisfied. Those who once took pride in their work in middle-level specialties are no longer as content to remain subservient to those in the elite track.

With a slower growth rate, political leaders must make more difficult decisions that require some groups to pull in their belt. Social cleavages will become more severe and the broad-based support for the conservative leadership will decline. The Liberal Democratic Party in the Diet is already eroding so that a coalition government is likely. As opposition parties and the disadvantaged groups they represent gain power, the great triad of leading politicians, elite bureaucrats, and big-business leaders will be unable to rule unilaterally. With a broader and more diverse base of rule, leaders will lose their capacity to achieve the consensus needed to act quickly. Government will be less effective.

Until now, Japan could selectively control imports of foreign ideas and customs, maintaining a tight national solidarity. With stronger foreign pressures on Japan to further open its import market, with increasing foreign contact and internationalization of Japanese companies, Japan will have more difficulty controlling foreign impact. It will become increasingly difficult to preserve the strong distinctive features of Japanese society and to prevent the spread of some of the less attractive features of Western society.

Japan, always fragile because of its dependence on the international system, faces even greater dangers than previously. Raw materials like oil could be cut off, European and American markets could be curtailed by protectionism, and the productivity of rising countries like Korea, Taiwan, and Brazil could destroy Japan's comparative advantage. Japan profited from a period of great stability in resources and great receptivity to its products, but this era is ending and future crises could have a devastating impact.

During growth the grand vision of catching up with and overtaking modern, affluent countries gave the entire society a sense of purpose. The victory won and the vision achieved, Japan no longer has any clear direction. The optimism, discipline, and hard work that resulted from the pursuit of these visions, according to the pessimists, will now go the ways of affluent Europe and America.

The above arguments embody very real fears and they are not without some foundation. Americans who are hopeful for an end to Japanese competitive power as well as Japanese spokesmen who are trying to counter foreign pressure on Japan to further relax import controls and to restrain exports are likely to repeat them often in a variety of forms. In making estimates about Japan's future, informed reasonable men do not entirely agree, and a scholar can do no more than offer his best professional judgment.

The Japanese for the last two decades have been caught up in a series of crises, shocks, disasters, and so-called "depressions" when growth rate goes down as low as five percent. Each time there was a wave of panic, and each time Japan rallied to astound the pessimists. According to the best estimates of Japanese and foreign economists, Japan in the decade ahead will still be able to maintain a growth rate of perhaps five to seven percent a year, substantially higher than the United States'. It is true that companies must repay loans to banks, but many are already finding ways to pay back some of their debts; and because of the policies of the Finance Ministry and the Bank of Japan, interest rates have already gone down far lower than during the rapid growth years. There are bankruptcies, but enough companies do well for the total employment to continue to rise; official unemployment is unlikely in the foreseeable future to reach three percent, and companies have expanded new product lines and further rationalized to control disguised unemployment. Companies have decreased seniority pay differentials and increased incentive pay systems without sacrificing the seniority system. Small and medium-sized enterprises are sometimes exploited by large manufacturers, but productivity and salary differentials between small and large firms continues to decline, and the small and medium-sized sector still continues to grow. Many large manufacturers want reliable subcontractors and therefore help modernize smaller companies; the result is that subcontractor workers are increasingly brought into a regularized employment situation similar to that of workers in large companies.

It is true that the service sector has grown relative to other sectors, but Japan is likely to turn this stage to its advantage as it has the stages of light industry, heavy industry, and high technology. As information processing becomes more important, Tokyo has the potential for becoming the information capitol of the world. Its six largest trading companies are probably each superior to any foreign company in range of economic and political information. Telephone facsimiles are already much more widespread in Japan than anywhere else. Because of its rapid advances in putting all published material on tapes and arranging patent and other laws to make this feasible, Japan is further along in having all library information integrated into a single system than any other country. Although part of its computer capacities still lag behind IBM, the national government's commitment to making Japanese companies superior in computer and telecommunication systems gives it distinct advantages over other countries where there is no such policy and where antitrust suits threaten to break up the strongest multinational companies of American origins. Meanwhile, Japanese investment overseas will bring Japan new opportunities. The Tokyo-based economist Tait Ratcliffe estimates that in 1980 Japanese investment overseas will have tripled in five years and will continue to expand. Purchase of foreign firms with high technology is growing.

It is true that the proportion of voters supporting LDP had been declining, but the decline now appears arrested and in local elections the LDP has been regaining power. Every opposition party that has grown in recent years soon peaked far short of a serious challenge to LDP supremacy. Since coalition government came to be considered a possibility, bureaucrats have become increasingly cooperative with key opposition Diet members, in preparation for working together if a coalition government is necessary. So many moderate opposition leaders are prepared to cooperate with the LDP that even with a coalition, the government is unlikely to be fundamentally changed.

It is true that young workers had been less enthusiastic about subordinating themselves to the group, but the fears of petroleum shortages after the oil shock and of foreign protectionism after Europe and America complained in 1977 has greatly strengthened discipline and has kept groups from different circles united.

It is true that Japan would be in great trouble if natural resources were cut off, but wise Japanese bureaucrats have managed to keep open many petroleum options (between the Middle East, Indonesia, Russia, China, Australia) and many coal and atomic energy options, all of which are supplemented by an excess supply of tankers and approximately ninety days on-shore petroleum storage capacity. With these efforts and their vigorous conservation program, the danger of a serious energy problem in Japan seems remote. With dollar devaluation, Japanese can now import oil so cheaply that some of the previous plans to reduce energy-intensive industrial production now seem unnecessary. As for international resistance to Japanese products, this will undoubtedly cause problems in certain selected industries, but the flexibility of the Japanese government's guidance, the capacity of the Japanese system to rapidly absorb information concerning trends, and the responsiveness of Japanese firms gives Japan many options. The fact is that the Japanese are likely to remain extraordinarily competitive in the world markets for a long time. What they reluctantly give up in labor-intensive industries like textiles and low-level electronics can more than be replaced by their rapidly growing capacity in new high-technology fields such as copiers, computers, and telecommunication equipment—a capacity that already threatens to weaken some of America's few remaining areas of competitive strength. Not only do exports of consumer goods continue to increase, but huge integrated Japanese construction projects in many parts of the world are growing rapidly, providing an outlet for Japanese production without attracting political reactions as do consumer products. Japanese investments throughout the world are already catching and surpassing American investments in many areas. Although investments in America have begun slowly, they can be expected to increase rapidly in the years ahead.

Within Japan, female temporary workers are generally the first laid off in times of economic difficulty, but in the "recession" year of 1977, for example, the number of women in the labor force increased almost two percent, far more than the growth of women in the population. The much heralded cleavages in Japanese society are sufficiently quiet that leftist political leaders still bemoan the low level of consciousness of Japanese workers. The Japanese fear of inundation by foreigners has receded as the value of the dollar has fallen because so few foreigners can afford to live in or visit Japan. In short, within the next decade at least Japan appears to have the leadership, cohesion, and group support necessary to maintain a highly effective postindustrial society without any great changes in its institutions.

CREATING AND BORROWING

Can the United States, with its strong tradition of individualism, acquire a system, however admirable and effective, that is based on very different premises? When Japan began borrowing from the West in the late nineteenth century, it had hoped it could get technology without giving up the Eastern spirit. In the end Japan had to change its own spirit and institutions far more than originally intended. Japan's ultimate success should not mask the turmoil of the process, but Japan found that it could effectively transplant institutions that, with its tradition, it had not been able to create. It is no accident that the early, basic discoveries of modern science, technology, and industry originated in Western Europe and the United States, where individuality and creativity flourished.

The first generation of industrialists in Europe acquired their skills through their own experiences, but the first generation of industrialists in Japan spent many years in training programs acquiring the experience of others. In the turmoil of the early Meiji period some great individual entreprenurs and charismatic leaders played a crucial role, but the dominant pattern for catching up was of central government planning and guidance, close government–business cooperation, and rapid creation of large, private institutions through centralized capital accumulation and formal training programs. As Ronald Dore put it, Japan, even more than Germany, is a "late modernizer," with a particular set of institutions designed for rapid catching-up. In the later part of the twentieth century these institutions, originally developed for providing central direction for rapid change, turned out to be better adapted to the complex problems of postindustrial society than the institutions of Western countries that were developed for creating industrialization. In the current era of rapid change, a highly politicized population, environmental pollution, and shortage of resources, the Japanese have found that institutions which provide more central direction, more flexibility, and more consensus outperform those which lack these capacities.

Until a few decades ago America's institutions, which grew out of the Western European experience, worked extraordinarily well. Doctrines of private enterprise, civil liberties, and states' rights allowed creative individuals and institutions to adapt to local situations. With its scientific and technological inventions, America was on the forefront of world creativity. Laws developed in response to European tyranny gave individuals their highly prized personal freedom. Benevolent charities and academic institutions provided a level of humanity and decency lacking in many nations. When these institutions were at the height of their success, Americans were proud of and devoted to their country.

By the 1970s, however, institutions that once served our country effectively have often been found wanting and have been strained almost to the breaking point. Organizations lost the power and flexibility to function effectively. In a loosely organized urban society, ordinary citizens are defenseless against crime and license. Government regulations have multiplied, creating endless litigation that burdens society financially and organizationally. Commitments made when resources were seemingly inexhaustible have created expectations that cannot be realized. Benevolent impulses and government programs have proliferated in a mass of confusion without adequate consideration of the financial burden on the taxpayer, of the divisiveness between taxpayer and recipient, of the motivation of the low-paid worker, and of the self-depreciation of the recipient in an achievement-oriented society.

The pace of economic change has accelerated and foreign trade increased, but America's institutions are not strong enough to guide these developments or to respond effectively to the problems of its declining economic competitiveness. When sudden dislocation can cause enormous human misery, as in the excessive migration from the rural south to northern cities in recent decades, the United States has had no migration policy. Our institutional practices promote adversary relations and litigation at a time when the complexity of our organizations requires greater consideration of overall goals and when divisiveness threatens to disrupt the society. As a result, judges are called upon to make complex rulings concerning social and economic situations, a task for which they are most often professionally unprepared.

Japan, with its greater sense of group orientation, more recent emergence from feudalism, and government-led modernization, has developed solutions for many of these problems that America, with its more individualistic and legalistic history, might never have invented. America's transition to industrialization did not require the central direction nor the high level of government and business cooperation required of a borrower. Now that postindustrial America, too, requires higher levels of cooperation and more central leadership oriented to a modern economic order, there is no reason why America could not borrow and adapt Japanese models which, with a different tradition, it could not have originally created.

No one should underestimate the difficulty of pulling out specific practices from their context. Nonetheless, while Japanese practices are in many ways significantly different from American ways, they are surprisingly consistent with America's basic values. America values free enterprise, and even more of Japan's gross national product is located in the private sector than America's. America is committed to freedom of speech and freedom of the press, and so is Japan. America strives for a more equal society, and although the Japanese have higher requirements for performance before granting underprivileged groups equality, they have exerted themselves in reducing differentials of opportunity and have achieved income differentials smaller than America's. Japan is group-oriented, but as George Lodge points out, communitarianism is an integral part of the American tradition, going back to the early New England village. America's many voluntary associations, its history of community organization, and the positive value it attaches to teamwork suggest that group-oriented activities, if not dominant, are at least not alien to the American tradition.

America's problem of recreating a sense of community now that group ties have been attenuated is infinitely more difficult than Japan's problem of maintaining group ties that were never dissolved. But there is no reason why, with greater central direction and sensitivity to the needs of various groups, to the mechanisms of maintaining solidarity, and to the practice of broad consultation, America could not adopt policies more suited to the postindustrial age and recreate a sense of community in a form adapted to postindustrial society.

It is not clear that Americans are ready to respond to the challenges now posed by Japan's success and that will soon be posed by the success of Korea and other Asian nations. Unlike other nations inundated by Western dominance, the Japanese beginning in the late nineteenth century moved with eagerness and speed to bring in foreign patterns rather than have them brought in; thus they became the masters of change rather than the victims. Other countries were devastated by foreign influence, but Japan was invigorated. This work is written with the hope that America, like Japan, can master the new challenges, that we will respond with foresight rather than hindsight, with planning rather than crisis management, sooner rather than later.

Bibliography
Index

Bibliography

CHAPTER 2

Abegglen, James C., Thomas Hout, and C. Tait Ratcliffe. *Japan in 1980.* London: The Financial Times, 1974.

Boston Consulting Group. *Trade between Japan and the United States.* Prepared for the U.S. Department of the Treasury, April 1978.

Financial Times, London, July 26, 1977. [Special issue on Japan.]

Gibney, Frank. *Japan: The Fragile Superpower.* New York: Norton, 1975.

Jorgenson, Dale. "U.S. and Japanese Economic Growth, 1952–1973: An International Comparison." Presented at the Fifth World Congress of the International Economic Association, Tokyo, August 29–September 3, 1977.

Patrick, Hugh, and Henry Rosovsky, eds. *Asia's New Giant.* Washington, D.C.: Brookings Institution, 1976.

Reischauer, Edwin O. *The Japanese.* Cambridge: Harvard University Press, 1977.

Scott-Stokes, Henry. *The Japanese Competitor.* London: The Financial Times, 1976.

[Statistical data is contained in annual government white papers published by various Japanese ministries (*White Papers of Japan,* Japan Institute of International Relations.) Various statistics are also summarized in such annuals as: *Japan Almanac*, Mainichi Newspapers; *Japan Statistical Yearbook*, Prime Minister's Office; *Nippon: A Chartered Survey of Japan*, Kokusei-sha; *Statistical Handbook of Japan*, Prime Minister's Office. Statistics are also frequently reported in international English weeklies such as *Japan Times* and *The Japan Economic Journal*.]

CHAPTER 4

Abegglen, James C. *Business Strategies for Japan*. Tokyo: Sophia University Press, 1970.

Amaya, Naohiro. "On Japan's Trade and Industrial Policies." MITI Report JR-1 (73-2). Tokyo, February 1974.

Campbell, John Creighton. *Contemporary Japanese Budget Politics*. Berkeley: University of California Press, 1976.

Frank, Isaiah, and Ryokichi Hirono. *How the U.S. and Japan See Each Other's Economy*. New York: Committee for Economic Development, 1974.

Fukui, Haruhiro. "Economic Planning in Postwar Japan." *Asian Survey* (April 1972) 12:327–348.

Johnson, Chalmers. *Japan's Public Policy Companies*. Stanford: AEI Hoover Institute, 1978.

Kaplan, Eugene. *Japan: The Government-Business Relationship*. Washington, D.C.: U.S. Department of Commerce, 1972.

Komiya, Ryutaro. "Planning in Japan." In Morris Bornstein, *Economic Planning East and West*. Cambridge, Mass.: Ballinger, 1975.

MITI. *Japan's Industrial Structure—A Long Range Vision*. Report BI-23. Tokyo, 1976.

———. *Japan's Industrial Structure—A Long Range Vision*. Report NR-140 (77-26). Tokyo, 1977.

OECD Secretariat. *Environmental Policies in Japan*. Tokyo, April 1977.

Ojimi, Yoshihisa. *The Industrial Policy of Japan.* Paris: OECD, 1972.

Sato, Hideo. "The Crisis of an Alliance: The Politics of U.S.–Japanese Textile Trade." Ph.D. thesis, University of Chicago, 1976.

Scalapino, Robert A., ed. *The Foreign Policy of Modern Japan.* Berkeley: University of California Press, 1976.

Tanaka, Kakuei. *Building a New Japan.* Tokyo: Simul, 1973.

Vogel, Ezra F., ed. *Modern Japanese Organization and Decision Making.* Berkeley: University of California Press, 1975.

Watanabe, Tsunehiko. "National Planning and Economic Development." *Economics of Planning* (1970) 10:21–51.

CHAPTER 5

Austin, Lewis, ed. *Japan: The Paradox of Progress.* New Haven: Yale University Press, 1976.

Baerwald, Hans H. *Japan's Parliament.* Cambridge: Cambridge University Press, 1974.

Curtis, Gerald. *Election Campaigning Japanese Style.* New York: Columbia University Press, 1971.

Destler, I. M., Hideo Sato, Priscilla Clapp, and Haruhiro Fukui. *Managing an Alliance.* Washington, D.C.: Brookings Institution, 1976.

Fukui, Haruhiro. *Party in Power—The Japanese Liberal Democrats and Policy-making.* Berkeley: University of California Press, 1970.

Langdon, Frank. *Politics in Japan.* Boston: Little, Brown, 1967.

Maruyama, Masao. *Thought and Behavior in Modern Japanese Politics.* London: Oxford University Press, 1963.

Morley, James W., ed. *Prologue to the Future: The U.S. and Japan in the Postindustrial Age.* Boston: D.C. Heath, 1974.

Patrick, Hugh, ed. *Japanese Industrialization and Its Social Consequences.* Berkeley: University of California Press, 1976.

Pempel, T. J., ed. *Policy Making in Contemporary Japan.* Ithaca: Cornell University Press, 1977.

Thayer, Nathaniel B. *How the Conservatives Rule Japan.* Princeton: Princeton University Press, 1969.

Watanuki, Joji. *Politics in Postwar Japanese Society.* Tokyo: Tokyo University Press, 1977.

CHAPTER 6

Abegglen, James C. *Management and Worker.* Tokyo: Kō-dansha, 1973.

Cole, Robert E. *Japanese Blue Collar.* Berkeley: University of California Press, 1971.

Dore, Ronald P. *British Factory–Japanese Factory.* Berkeley: University of California Press, 1974.

Marsh, Robert M., and Hiroshi Mannari. *Modernization and the Japanese Factory.* Princeton: Princeton University Press, 1976.

Okochi, Kazuo, Bernard Karsh, and Solomon B. Levine. *Workers and Employers in Japan.* Princeton: Princeton University Press, 1974.

OECD. *Manpower Policy in Japan.* Paris, 1973.

Pascale, Richard Tanner. "Personnel Practices and Employee Attitudes: A Study of Japanese- and American-Managed Firms in the United States." *Human Relations* (1978) 31:597–615.

Ratcliffe, C. Tait. *Japanese Corporate Finance, 1977–1980.* London: Financial Times, 1977.

Rohlen, Thomas. *For Harmony and Strength.* Berkeley: University of California Press, 1974.

Tsurumi, Yoshi. *The Japanese Are Coming.* Cambridge, Mass.: Ballinger, 1976.

Yoshino, M. Y. *Japan's Multinational Enterprises.* Cambridge: Harvard University Press, 1976.

―――. *The Japanese Marketing System.* Cambridge, M.I.T. Press, 1971.

―――. *Japan's Managerial System.* Cambridge: M.I.T. Press, 1968.

CHAPTER 7

Bereday, George Z. F., and Shigeo Masui. *American Education through Japanese Eyes.* Honolulu: University of Hawaii, 1973.

Comer, L. C., and John P. Keeves. *Science Education in Nineteen Countries.* New York: Halsted, 1973.

Cummings, William K. *Education and Equality in Japan.* Princeton: Princeton University Press, 1979.

―――. "The Effects of Japanese Schools." In Antonina Ktoskowska and Guido Martinotti, eds., *Education in a Changing Society.* London: Sage, 1977.

Glazer, Nathan. "Social and Cultural Factors in Economic Growth." In Hugh Patrick and Henry Rosovsky, eds., *Asia's New Giant.* Washington, D.C.: Brookings Institution, 1976.

Halloran, Richard. *Japan: Images and Realities.* New York: Random House, 1969.

Kobayashi, Tetsuya. *Society, Schools, and Progress in Japan.* New York: Pergamon Press, 1976.

Ministry of Education. *Course of Study for Elementary Schools in Japan.* Tokyo, 1976.

―――. *Course of Study for Lower Secondary Schools in Japan.* Tokyo, 1976.

―――. *Educational Standards in Japan.* Tokyo, 1970.

Monbushō. *Chihō kyōikuhi no chōsa hōkokusho* (Survey of local educational expenses). Tokyo, 1976.

————. *Waga kuni no kyōiku suijun* (Educational standards in Japan). Tokyo, 1976.

OECD. *Reviews of National Policies for Education: Japan.* Paris, 1971.

Passin, Herbert. *Society and Education in Japan.* New York: Columbia University Teachers College, 1965.

Singleton, John. *Nichū.* New York: Holt, Rinehart & Winston, 1967.

Vogel, Ezra F. "Infernal Entrance Examination." In *Japan's New Middle Class.* Berkeley: University of California Press, 1963.

CHAPTER 8

Bennett, John W., and Solomon B. Levine. "Industrialization and Social Deprivation." In Hugh Patrick, ed., *Japanese Industrialization and Its Social Consequences.* Berkeley: University of California Press, 1976.

Campbell, John C. "Entrepreneurial Bureaucrats and Programs for Old People in Japan." Presented at the American Political Science Association, New York, August 31–September 3, 1978.

————. "Programs for the Aged in Japan." Presented at the Midwest Regional Seminar on Japan, December 3, 1977.

Japan Institute of Labor. *Japan Labor Bulletin.* Tokyo, monthly.

Kōseishō. *Kōsei hakusho* (Welfare white paper). Tokyo, 1975.

Kōsei Tōkei Kyōkai. *Kokumin eisei no dōkō,* "Kōsei no Shihyō" (Social welfare indicators). Tokyo, 1976.

Husby, Ralph D. "Public Assistance (*Seikatsu Hogo*) in Japan." Unpublished manuscript, 1975.

Nihon Keieisha Dantai Renmei Jimukyoku. "Fukuri Kōseihi chōsa kekka hōkoku" (A survey of [employee] welfare benefit payments). Tokyo, 1976.

Nishimoto, Kōichi. "Nōkyō" (Agricultural cooperatives), *The Japan Interpreter*, 1972, 321–331.

Palmore, Erdman. *The Honorable Elders*. Durham, N.C.: Duke University Press, 1975.

Plath, David. "Japan: The After Years." In *Aging and Modernization*, ed. Donald Cowgill and Lowell Holmes. New York: Appleton-Century-Crofts, 1972.

Social Insurance Agency, Japanese Government. *Outline of Social Insurance in Japan*. Tokyo, 1977.

Yamaguchi Shin'ichirō, ed. *Nihon no fukushi* (Japanese welfare). Tokyo, Zaikeishōhōsha, 1976.

CHAPTER 9

Ames, Walter L. "Police and Community in Japan." Unpublished manuscript, 1978.

Bayley, David. *Forces of Order: Police Behavior in Japan and the United States*. Berkeley: University of California Press, 1976.

Clifford, William. *Crime Control in Japan*. Boston: D.C. Heath, 1976.

Hōmushō. *Hanzai hakusho* (Crime white paper). Tokyo, 1976.

CHAPTER 10

Lodge, George C. *The New American Ideology*. New York: Knopf, 1976.

Index

Activity clubs, student, 99–100
Agricultural associations, 106–107
Agricultural Cooperative, 194
Agricultural exports, American, 12–13
Agriculture, Ministry of, 80, 123
Airlines, 79
Alienation in Japanese society, 217
Allied Occupation, 5, 153, 167
All-Japan Airways, 79
Antitrust laws, American, 236–237
Apprenticeship, ministry training, 57
Asian Development Bank, 72
Automotive industry: merger attempts
  in, 77; pollution standards for, 82;
  protection of, 11–12, 241; trade
  restraints in the United States, 14

Bank of Japan, 75
Banks: company indebtedness to, 73,
  75, 135, 137–138, 246; government
  influence on, 73, 75, 78
Baseball, 32–33
Bayley, David, 204, 208, 209
Bell, Daniel, 44
Bonuses, incentive, 138–139, 147
Bowling, 35
Budget, national, 67–68
Burakumin, 198, 239
Bureaucracy: commitment to employ-
  ees, 51; in contrast to American
  system, 233–234; deliberative coun-

cils of, 87–89; Diet's relationship
  with, 87; education of members,
  36–37, 55; errors of, 93, hierarchy
  of members, 56–58; politicians' relations with, 57, 60; press relations
  with, 85–86, 125–126; private sector cooperation with, 85, 89; responsibility of, 65–66; role of elite
  members, 83–84. *See also* Government
Business: bank financing of, 73, 75,
  135, 137–138, 246; Chamber of
  Commerce representation, 112; determination of market share in, 10–
  11, 136–137; development of company system for, 132–137; employee
  benefits from, 149, 190–193; employee identification with, 131–132,
  146–148, 152–153; future of, 250–
  251; government benefits for, 122;
  health care provided by, 190, 192;
  hierarchy of officials in, 141–144;
  hiring practices of, 140–141, 149;
  information gathering by, 43–49;
  joint study session use by, 48–49;
  Keidanren representation, 113–116;
  labor union encouragement by, 153,
  154; ministry concern for, 70–78,
  138; political contributions of, 118,
  123; promotion systems in, 149–
  150; recession practices of, 138–

267

Index

Index